The Middle East At The Crossroads

The Middle East At The Crossroads

REGIONAL FORCES & EXTERNAL POWERS

—— Edited By ——
JANICE GROSS STEIN
DAVID B. DEWITT

MOSAIC PRESS

Canadian Cataloguing in Publication Data

Main entry under title:
The Middle East at the crossroads

Bibliography: p.
Includes indes.
ISBN 0-88962-202-7 (bound).
ISBN 0-88962-201-9 (pbk.)

1. Near East - Politics and government - 1945-
2. Near East - Foreign relations. I. Stein, Janice. II. Dewitt, David Brian, 1948-

DS63.1.M53 1983   956'.04   C83-098976-5

Published by Mosaic Press, P.O. Box 1032, Oakville, Ontario, L6J 5E9, Canada.

Published with the assistance of the Canada Council and the Ontario Arts Council.

Copyright © Janice Gross-Stein and David B. Dewitt, 1983

Typeset by Speed River Graphics.
Design by Doug Frank.
Printed and bound in Canada.

ISBN 0-88962-202-7 cloth
ISBN 0-88962-201-9 paper

Distributed in the United States by Flatiron Books, 175 Fifth Avenue, Suite 814, New York, N.Y. 10010, U.S.A.

Distributed in the U.K. by John Calder (Publishers) Ltd., 18 Brewer Street, London, W1R 4AS, England

Distributed in New Zealand and Australia by Pilgrims South Press, P.O. Box 5101, Dunedin, New Zealand.

to all those who struggle for
a just and lasting peace in the Middle East

Acknowledgements

The Canadian Professors for Peace in the Middle East was established in 1973. Over the years many people from across Canada have contributed their time and energy to the central concern of the organization — education about and support for the pursuit of peace in the Middle East. None gave more than the late Harry Crowe. First as national co-chairman with Irwin Cotler and then on his own, Harry set the direction and the tone of CPPME. He stimulated controversy and debate while, at the same time, he engendered commitment from those he reached, and his reach encompassed most universities from coast to coast. His honesty and fairness, his intellectual rigour, and his passion drove him to speak forthrightly on the fundamental issues of peace, war, and justice in the Middle East. The memory and principles of this man, a man who epitomizes the epithet of "scholar and gentleman", inspired this collection.

The chapters of this volume were written by participants in the annual CPPME conference held at Glendon College, York University, in May 1982. Dr. Eva Dessen, CPPME Executive Director, with the assistance of the office staff, and Professor Irving Abella of Glendon College, made superb arrangements for the meetings. As convention co-chairpeople, we would like to thank the participants and the organizers who, together, contributed to discussion and debate that was lively, provocative, and informed. Through the active interest, determination, and extraordinary editorial assistance of Howard Aster at Mosaic Press, we are now able to disseminate to a much wider audience this collection of essays which treats some of the fundamental issues affecting peace in the Middle East.

Janice Gross Stein and David B. Dewitt,
Co-editors and Conference Co-Chairpeople,
January 1983

TABLE OF CONTENTS

9

INTRODUCTION

Janice Gross Stein
Department of Political Science
University of Toronto

The Middle East is often the focus of the world's attention, curiosity, and alarm. Although it has long been important in international politics, in the last decade its resources and its struggles have impinged directly on the interests of many who are remote geographically, politically, and even spiritually from the Middle East. The Arab-Israel conflict, the ongoing war between Iraq and Iran, internecine quarrels among Arab leaders, all these have drawn the powerful and the weak, the arms merchants and the mediators, to the politics of the region. And the singular importance of oil to the economies of the older industrialized states, those of the newly industrializing, and to those struggling at the margin, has made the Middle East, its economics and politics, its conflicts and its stability, a primary international concern. The Middle East is now the object of intense scrutiny by developed and underdeveloped societies, by industrialized and agrarian economies, and by eastern and western polities. This interpenetration of outside interests and forces from within has tied the peoples and politics of the Middle East to the wider international arena.

This volume speaks to the interplay of regional forces and outside interests which shapes the politics of the Middle East. It begins with an examination of OPEC, the highly visible energy coalition which came to international prominence in this last decade. The revolution in the price of energy which began in 1973 and continued in 1979-80, had profound consequences for the politics of the Middle East and the economies of the rest of the international community. Oil diplomacy and petrodollar politics became the codewords for the new realities of international economic and political power, but perhaps most remarkable was the expectation that the oil producers might be in the vanguard of a fundamental change in the international hierarchy.

Sally Zerker looks at the past, present, and future of OPEC as a manager in the international energy market. She pays particular attention to the growing rivalry between Iran and Saudi Arabia for principal authority in the coalition and examines the implications of their distinctive economic objectives and needs as well as their political and religious differences. The future of OPEC cannot be understood apart from the ongoing war between Iran and Iraq and the political rivalry between Iran and Saudi Arabia, the revolutionary Shi'i republic and the conservative Wahhabi monarchy. Yet OPEC's viability will in turn affect the war between Iran and Iraq which again shapes the dynamics of the coalition opposed to Israel. This nexus of political and economic forces which cuts across national boundaries within the region, is critical to our understanding of the contemporary Middle East. At the same time, it is precisely this linkage of forces which draws outsiders into the vortex of Middle Eastern politics.

The second important transnational force which crosses the political boundaries of the Middle East are the groups of armed fighters who strike at civilian as well as military targets to capture international support for their political objectives. D.J.C. Carmichael poses a critical question for discussion: how is a leader of civilized conscience to judge and respond to such acts? As Ross Rudolph argues, however, in political discourse there are no rigid designators: one person's 'terrorist' is another's 'freedom fighter'. There is simply no general consensus on the appropriate standards for the use of force on behalf of a community. Precisely because of the ambiguity of relevant ethical principles, much has been written about the requisites of guerrilla strategy and the political realities of international terrorism, but little has been said about the ethical dilemmas which confront those who must make the very difficult choice of an appropriate response. It is these very difficult dilemmas, dilemmas whose consequences range far beyond the Middle East, that Carmichael and Rudolph address. Their debate is far from abstract, however, for both look at the relevance of moral principles to the bitter conflict between Israel and the Palestine Liberation Organization, a conflict which culminated in a devastating war in Lebanon in the summer of 1982. Their analysis leads inevitably to a consideration of the principles of legitimacy, peace, and justice between the two peoples.

The third important force that crosses the Middle East is the little understood but extraordinary phenomenon of Islam as a political factor within the broader context of development and change. Religious militancy in the Middle East has intensified dramatically in the last decade: it overthrew the Pahlavi dynasty in Iran, threatens the fragile political regimes along the Gulf, and provoked the seizure of the Grand Mosque in Mecca. Saleem Qureshi examines the nature of this religiously inspired political militancy in the arc from Turkey to Iran. He locates Islamic fundamentalism both in time and in space by exploring parallel movements within the Islamic world, looks at the causes of its development and the scope of its impact, and then assesses its political implications for the future of the region. Qureshi questions whether Islamic fundamentalism, which appeals to the underprivileged, the deprived, and the alienated, the underclass in the Middle East, will be able to transcend the overlapping conflicts between tradition and modernity, religion and secularism, conspicuous consumption and deprivation.

In the second part of the volume, we turn to the impact of outside forces on the management of conflict within the Middle East. Of obvious importance are the United States and the Soviet Union, the two superpowers who have competed for influence in the region for the last three decades. Indeed, it is little exaggeration to suggest that the two have practiced the politics of mutual exclusion as each has armed and supplied one or another of the protagonists in the Arab-Israel conflict.

Yet, the last few years have witnessed important changes in the role each power has played. The Soviet Union lost its most important ally in the Arab-Israel conflict, Egypt, and has been markedly reserved in its support of the PLO, Syria, and Iraq. Caught in the web of inter-Arab struggles, quiescent in its diplomacy, the Soviet Union has been relegated to the margin in the core of the Middle East even though it has emerged as a power to be reckoned with in the northern periphery. Or has it? Paul Marantz addresses these questions when he looks at the impact of internal Soviet forces on foreign policy in the years to come. His essay explores Soviet petroleum shortages, the growing Muslim population, the decline in the growth of the Soviet economy, and the difficulties Andropov will encounter in the consolidation of power. Marantz suggests that it may be somewhat premature to conclude that the low Soviet profile in Lebanon this past summer is a model of the future. On the contrary, the Soviet demand for recognition as a great military power may well limit its willingness to engage in constructive search for even-handed solutions to the deep-rooted conflicts of the Middle East.

Even more striking is the prominence of the United States in the last several years as a conflict manager and a mediator actively engaged in the search for solutions to the Arab-Israel conflict. As Blema Steinberg demonstrates in her analysis of the mainsprings of American foreign policy, this high profile grows out of the intersection of complex economic, political, and international interests. Her essay looks particularly at two dimensions of American foreign policy in the Middle East: the role of the United States as a conflict manager and the scope of its military commitments expressed through arms sales and formal treaty arrangements. To explain the complex interests that give rise to active American involvement in managing the conflict, or, alternatively to periods of 'benign neglect', Steinberg looks back at the history of American policy to predict its future. Surprisingly, she finds that pursuit of detente with the Soviet Union did not lead to any particular strategy to manage the Arab-Israel conflict nor was it a better predictor of American military commitment in the region. However, when the United States regarded Soviet ambitions with hostility and expressed a strong interest in containing the Soviet Union, it generally did not commit itself to mediating the Arab-Israel conflict. Regional interests were also important in shaping American policy: as the importance of Arab oil and petrodollars grew, the scope of arms sales to both Israel and the Arab states increased dramatically. Steinberg suggests that if the Reagan administration moves away from confrontation politics with the Soviet Union, American diplomacy may enter a new and more vigorous phase of conflict mediation.

The United States and the Soviet Union are not the only major powers with strong interests in the Middle East. Western Europe in particular, with a long history of involvement in the region, has important political and economic interests at stake in the Middle East. Heavily dependent on oil, far more so than the United States, the West Europeans and the Japanese have focused their attention on ameliorating the Arab-Israel conflict to guarantee a secure supply of energy. Some observers suggest that the politics of oil have substantially altered policy toward the Arab-Israel conflict and exacerbated tensions within the alliance. The optic of energy-dependent Western Europe, they argue, is considerably different from that of the superpower and leader of the western alliance, and it is not at all surprising to find exasperation and temper on both sides of the Atlantic. The Arab-Israel dispute has become an issue in alliance politics.

Janice Gross Stein disputes these contentions in her look at the politics of alliance policy toward the Arab-Israel dispute. In a retrospective review of Canadian, European, Japanese, and American approaches to the management of the conflict in the last decade, she finds that substantive differences in policy and reputed tension within the western alliance were considerably exaggerated. Rather, similarities among alliance members were greater than their differences, this despite the varying degrees of energy dependence on and political involvement in the Middle East. The change in policy that did occur focused on the Palestinian dimension of the Arab-Israel conflict, but policy evolved on both sides of the Atlantic. More controversial were the different perspectives toward the management of the conflict. Europe and Japan emphasized comprehensive settlement and comprehensive participation in the negotiating process while the United States led the way in engineering settlement by stages with selective participation. Even these differences narrowed in the 'eighties, however, as the Reagan administration outlined its proposals for a settlement of almost all the outstanding issues in the dispute.

The final two essays in the volume take a closer look at the roots and the thrust of Canadian policy toward the Middle East. David Dewitt and John Kirton argue that Canadian policy has changed its focus, that it no longer responds to the dictates of liberal internationalism and the collective good. On the contrary, domestic factors have become far more important in the determination of policy and reinforce the pursuit of national interest through active bilateralism. Canada may well be one of many states, they suggest, who try to by-pass the Arab-Israel conflict and exploit the available opportunities in the Middle East. The active pursuit of self-interest is likely to shape policy in the 1980s.

The detailed examination of Canada's policy making process on anti-boycott legislation, by Howard Stanislawski, lends support to the central argument of Dewitt and Kirton. Canadian mandarins were unprepared for the intense interest of ethnic and business groups on an issue that encompassed both foreign and domestic policy. The alliance of interest groups calling for anti-boycott action constituted an unprecedented challenge to elite domination of the foreign policy process in Canada. Political leaders were forced to deal with a wide array of complex, intersecting, and competitive interests struggling to shape policy. The new emphasis by Canadian leaders on the pursuit of self-interest, defined largely in economic terms, Stanislawski argues, marks a fundamental shift in the thrust of Canadian foreign policy in the Middle East.

The conclusion to the volume looks at the range of forces that link the Middle East to the wider international community. Energy, collective military action that cuts across the borders of the region, and a resurgent Islam, all create new challenges to the creation of a stable and peaceful order in the Middle East. The two superpowers have been more active in clarifying the limits of acceptable military action within the region than in creating a shared consensus on the dynamics and determinants of peace. The major powers — the West Europeans, Canada, and Japan — are increasingly assertive, however, in the pursuit of their own interests in the region and, consequently, provide some alternative to the sharp conflict between the superpowers of the last two decades. Ultimately, however, peace rests on the capacity of the parties in direct confrontation, the Israelis and the Palestinians, to recognize each other's national existence. Leaders within the Middle East must come to recognize and pursue the enormous promise of peace, prosperity, and justice.

Part I
REGIONAL FORCES

OPEC: PAST, PRESENT AND FUTURE

Sally F. Zerker
Division of Social Science, York University

History rarely provides an instance of distinct discontinuity, a moment where an event of weighty significance sharply demarcates economic and political realities as they exist before and after the occurrence. But just such a moment of discontinuity did occur in October 1973, when an upheaval in international trading relations, as the Shah of Iran put it, ended "the era of cheap oil for the industrialized world". For those whose social and industrial efficiencies were premised on low cost petroleum energy, the impact of a sudden expiration of cheap oil was decidedly disturbing. Its cause, however, was by and large a mystery, which magnified the fear and confusion prevalent at that time.

The one irrefutable reality which impressed itself on oil consumers was the escalating pace of oil price increases, from $3.01 per gallon at the start of the transformation in mid-October, to $11.65 on 1 January 1974, increases which seemed to have cyclonic and uncontrollable force. The severe economic consequences of the escalating prices brought the price-maker to the forefront of media and broad public attention for the first time. It quickly became known that the instrument behind this price revolution was an alliance of oil producing nations called the Organization of Petroleum Exporting Countries (OPEC). Although knowledge about OPEC's existence and activities had been previously available, as an institution it had been largely ignored, not only by the lay public but also by many scholarly and industrial specialists who had assessed it as a vociferous, pretentious, and generally innocuous organization.[1] Clearly that appraisal was no longer valid, if ever it had been. Moreover, this organization was also linked to political and military events in the Middle East through coincidental tactics undertaken by a sub-group within OPEC, called the Organization of Arab Petroleum Exporting Countries (OAPEC). Indeed it was these Arab members in OAPEC who helped trigger the crisis when they imposed an embargo against the United States and the Netherlands following their oil ministers' meeting in Kuwait on 17 October.[2] These two states were singled out for special punitive treatment because of their support for Israel prior to and during the October War which was then raging. All other consuming nations were also subjected to a program of supply constraint, as OAPEC nations pledged themselves to cut production by 10% the first month and then by 5% each subsequent month until they altered their policies to support Arab demands in their conflict with Israel.

Thus, Arab political objectives created short-run oil shortages which aided OPEC as a steep price escalator. Of course OPEC's success, then and later, was not merely a function of its own co-ordinated actions. Rather, it was due to world — and particularly U.S. — consumption of petroleum products, which by 1973 had grown to depend on OPEC output for more than 60% of its requirements.[3] Nevertheless, after the oil crisis, commentators devalued the importance of probable changes in demand resulting from the price revolution, and concentrated instead on OPEC's internal strengths as an effective "cartel". Analysis had swung to the opposite extreme. Limited attention to OPEC was replaced by widespread and ready identification of OPEC as an agency of wealth and power. But such stereotypical identification was, in some sense, not much better than the earlier state of ignorance, since both precluded careful and informed analysis. Therefore, it is not surprising that, almost a decade after the oil convulsions, outside of a select circle, knowledge about the nature, structure, and operation of OPEC remains painfully superficial.

Moreover, because of inadequate and often superficial analyses, we have recently been treated to yet another revaluation of OPEC, one which reverses the previous view, again without substantive foundation. Beginning early in 1982, as it became evident that world demand for petroleum, which had fallen 5½% in 1980 and an additional 4½% in 1981, was expected to continue to fall through 1982,[4] the prevailing prediction was that of OPEC's imminent demise. Analysts now stress the exogenous forces as the determining elements and portray OPEC as a helpless body, rendered powerless by forces beyond its control.

The question at issue is not whether the forecasters are right or wrong this time. The problem is that energy forecasting has been wrong most of the time and that the record has been "atrocious", as one expert asserted recently.[5] What is important is to discover the origin of the failure, since faulty forecasts have very serious consequences given the importance of energy costs and availability to production and distribution of material wealth. Clearly some enormous methodological failure must be corrected if we are not to replicate past errors. More narrowly, with respect to OPEC's role and prospects, we must carefully scrutinize the organization's structure and operation within a framework of real resource and demand conditions.

World Resource Base

Because oil is understandably seen as a finite resource, it has not been difficult to persuade the public that the oil consuming world is in critical danger of losing its main source of fuel and power. That is exactly the message which emanated from OPEC diplomats and oil company advertisements, starting with the price revolution in October 1973 and continuing throughout the remainder of the 1970s. Spokesmen justified higher oil prices — which quadrupled in the first few months and tripled again between 1979-1980 — on the grounds that they forced the conservation of a valuable and vital raw material which was approaching the end of its exploitable lifespan if consumption continued at the current rate.

Had that perspective on the future of oil come only from those directly involved in the industry, it might not have carried the weight it did because of the obvious conflict of interest. However, their position was supported by seemingly disinterested parties, by economists, government spokesmen, and consulting firms. In fact, such authorities, along with major oil company representatives, were recently the subject of a DELPHI-type poll which canvassed expert opinions as a basis for estimating ultimately recoverable conventional oil. The results of that survey upheld the view of imminent oil depletion, suggesting that the peek of world oil production had either already been passed, or at best, might be stretched to the year 1992.[6]

It is necessary here to distinguish between the concept of "proven reserves" and "ultimate resources". Pollsters addressed only the latter concept in their questions. Too often these two measurements are confused, and "proven reserves" are incorrectly used as a guide for evaluating future world resources. But "proven reserves" represent only *known* in-ground pools which have been identified by actual drilling operations and which are recoverable with known techniques at current levels of prices and costs. Therefore, they do not and cannot measure "ultimate resources", which refers to the proportion of a resource base (world-wide) producible under a specific set of technical and economic conditions. In Peter Odell's words, proven reserves represent "the working inventory of the industry and do not give any indication of the quantity of oil available for future use".[7] Our assessment of oil's future prospects must therefore deal with the much more difficult and uncertain dimension of ultimate resources.

Ferdinard Banks, an economist specializing in the resource field, argues the case of oil's early exhaustion and predicts the decrease of the world production of oil when there is still a large amount of recoverable oil in the ground.[8] He bases his analysis on the r/p ratio, which is the relationship between reserves to production. Banks explains that each oil field has a potential production rate that depends upon the size of the field, its geology, and its facilities for lifting and transporting oil. As a general rule it is uneconomical to produce more than 15% of the total recoverable oil in the fields of a country or region in any one year; to go beyond this would result in permanent damage to the usable life of the fields. This economic constraint then is fundamental to the exploitation of oil. Using a hypothetical construct, and assuming an r/p ratio of 15, Banks shows that production must fall below intended production within a few years of a field's operation, and that when production starts to fall, less than half the reserves are used up.[9] He then applies his hypothetical model to the real world. The resource data which Banks uses comes from a 1977 World Energy Conference where ultimate world resources were estimated at close to 2,000 billion barrels (bb).[10] At the time of that accounting, 361 bb had already been produced, 652 bb were listed as proven reserves, and 997 bb were in the probable-reserves category. It is significant that Banks takes this tabulation as final, asserting that thus far (1980) the results had not been challenged. (He erred, of which more later!) Banks concluded, after applying the principles derived from the r/p ratio and the lessons of his hypothetical model, that at best the world is approximately two decades away from the height of oil output (the year 2000), although it is more likely that we are less than one decade away (the late 1980s). His analysis leads to a very pessimistic outlook for continued expansion of oil output. Even at current rates of consumption, oil scarcities are on the horizon, and with economic recovery and higher rates of consumption, scarcities will develop more quickly. This analysis depends upon the assumption that the world's oil resource base and ultimate resources have been scientifically established and that their well-defined and small size precludes expansion of production beyond a few more years. Yet such confirmation is simply not available. On the contrary, the world's most active investigators of this problem and the source of most of our information over the past four decades since oil came into its own as a fuel, that is to say, the major international oil companies, have revealed not only their uncertainty on the question of ultimate resources, but have produced an inconsistent record of estimates over time.

An important new study looks closely at the profile of the oil companies' prognostications regarding the world resource base from 1950 to the present.[11] Peter Odell and Kenneth Rosing demonstrated both the variability and the contradictory character of the industry's evaluation of future supplies. From 1950 until the early 1970s, the majors considered the world's oil resource base to be so large as to be irrelevant to the question of the development of the oil industry.[12] "As far as the companies in the late 1960s and the early 1970s were concerned, the expansion of the industry's resources to whatever levels were required was essentially a function of their continued investment in the search for oil and their confident expectation that they would not only find more new petroliferous regions and more new fields in existing regions, but that recovery rates would steadily improve through both technological developments and the impact of improved economics...".[13] Then, in 1973, without explanation or justification, the industry's forecasters made a complete turnabout, changing from enthusiastic optimists to gloomy pessimists almost overnight. Significantly, that transformation coincided, more or less, with the price revolution. Since that time, the prevailing view within the industry, presented to the public by means of "public service" advertisements, is the currently-favoured proposition that the world hangs on the edge of an oil precipice; the beginning of the end is upon us.[14] This set of estimates by the oil companies — like that of Banks' — is also based on the very conservative estimate of world oil resources approximating 2,000 bb.

Odell and Rosing challenge that conservative figure and point to the fact that this estimate of 2,000 bb is not generally conceded except by those directly affected and influenced by the oil companies.[15] Alternate estimates have been made, however, by the Institut Français du Pétrole (1948), the International Institute for Applied Systems Analysis (1977), and the Soviet Union, among others. What emerges is a range of estimates in which 2,000 bb represents the lowest, most restricted concept of the world's ultimate resources. The middle range suggests conventional resources at between 4,000 and 6,000 bb, depending on the price consumers can afford to pay.[16] If one adds non-conventional oil to this volume, amounting to between 2,000 and 5,000 bb which should be recoverable in the near-future, the upper limit to this series of estimates reaches an expansive total of 11,000 bb. Significantly, the technology of non-conventional oil, which is usually mined rather than drilled, and where reserves relative to production are extremely large (e.g. Canadian tar sands), makes the concept of an r/p ratio completely irrelevant.

The authors have taken account of this series for their own calculations of the future of oil. They devised a complex mathematic model of analysis which interrelates and integrates three essential factors which bear on the potential production of oil: ultimate resources, annual additions to reserves, and cumulative uses. Their approach stresses the inter-dependence of contributing factors and also utilizes all the data available on ultimate resources. They represent their conclusions in the form of likelihoods rather than hard and fast forecasts, an approach which seems eminently reasonable, given the uncertain knowledge which characterizes the basic estimates. Odell and Rosing demonstrate that even with the most restrictive estimates for resource potential there is a far longer life for oil production than that currently suggested by the industry. They calculate a 90% chance that oil production will continue to grow until the year 2001, a 50% chance that it will grow until 2033, and a 10% chance that the peak will not arrive until 2072.[17]

It should be stressed that the size of the world's oil resources matters a great deal to the fortunes of OPEC. That organization's continuing success as an economic and political alliance will be directly affected by the quantity of oil in the ground and its availability. If total resources are small, OPEC's present holdings of oil reserves are clearly relatively more valuable than if the raw material can be expected to become more abundant. Today, OPEC reserves of roughly 450 bb account for approximately 60% of total world proven reserves.[18] Assuming the conservative resource case — i.e., 2,000 bb and peak production within a few years — OPEC's known raw oil assets represent almost 30% of ultimate resources (see Banks' figures above).

Whether or not OPEC's share of world reserves will rise or fall in the future will depend on the rate of new discoveries, but in all events the value of its present holdings will inevitably increase as it becomes more difficult and more costly to locate marginal deposits. Furthermore, according to this line of argument, there is no ground for believing that all new

23

discoveries will be external to OPEC; on the contrary, there is good reason to expect the Middle East and North Africa to remain a region with favourable potential.[19] Thus, the pessimistic resource case indicates a very strong bargaining position for a united OPEC, now and in the years ahead, especially once the peak production point is passed.

On the other hand, if the middle range rather than the minimal level of estimates are correct — i.e., 4,000 to 6,000 bb — OPEC's likelihood of continued predominance is more doubtful. Under such circumstances, probable-reserves represent 75% or more of ultimate resources. That means that far more oil is waiting to be found than has already been found. Some might contest reliance on these estimates for analysis, arguing that the largest and most accessible finds are the ones already discovered, and that even if much more oil remains hidden under the earth's crust, the cost of its exploitation rises with increasing difficulty in its extraction and as distances from established markets lengthen. However, the prospects for oil discovery are not quite that simple. In part, oil company estimates are as conservative as they are because historically oil companies have avoided development projects in politically sensitive areas; this is quite understandable, since capital always tries to minimize risks. But that is why, by and large, Latin American and third world countries have been neglected until now as areas of active exploration.[20] In turn, the existence of vast untapped regions in the world reinforces the position of those who estimate moderate or even large ultimate resources, estimates which suggest lower cost and less prohibitive barriers to future exploration and development.

No one can say with certainty whether more or larger new finds will be made in OPEC territories or in non-OPEC territories. At the present time, investment in the search for oil is rising in non-OPEC areas and falling in OPEC regions[21], and although there is no one-to-one relationship between investment dollars and additions to proven reserves, the probability of discovery is greatest where the money is being spent. For obvious reasons, the odds favour geologically-appropriate, previously unexplored regions, where investment in exploration is occurring. If the laws of chance hold, OPEC's share of oil reserves has a greater probability of falling as a proportion of the world's known petroleum.

Unfortunately we can never be exact about ultimate resources, since enormous expenditures of capital are required to identify reserves. Such expenditures are made either by private or by public enterprises. Private investors act in accordance with their profit maximizing objectives and therefore expend capital only as demand and supply conditions dictate. Public enterprises may have different goals from those of private corporations — they may, for example, look to petroleum production as a national economic stimulant or seek to develop their own resources for security reasons — but even public undertakings are constrained by such considerations as development costs, market prices for petroleum products, and opportunity costs for capital. Therefore, completely verified data regarding ultimate resources are not possible. In estimating ultimate resources, one must work with probabilities, which are appropriate as well for evaluating OPEC's supply situation in the future.

As we saw, Odell and Rosing have adopted just such an approach. They have pointed to a very strong possibility for continued growth in oil production over the next three decades, a moderate or even chance for expansion for six decades, and a very small chance in the longer term. How does this analysis relate to OPEC's prospects? Ultimate resources and OPEC's fortunes are inversely related; that is, the higher the probability of greater world oil supplies in the future, the less the likelihood that OPEC's current predominant position will remain intact. In addition, one must include in the analysis OPEC's growing internal consumption of hydrocarbons, which is expected to rise to six million barrels per day (mb/d) by 1990, and to three times that much by the year 2000, making OPEC countries comparable to current levels of U.S. consumption.[22] Rising consumption cannot fail to have an impact on the organization's capacity to export. These two developments — increased domestic use and expanded non-OPEC sources — translate into a general long-run weakening of the combine's bargaining power, which will undermine its ability to unilaterally determine prices for the international oil industry. It is against this background that we turn our attention to OPEC itself.

OPEC's Rise to Power

When the Organization of Petroleum Exporting Countries was established in 1960, its founders defined its functions in strictly economic terms. However, its roots derive from Arab political institutions; it was the Political Committee of the Arab League — organized in 1945 to resist the creation of a Jewish state in Palestine — which pioneered co-operation in oil policy by sponsoring a Committee of Oil Experts, a committee which met for the first time on 14 June 1952.[23] The Arab League created a committee on oil to co-ordinate Arab oil policy as a complement to the League's economic boycott of Israel; it was designed to prevent the export of oil to that country. To assist the Committee of Oil Experts, the League introduced a permanent Department of Oil Affairs, and tellingly, that department remained a subordinate of its Political Committee until 1964. The Oil Department subsequently initiated and sponsored Arab oil congresses to discuss issues related to petroleum production and export. Thus, the incentive for initial collaboration on oil policy by Middle Eastern countries was primarily political.[24]

The first Arab Oil Congress was held in Cairo in April 1959, at a time when leaders of the oil exporting countries were incensed over the recently announced reduction in posted or reference prices which had been unilaterally imposed by the major oil companies. These prices were set by the companies and used as the basis for calculating payment of income tax and royalties to the host governments.[25] In February, just two months before the oil congress met, this reference price was dropped by 18¢ a barrel, amounting to 8% of the current rate.[26]

Why did the companies arbitrarily — and some would say arrogantly — take measures certain to arouse resentment among oil producers? A number of interpretations have been offered to explain the depression of prices in 1959 and again in 1960 by the oil companies. Venezuelan leaders argued that the companies had reduced their prices to retaliate against its tax increase on its domestic oil concessionaires. Venezuela had raised its tax from 52% to 65% on 19 December 1958.[27] Then-President Romulo Betancourt subsequently wrote that the U.S. government was prompted by the oil companies when it instituted an import quota system on 11 March 1959, thereby drastically limiting Venezuelan exports to its major market. One should note, however, that whatever the effect of the new regulation on Venezuelan interests, no serious student of the subject would agree that those new U.S. regulations were undertaken as a punitive measure against that country. Indeed, they were designed to limit the competition of cheap Middle Eastern oil and thereby protect domestic American producers.[28] Nevertheless, Betancourt's analysis of American action as punitive induced him, as he said, to seek closer ties with the Arabs, "with a view to setting up not what might be called a cartel but an agreement between producing countries to turn against the cartel of oil companies."[29] Both Venezuela and Iran were invited to participate in the first Arab Oil Congress, and the invitation coincided with Betancourt's estimate that inter-country co-operation was the best alternative to company domination.[30] For their part, the Arab producers also recognized their interdependence with other exporting nations. At no time had their output exceeded 30% of world demand; alone they could not command the international market. They understood that they had to look beyond the framework of the Arab League.

Oil company executives were also present at the congress. But representatives of Iran, Venezuela, Iraq, Kuwait, and Saudi Arabia slipped away during the Congress — to escape the notice of company men — ostensibly to enjoy the pleasure of a sailing party on the Nile. While on board they signed a "top secret agreement" regarding mutual co-operation. That pact was the precursor to the founding of OPEC the following year, for as Abdullah Tariki, the Saudi oil minister of that era conceded, the idea of OPEC owes its existence to the first Arab Oil Congress.[31]

This analysis of the motives behind company-imposed price reductions and the responses of the host governments to the reductions stresses concentrated power and its exploitive use by the companies for unrestrained gain. A second interpretation emphasizes the demand and supply conditions which the industry faced after 1957, when posted price for the market crude was raised from $1.97 to $2.12.[32] The record shows that this higher price did not hold, as competition forced the companies to offer discounts and other concessions to attract business. A number of factors account for the introduction of competitive forces after 1957. Some analysts suggest that it was the entry of newcomers into the international oil industry, principally American independents beyond the majors' control, whose invasion of foreign markets disrupted the "well-ordered" operation that had prevailed until then.[33] However, M.A. Adelman, a prominent authority on the oil industry, argues that the newcomers' share was too small in the late fifties and early sixties to have any impact on prices; rather it was the old internationals who cut prices.[34] This interpretation is supported by the admission of an Exxon executive that the majors began offering sizeable discounts below posted prices.[35]

But other developments in the industry cumulatively influenced the price downward. The Soviet Union was trying to break into markets outside of the Soviet bloc through price competition, forcing the majors to defend their share of the market with cash discounts. The Japanese market also experienced some stiff competition as Nippon Oil, a joint venture with Caltex, became more important. The majors could not reduce their output in the Middle East because the host governments were intent on maintaining and expanding their national revenues. And finally, the U.S.A. closed all but 10% of its market to foreign imports (other than Canadian) when it instituted the quota system. The American government's protectionist policy softened world prices in 1959-60, both because it lowered demand and because the eight majors could no longer use U.S. prices to administer Middle East prices in unison.

These were the conditions that prevailed when the first reduction in posted prices was imposed in February 1959 and, with no relief from competitive pressures, the majors implemented a second unilateral reduction of 10¢ a barrel in August 1960.[36] It is not difficult to imagine how the host countries felt about this additional loss in income and affront to their sovereignty. With the groundwork already laid during their sail on the Nile, they prepared to take more combative steps. Annoyed more by the lack of consultation than by the price cut itself, even the Shah of Iran overcame his usual objections to participation in an organization dominated by Arab countries and joined the world's four other largest oil exporters — Iraq, Kuwait, Saudi Arabia, and Venezuela — to establish a permanent organization "with a view to co-ordinating and unifying the policies of the Members."[37]

These five founding members understood that their collective bargaining power was directly related to the share their joint production had of world demand. They were anxious therefore, to bring other exporters with significant volume into the organization, on condition that they were unanimously approved by the original members. OPEC quickly expanded to its present complement of 13 members: four additional non-Arab participants — Indonesia, Nigeria, Ecuador, and Gabon — and four new Arab members — Qatar, United Arab Emirates, Algeria, and Libya — joined in subsequent years.

One might say — and many have — that OPEC was born of resistance to oppression and exploitation. These terms, however, need definition and clarification. If oppression and exploitation refer to limited sovereignty and restricted control of national resources, there can be no dispute about the correctness of that assessment. If, on the other hand, these terms suggest increasing material deprivation, the argument would be very difficult to sustain. The evidence does not show that the share of producing countries was squeezed more and more and that they earned less and less, either relatively or absolutely.

Data for all the majors' payments are not available for all the relevant years, but available information does suggest a definite trend, a dramatic increase in both per unit returns and total revenues for the host countries in the decade prior to the establishment of OPEC. From the time that a 50:50 profit sharing formula was introduced in 1950, producers realized a sharp improvement in their take. Thus, Aramco's payment to Saudi Arabia represented only 17¢ per barrel of oil in 1946-7, rose to 28¢ in 1950-1, advanced steadily to a high of 96¢ in 1955, slipped back to 80¢ during 1957-8 and 74¢ in 1959.[38] However one reads these data, even taking the worst return at the end of the decade, on a per barrel basis, Saudi Arabia's earnings almost tripled from the beginning to the end of the decade. This expansion occurred while the price of oil changed only slightly; posted prices for 36° API crude were set at $1.75 in 1949, $1.97 in 1953, $2.12 in 1957, and $1.94 in 1959.[39] Nor did the general price level inflate commensurately with per barrel advances; wholesale prices rose in the United States by 19% between 1949 and 1960, by less than 20% in Germany, and by 65% in the United Kingdom where inflationary problems were more intense.[40] In addition, overall company payments to the four Middle Eastern governments expanded by 400 to 500 % through the decade of the 1950s. Table I supports this claim.

Payments to Host Governments Under 50-50 Profit Sharing, 1950-64 (/ millions)

Year	Aranco (Saudi Arabia)	IPC/MPC/BPC (Iraq)	KOC (Kuwait)	Consortium (Iran)
1950	20.2			
1951	39.3	15.2	6.4	
1952	75.8	40.7	20.4	
1953	60.6	51.4	60.4	
1953	83.9	68.5	69.3	3.1
1955	120.8	73.8	100.7	32.3
1956	102.4	69.2	104.6	54.8
1957	102.3	51.5	110.0	76.0
1958	102.6	84.6	126.4	88.3
1959	105.5	86.8	146.1	93.7
1960	111.7	95.4	147.1	101.9
1961	125.8	95.1	156.7	107.6
1962	136.3	95.1	160.0	119.2
1963	149.5	110.0	177.5	137.4
1964	172.2	126.1	184.2	171.5

Source: **Mikdashi**, *A Financial Analysis of Middle Eastern Oil Concessions: 1901-65, p.177.*

Moreover, the host governments' share of profits actually was greater than the established 50:50 ratio; it was closer to 55:45 or even 60:40 in their favour, and the trend in this direction began before the founding of OPEC.[41]

One must conclude that the producers' incentive and ability to organize came not from weakness but from strength, which should surprise no one familiar with the history of workers' collectives.[42] Adelman wrote that "it is axiomatic that a good discovery means a dissatisfied landlord who wishes he had held out for more. He will look around for any possible way of getting more."[43] Those "good discoveries" in the Middle East and Venezuela, combined with augmented returns, transferred significant potential power to the landlords, power which could be mobilized through combination and unified policy.

OPEC had a beneficial effect on its members' welfare from the start, both in terms of their ability to intervene in the international decision-making process on petroleum and in their total incomes from oil (see Table I). Firstly, the emergence of a collaborative institution froze prices at their August 1960 level; there are strong indications that the downward thrust would have continued in its absence.[44] Secondly, in 1962, OPEC began renegotiating the terms for royalty payments, requiring as part of a package of demands that royalties be treated as company costs of production rather than, as was the case until then, as credit against company income tax liability. That is to say, OPEC proposed to expense royalties rather than to treat them as income tax, a procedure which would have meant a 12% rise in company payments while other factors — such as posted price and royalty rate — remained the same.[45] Most members of OPEC were satisfied with the results of these negotiations, which stretched over a number of years,[46] and as a result, payments per barrel rose in the mid-1960s throughout the Middle East.[47] Thirdly, another round of OPEC/company negotiations in 1966-7 provided for phasing out of allowable discounts through to 1973; this would have added another 7 (+/- 2)¢ to the company per barrel charge.[48]

One must use the subjunctive to describe the benefits of these negotiations because OPEC took additional steps three years before all the benefits were due in full. OPEC approached the 1970s with a much clearer sense of its potency, and a much better understanding of market forces. Both from a psychological point of view and with respect to the realities of the international petroleum market, 1970 was a turning point. The organization had a decade of experience and confidence, just as the U.S. became a net importer of oil rather than a net exporter, putting great strains on existing capacities.[49] During 1969-70, demand in Western Europe for oil products also increased more rapidly than anticipated. In addition, Tapline, the pipeline carrying oil from Saudi Arabia through Syria, was sabotaged and shut down.[50] All these elements created a sellers' market, and the sellers were organized and ready to manipulate the new situation to their advantage.

It took a maverick, however, to shatter traditional approaches to the oil companies and Libya's Qaddafi was that maverick. After a series of threats, he won higher payments from his concessionaires in September 1970, and other Middle East rulers immediately followed. This was an instructional experience of immense significance, for it taught the producers who held the levers of power. When OPEC's 21st conference convened in December 1970, the lessons learned earlier that year were translated into firm demands for higher prices and taxes as well as an inflation escalator. This time negotiations did not drag on for years. On the contrary, only two months later, on 14 February 1971, a deal was signed between 22 western oil companies and the Persian Gulf producing countries. Leapfrogging methods won even better terms for Libya in an agreement signed in Tripoli on 2 April.[51] These new packages meant a combined royalty plus tax increase to the Gulf producers amounting to 47¢ per barrel (from June 1971 to December 1972), and a rise of between 65¢ and 80¢ to Libya.[52]

The Tehran-Tripoli experience demonstrated to OPEC, as nothing before had done, the power of unified action. Collective action seemed so successful that it was possible to overlook or discount the significance of the existence of a sellers' market. Meanwhile, the companies found themselves in a transformed world and they did not know quite how to behave. They wavered, they vascillated, afraid to challenge the producers for fear of losing desirable supplies, and were unable to forge a common front. Perhaps it would not have mattered if they had managed to work in concert, or perhaps they had no desire to interfere in OPEC's price inflation because it organized the market for them and raised their profits. In any case, the oil world had shifted in favour of those who owned this seemingly scarce resource. John Blair believes corporate weakness made a difference. "The real impact of this unsuccessful effort at corporate solidarity", he wrote, "was not economic but psychological. Faced with a determined show of opposition, the companies had for the first time capitulated not once but twice...a lesson whose significance was not lost upon the colonels of Libya or the kings and sheiks of the Middle East."[53]

These rulers, thus enlightened, proceeded to elaborate and increase demands for producer participation and additional rounds of price hikes, one in January 1972 and another of 11.9% in June 1973. In September 1973, a month before the October War broke out, Sheik Yamani, Saudi Arabia's oil minister, declared the Tehran-Tripoli agreements void. This was a blow to the companies and to the U.S. State Department which had drafted teams of negotiators to help keep the oil market "orderly". Yamani's announcement was even more shattering, however, for he made it clear that prices would once again be unilaterally determined, but henceforth the price-maker would be OPEC rather than the companies. Thus OPEC had taken over the reigns of power in the international oil industry, and the stage was set for the OAPEC boycott and the price revolution.

OPEC in Operation

It is convenient to refer to OPEC as a cartel. It seems like a cartel, especially because it has managed to establish prices which are an approximation of the monopoly price.[54] Yet OPEC is not in fact a cartel because it does not function like one. Cartels raise prices by some form of co-ordinated output controls, by quotas or prorationing which are agreed upon by all parties to the compact. Once there was such a formal cartel in the oil industry, from 1928 to about 1939, when the big three of that era — Standard oil of New Jersey, (Exxon), Shell, and BP — divided the oil markets through a series of written agreements.[55] But the combine we know today as OPEC does not manage its affairs in that way.

In the 1960s, under the leadership of Saudi Arabia's Tariki and Venezuela's Alfonzo, an attempt was made to set up a prorationing scheme, but by 1966 it was obvious to its supporters and opponents alike that the plan had failed.[56] Apportioning shares among countries is an enormously difficult task, as one might well imagine. By what criterion, for example, should shares be distributed? The countries with large reserves argue that quotas should be calculated as a percentage of proven reserves, while countries with large populations and heavy economic burdens want shares to be based on some criterion of need. When OPEC rose to prominence in the early 1970s, the organization could well afford to leave such troublesome questions aside, since world demand was large enough to absorb the desired output of every producer and the production capacity of OPEC crude constituted over 60% of the non-communist world's capacity.[57] Consequently, the combine did not need to and indeed did not designate any system of quotas for its participants. On the contrary, reliable evidence points to great variability of market shares among members of OPEC following the price revolution.[58] Therefore, it is clear that OPEC did not have the characteristics of a cartel.

How then has it managed to keep prices well above the competitive price? Edward Erickson and Herbert Winokur argue that OPEC operates like an oligopolistic industry with Saudi Arabia as the price leader: "Dominant price leadership, as with a cartel, also results in a restriction of output. But unlike a cartel, the restriction is passive rather than active. No quota system is required. There is no explicit allocation of market shares among firms. Concerted and co-ordinated action to prorate output is not a part of the behaviour pattern because it is unnecessary. The dominant firm, or the balance wheel of the system, takes up the slack."[59]

Saudi Arabia is admirably suited to assume the role (or carry the burden, as the case may be) of price leader. As with oligopolistic industries, the price leader should be the participant with the lowest costs and the largest capacity. Saudi production costs have historically been amongst the lowest in the world,[60] and its technical ability to expand and contract output rapidly has been particularly evident in recent months, when its output reached 10.3 mb/d in August 1981 and fell to 5.5 mb/d exactly one year later.[61]

Price leaders are not chosen by the others in the industry or combine; this is not a democratic procedure. Rather, it is a question of the leader's ability to set a price and make it stick. The leader fixes the price which in turn determines total demand. Each member takes that share of the total which it can or is willing to handle. How each one determines its appropriate volume will depend on a host of factors including contractual arrangements, production capacity, long-term resource maximization, and revenue requirements. Once all the participants make their commitments, Saudi Arabia must be willing to make up the residual, aiming to create the most desirable situation where supply is just short of demand.[62] If the demand for oil is so great that the followers producing at full capacity cannot satisfy consumers, the leader must expand its output to fill the gap (almost) between total demand and the others' volume of production. In that way the market stays stable and calm, even at prices much higher than competitive price. On the other hand, if for any reason demand slumps — the price may have been set so high that levels of consumption drop — Saudi Arabia must be prepared to produce less and earn less, again matching its output to the difference between the volume sold by all the followers taken together and total demand. In other words, the price leader makes its leadership stick by being the supplier of last resort.

At this point in the discussion, one could suggest that distinguishing between one manner of monopoly price-setting and another is quibbling over semantics. However, these differences are enormously important both in the analysis of why and when a particular system runs into difficulties and in the assessment of possibilities for redress. For OPEC and Saudi Arabia, the oligopolistic model worked extremely well as long as the price level did not cut into their joint preferred volumes. There are generally very few problems on the upside; the problems which arise when all the partners are working to capacity are the kind nobody minds very much. But when consumption contracts and the system has to adjust to lower volumes, the lot of the price leader becomes much more burdensome. Suppose the price leader establishes a price so high that the total demand for OPEC exports is less than the group's minimum target. Then Saudi Arabia, as the balance wheel, has the choice of either lowering prices or reducing its own share. If the leader attempts to hold the higher price and continues to sell more than the residual demand, some members will have to shade their own prices — by offering discounts or entering the spot market — in order to receive the revenue they regard as essential. Obviously, that development fractures the organization's solidarity and threatens the basis of its power.

32

A cartel faces these contingencies in a totally different way. Its survival depends on retaining and protecting the quota system, which also can be a formidable assignment; with prices above the marginal cost of production there are powerful incentives to cheat.[63] But the weight of the burden of adjustment is distributed throughout the system, and whether the market is expanding or contracting there must be the same degree of vigilance to defend against the disrupting chiseler.

In theory, the oligopolistic price leader must be prepared to reduce its own output to zero, at least until such time as downward price flexibility returns consumers to the market. In practice, neither price nor output are that adaptable. The leader's authority is in the balance on the one hand, and its income is at issue on the other. It has no wish to see its traditional markets taken over by other producers and there are contractual arrangements with marketing firms which should be honoured. Moreover, reducing the over-inflated price may not garner the desired new buyers of oil because, in the interim, structural changes have been made on a wide scale to alternative forms of energy. The essential weakness of the oligopolistic model is its leader's and followers' attraction to a destructively high price on the upside which cannot easily be mended on the downside.

Additionally, the oligopolistic approach does not entirely avoid complications resulting from its members' varying production capacities and revenue requirements, even when there is no attempt to establish quotas. One study distinguishes between OPEC participants on the basis of the respective degree of their market power, their individual need for revenue, and their reserve holdings.[64] Those with strong market power — holding approximately 20% of total OPEC output — include Saudi Arabia and, until the Iranian revolution, Iran as well. Those with moderate market power — who account for between 5 and 10 percent of OPEC's sales — include Kuwait, Libya, Iraq, Venezuela, Nigeria, Indonesia, UAE, and now Iran. Four countries have weak market power — Qatar, Gabon, Ecuador, and Algeria — with less than 5 percent of OPEC production.

Market power indicates physical and technical potential. Need for revenue reflects the individual participant's ability to absorb export earnings. Thus for example, Saudi Arabia, with a population of approximately 8 million, has a very different and much lower capacity to absorb revenue than does Iran, with its population of 33 million. Kuwait and UAE also have high reserve to population ratios and therefore low absorptive capacities, while Indonesia and Nigeria have the opposite profile. Therefore, there can be no uniform opinion within the group about the best level of price and output. Saudi Arabia, with reserves of approximately 146 bb (33% of OPEC's total reserves) and a low absorptive capacity, has an interest in long-term stable commitment to oil by consumers and therefore prefers a lower price and larger output. But Iran, with its high absorptive capacity and smaller reserves, opts for higher

33

prices and lower volumes. Kuwait and UAE should easily fall into line with Saudi Arabia, given their respective reserve/absorptive capacities, while Nigeria and Venezuela should share Iran's preference structure.

Thus it is a mistake to view OPEC as a monolith. To do so is to miss the extremely significant internal variants which pull members in different, at times opposite, directions. A pricing policy which suits a country with large reserves and low absorptive capacity will not satisfy one with small reserves and a large population in dire need. Frank Wyant believes that OPEC worked as well as it did for a decade because those countries which needed more revenues and had the absorptive capacity tended also to be the ones with the least potential to expand production. Conversely, members who preferred less than maximum current earnings were also the ones who were most adaptable in terms of output. That is to say, the need to have and the ability to absorb oil revenues was inversely related to the desire and capacity to increase production.[65]

The OPEC formula, which was so effective through the 1970s, will not necessarily function with the same ease or success once conditions change in response to that success. However, one errs if one assumes that a new economic environment inevitably means the collapse of the organization. Whether or not OPEC continues to be as powerful in the 1980s as it was in the last decade will depend on its adaptability, either within the framework of its present structure, or its capacity to move to an alternative model of internal control, one more closely allied to the operations of a cartel. Moreover, OPEC's future will also be shaped by the physical, technical, and economic factors which will determine the size of ultimate resources and the potential for continuing high levels of petroleum exploitation.

OPEC Today and Tomorrow

Pressure on the organization to become more flexible intensified toward the end of the 1970s. Severe convulsions in petroleum markets began at the end of 1978 when political turmoil in Iran sent a nervous spasm through the entire oil world. Iran was then the world's second largest crude exporter and fourth largest producer, averaging an output of 5.5 mb/d or just over 9% of world crude oil. Industry publications reported speculation that there might be a 60% shortfall in Iranian crude liftings.[66] A general uneasiness set in as buyers worried that Iranian deficiencies could not be compensated for from other sources, especially since global (non-communist) consumption was already at a record 49.6 mb/d.[67]

The industry's most pessimistic prognosis, however, understated the dislocation in oil markets that did occur. Iranian oil fields were shut down by striking workers in support of the exiled Ayatollah Khomeini, and the country's exports fell to nil by the end of the year. The shock waves spread. Saudi Arabia did cushion the shock at least partly; it performed as a balance wheel should and boosted its output from 9.3 mb/d in August

34

1978 to 10.3 mb/d in November 1979, and still higher again in December.[68] That year, the Saudis surpassed the ceiling of 8.5 mb/d they had originally set.

Although OPEC production proved to be very flexible, increasing from 29.88 mb/d in 1978 to 31.22 mb/d in 1979, buyers, acting in fear, nevertheless scrambled for supplies. Their actions became a self-fulfilling prophecy, as merchants and traders jousted for oil on the spot market in anticipation of shortages, thereby ensuring the shortages they sought to avoid. A pricing frenzy followed, and oil companies, governments of importing countries, and independent traders built up their stocks to hedge against further price escalations.[69]

By the end of the year, official OPEC pricing was irrelevant. The organization's target for 1979 had been a 14.5% increase, raising the $12.70 per barrel market price for 34° Arabian light to $14.54 over four quarterly installments. But by mid-year those targets had been surpassed. Saudi Arabia agreed to a new level of $18 and officially announced that all the parties would hold the line at $23.50. The unified structure — if not completely abandoned — was modified and the price leader stressed only the maximum allowable charge.

Unfortunately for the solidarity of OPEC, individual members chose to go their own way and to sell at the highest prices offered. By the beginning of 1980, Arab light was valued at $39 a barrel in the spot market and governments were sending more and more of their output into that attractive market; between 15 and 20 % of the world's oil moved through such arms-length deals compared to 5% earlier. The international oil market developed a three-tier pricing structure, with a lower tier represented by so-called moderates, including Saudi Arabia, a middle-tier of sellers asking official prices plus premiums, and an upper-tier established by spot prices. The market was chaotic, with oil refiners paying anywhere from $20 to $40 a barrel, depending on the quality, the country of origin, and whether the purchase was through contract or at arms-length.[70]

Throughout this rapid escalation in prices, OPEC producers seemed little concerned about the short- and long-run consequences. Most participants objected to Saudi Arabia's desire to restrain prices at $32 a barrel for the marker crude. In its "moderate" policy, Saudi Arabia was clearly pursuing its best short- and long-run interests, given its reserve/absorptive capacity situation. Other OPEC members preferred another strategy: they believed that together they could easily implement counter-measures to handle the curtailment in consumption which could result from the tripling of prices between 1979-80. This view was strengthened when the war between Iran and Iraq broke out in September 1980. Because of the fighting, not only would Iran not return quickly to its former market strength, but Iraq would inevitably reduce exports as well. Also, OPEC earnings per unit had multiplied manifold, so that even the countries with high absorptive capacity could afford to reduce production and exports. OPEC members decided that each would contribute to overall well-being by committing itself to a production cut. Saudi Arabia agreed to reduce by 1 mb/d, Kuwait by 0.8 mb/d, Iraq by 0.6 mb/d, and so on. OPEC analysts estimated that the fall-out from the latest price escalation would effect a 2 to 3 mb/d drop in demand, an amount that was quite manageable given OPEC's constraining tactics.[71]

As the Gulf War intensified, internal optimism about OPEC's future prospects soared and members grew more confident about their ability to contain supply. OPEC production data for 1980 show that its total output was on average 6 mb/d less than the previous year, reduced to 25.4 mb/d. Only Saudi Arabia increased its exports, in an effort to compensate for losses from the war zone, reaching a high of 10.4 mb/d in October 1980.[72]

But to almost everyone's surprise — both OPEC analysts and forecasters of consuming governments — the demand side of the equation was sliding far below expectations. By the end of 1981, OPEC tried to stem the tide by unifying the price once again at a compromise $34 a barrel Arabian light.[73] But it was too little, too late. Even with OPEC's reinstated unified price structure, consumption continued to tumble. The industrial economies were struggling with high energy costs and the related problems of rapid inflation and exorbitant interest rates. Governments tried to cope with the economic crisis through tight money policies, which compounded the crisis and pushed the western world into an economic recession.

The severe consequences of the seventeen-fold price increase in oil prices since 1972 should now have been apparent for all to see. In the short-run, when consumers are locked in through earlier expenditures for equipment and transport facilities to a particular kind of energy, a steep increase in its price will have a less than proportional impact on demand (i.e. inelastic demand in the short-run). But over a longer period, defined as the time required to adjust technology to use of lower-cost fuel, the effects of such dramatic price rises are neither temporary nor small. At the beginning of 1981, it should have been apparent to OPEC observers and oil company analysts that the short-run influence of the recent escalations coincided with the long-run responses to earlier price developments. The oil market was undergoing widespread and deep structural changes,[74] reduced demand for petroleum products, and the development of non-OPEC petroleum for production and export.

However, neither OPEC nor company executives read the signals right. OPEC's Long-term Strategy Committee continued to see its own maximum capacity of 35 mb/d as well below that required to satisfy the West's demand.[75] Oil company forecasters, at the beginning of 1982, conceded a slowing down of growth in demand for oil but did not recognize an absolute decline. Exxon, Texaco, Socal, BP, and Royal Dutch/Shell all scaled down their expectations drastically, but still anticipated that world demand would move steadily upward from 47 mb/d to 50.7 mb/d in 1985, and 52.5 mb/d in 1990. These predictions were based on estimates of between 2.5 and 3.5 % growth in GNP.[76]

By all the indicators, these estimates were overly optimistic. Economic growth for the industrial countries as a whole was 1.8% through 1981.[77] World oil consumption had fallen absolutely by 9% over the two previous years, while U.S. use dropped by 6.2% and its imports fell even more.[78] A few analysts cautioned that such sanguine hopes for the oil industry and OPEC were self-delusionary, but their voices fell on deaf ears.[79] When OPEC members convened their 62nd Conference in December 1981, they made minor revisions to the price structure, but they paid almost no attention to the inescapable market realities.[80] Yet, within three months, non-OPEC producers were offering oil at $4 discounts and Iran, Iraq, and Venezuela were doing likewise.[81]

How was the balance wheel responding to these new developments? In one sense Saudi Arabia performed well. Quietly and without fanfare it reduced its output to under 8 mb/d by January 1982 and continued cutting beyond that.[82] But in another respect, it was unrealistic in its insistence on solidarity at the $34 benchmark rate even while price desertions were evident and ongoing. Saudi Arabian reduction in its output was no longer sufficient to make room for its partners' preferred or necessary shares, particularly as Iran re-entered the oil market in force to pay for its lengthy and costly war with Iraq. As OPEC sales plummetted (from 31.3 mb/d in 1977 to 19 mb/d in early 1982),[83] Saudi Arabia was taking almost half the total demand. The Saudis tried to reassure their collaborators in OPEC by announcing a cut in production to 7.5 mb/d, but this gesture was greeted with cynicism for, as one trader commented, "Who are they kidding? Everyone knows they aren't producing all that much anyway."[84]

The weakest link in the OPEC chain was Nigeria, with its population of 80 million and a five-year development plan committing the country to expenditures of $125 billion, to be paid for almost entirely from oil export earnings.[85] Saudi Arabia could try to force its traditional customers in Aramco to buy Nigerian oil at high rates — which it did — but it was a stop-gap approach and ultimately insufficient.[86] The Nigerian issue was only a manifestation of a far more serious problem.

OPEC members convened an emergency meeting in March of 1982; at that meeting they took steps to become a cartel by introducing a production ceiling for all members of 17.5 mb/d, establishing shares for each country, and instituting a monitoring committee. Immediately, however, friction surfaced, for the Saudi share was set at 7 mb/d, leaving only 10.5 mb/d for all the others, and Iran refused to accept its quota of 1.2 mb/d.[87] Iran insists that Saudi overproduction is the cause of OPEC's difficulties and that it is entitled to part of Saudi Arabia's large production quota.[88] Iran has some sympathy among Arab members of OPEC. Even some Arab leaders, who fear and resent Iran's military actions and its successes against Iraq, nevertheless support Iran's stand on production shares and argue that Saudi Arabia should limit its sales and earnings.

Under the best of circumstances — that is, when all the participants agree to the terms of the compact — cartels are difficult institutions to manage and hold together. OPEC attempted cartelization over the opposition of some of its members and therefore it comes as no surprise that those who opposed their quotas soon rebelled. Libya, Nigeria, and Venezuela, as well as Iran, had produced more than their respective quotas by June.[89] The monitoring committee had no power to act. The attempt at cartelization did not succeed in equipping OPEC's members to face the new economic realities.

At the present time, OPEC faces very difficult choices between policies which are not very attractive. They might lower prices hoping to reverse earlier conversions away from oil and to stimulate the economies of their customers. But because so many of the poorer members face an economic crisis of their own — Nigeria, Ecuador, Venezuela and Indonesia have all been gravely affected by the recession and the collapse in the oil market — it would be very difficult to persuade them to reduce their export earnings still further. The richer participants also reject this approach because it exposes the organization's weakness and undermines its claim to compensation in accordance with the inflation rate in industrial countries. A more popular alternative requires Saudi Arabia to respond responsibly as price leader to the appropriate residual supply. Saudi Arabia, of course, does not appear ready to reduce its own output to that of other moderate producers; its current level of 5.5 mb/d still takes over 30% of the group's sales.

Whether OPEC chooses to continue along the oligopolistic path or tries to transform itself into a cartel that works, Saudi Arabia is the key. In either case, until the world demand for oil recovers (if it does in the near future), the Saudis must shoulder the burden and agree to a distribution that the other members of OPEC consider fair. At this writing, Iran, Iraq, and Libya who all insist that the Saudi share is too large, are trying to enlarge their share by undercutting the Saudi Arabian price ($34).[90] The surplus countries, with low absorptive capacities — that is, Saudi Arabia, Kuwait, and UAE — are pitted against the African countries, the warring Gulf countries, and Venezuela; the growing rift within the organization is becoming obvious to all.[91] Undoubtedly, the weak market for oil is the external source of friction, but the rejection by the followers of the leader's current price and indigenous production schedule suggests deep-rooted internal division as well.

If Saudi Arabia is unwilling to compromise, neither oligopoly nor cartel will produce the solidarity which is essential to a collective bargaining institution and was a significant factor in OPEC's original rise to power. Without that kind of major adjustment, logic points to a continued waning of its earlier prominence. OPEC's position has already slipped to less than 45% of (non-communist) world consumption.[92] Moreover, since OPEC's political influence on the international scene varies directly with its economic power, the quality of Saudi Arabian leadership within the organization will affect not only economic policy but Arab political options as well. Libya's recent call for an oil boycott to punish the United States for its support of Israel during the war in Lebanon, for example, was treated by other OPEC members as yet further evidence of Qaddafi's unreliability. For the moment, the Arab oil weapon is dead; OPEC producers now need oil revenue more than the United States needs oil.[93] Undoubtedly, Saudi Arabia's petrodollar surplus will continue to attract and influence American policy-makers, but ultimately Saudi Arabia's power base rests on its leadership of OPEC, and if it is to maintain that base, it must be prepared to deny itself if necessary. If Saudi Arabia does not, it jeopardizes its own power as well as the future of OPEC.

FOOTNOTES

1 John M. Blair, *The Control of Oil* (New York: Vintage Books, 1978), p.262.

2 Robin C. Landes and Michael W. Klass, *OPEC: Policy Implications for the United States* (New York: Praeger Publishers, 1980), p.33. Abu Dhabai was first to announce the embargo on 18 October, followed by Libya on the 19th, Saudi Arabia and Algeria on the 20th, and Kuwait, Bahrain,Qatar, and Dubai on the 21st.

3 Arnold E. Safer, *International Oil Policy* (Toronto: Lexington Books, 1979), p.22.

4 E. Stanley Tucker, "End of a Slump in Demand?", *Petroleum Economist*, September 1982, p.353.

5 See *Petroleum Economist*, August 1982, p. 310, and September 1982, p.355; also *Wall Street Journal*, 5 May 1982, "More or Less Oil Will Go Up or Down or Maybe It Won't."

6 Proceedings of OPEC Seminar, *OPEC and Future Energy Markets* (London: Macmillan Press, 1980), see E. Ruttley, "World Energy Balances: Looking to 2020", pp. 55-57.

7 Peter Odell, *An Economic Geography of Oil* (London: G. Bell and Sons, 1963), p.4.

8 Ferdinard E. Banks, *The Political Economy of Oil* (Toronto: Lexington Books, D.C. Heath and Co., 1980), pp.46-51 and passim.

9 *Ibid.* p. 47. Assume two cases, both with reserves = 220 units; in case 1 production is to be held at 10 units per period; in case 2 production is to grow at a rate of 10% per year. Notice that in both cases when production carries on from year to year, when it starts to fall, less than half the reserves are used up.

10 See the report on the conference in Romulo Betancourt, *Venezuela's Oil* (London: George Allen & Unwin, 1978), pp. 243-52. The two basic

conclusions which emanated from the conference were a) the world's oil will be exhausted by the year 2000, given the existing rate of consumption and growth (1977), b) this development will pose a serious threat to all mankind before the end of this century.

11 Peter R. Odell and Kenneth E. Rosing, *The Future of Oil* (London: Kogan Page, 1980).

12 *Ibid.*, p. 24 and ch. 3.

13 *Ibid.*, p. 125.

14 *Ibid.*, p. 126 and ch. 4.

15 See *Petroleum Economist*, March 1982, p. 82, for a gloomy view of the prospects for the world in the year 2000 as reported to U.S. Presidents Carter and Reagan. This analysis is based on the same conservative estimation of ultimate resources.

16 See also Russel S. Uhler, "Economic Concepts of Petroleum Energy Supply", in C. Watkins and M. Walker (eds.), *Oil in the Seventies* (Vancouver: The Frazer Institute, 1977), for a discussion of the role of price in determining oil supplies.

17 Odell and Rosing, chs. 5 and 6 passim.

18 *International Petroleum Encyclopedia 1974* (Tulsa, Okla: Petroleum Publishing); Hussein K. Abdel-Aal and Robert Schmelzlee, *Petroleum Economics and Engineering*, pp. 8-10.

19 See *Petroleum Economist*, November 1981, p. 465, for a report of five new finds in Saudi Arabia in 1980.

20 Odell and Rosing, p. 29 citing R.A. Sickler (Royal Dutch/Shell Exploration and Production Division) *Methods and Models for Assessing Energy Resources.*

21 Edward H. Erickson and Herbert S. Winokur, Jr., "Nations, Companies and Markets: International Oil and Multinational Corporation", in *Oil in the Seventies*, p. 190.

22 Rene G. Ortiz, "The World Energy Outlook in the 1980s and the Role of OPEC", in Ragaei El Mallakh (ed.), *OPEC: Twenty Years and Beyond* (Boulder, Colorado: Westview Press, 1982) , p.9.

23 Zuhayi Mikdashi, *The Community of Oil Exporting Countries* (London: George Allen and Unwin Ltd., 1972), p. 28.

24 Nazli Choucri, *International Politics of Energy Interdependence* (Toronto: Lexington Books, 1976), p. 37.

25 The system of posting prices for Middle Eastern oil, which was introduced in 1950, began with the introduction of the 50:50 profit sharing scheme, where profits were to be calculated on the basis of costs on the one hand and posted price on the other. Posted prices were to represent a "fair" price which would be acceptable to host governments as a basis for calculating taxable profits. See Shell Transport, *Annual Report*, 1961, p. 16.

26 Zuhayi Mikdashi, *A Financial Analysis of Middle Eastern Oil Concessions: 1950-65* (New York: Frederick A. Praeger, 1966), p. 172.

27 Betancourt, p. 51.

28 Blair, pp. 171-83.

29 Betancourt, p. 36.

30 Venezuela was vulnerable to the pricing policy applied to Middle Eastern producers because of its relatively high costs compared to the costs of exploration, development, and production in the Middle East. For relative costs see Landes and Klass, p. 197; Mikdashi, *Financial Performance*, p. 94. Venezuela feared that a reduction in Middle East prices would undercut and invade its established markets. In 1958 and 1959 there was evidence that such a diversion of markets to Middle Eastern output did take place. See George W. Stocking, *Middle East Oil* (Kingsport, Tennessee: Vanderbilt Press, 1970), p. 381.

31 Mikdashi, *Community*, p. 31.

32 Mikdashi, *Financial Performance*, p. 172.

33 *Ibid.*, p. 170.

34 M.A. Adelman, *The World Petroleum Market* (Baltimore: Johns Hopkins University Press, 1972), p. 199.

35 *Oil and Gas Journal*, 15 August 1960, p. 15.

36 Mikdashi, *Financial Performance*, p. 172.

37 Mikdashi, *Community*, p. 33; Stocking, p. 353.

38 Adelman, p. 208.

39 Mikdashi, *Financial Performance*, p. 172.

40 *Petroleum Press Service*, November 1959, p. 410.

41 Mikdashi, *Financial Performance*, p. 176.

42 Everywhere, it was skilled workers who, by virtue of their prized talents, were first able to organize labour unions. Ordinary unskilled workmen were too weak and too easily replaced to organize as collective bargaining units until after the pioneer work had been done by the stronger sector of the workforce.

43 Adelman, p. 207.

44 Stocking, p. 357. Abdullah Tariki claimed that the oil companies had conspired to push prices down. Shell Transport, *Annual Report*, 1961, p. 16.

45 Stocking, p. 364. See also Adelman, p. 207, footnote. Royalties were calculated at 12.5% in 1962 for all but Saudi Arabia. Assume receipts over and above costs = 100 and royalties = 12.5. Royalties as income tax meant that companies paid an additional 37.5 to bring it to 50, or half the profits. Royalties expensed meant gross profits are 100, 12.7 = 87.5, tax due = 43.5, making host governments' take = 43.5 + 12.5 = 56.

46 Stocking, pp. 365-71. Iraq was dissatisfied and Kuwait's parliament surprised its rulers by objecting and holding up approval.

47 Adelman, p. 208, Table VII-2.

48 *Ibid.*, p. 209. Adelman believes that by 1969 the actual split was 83:17 in favour of the governments, a rather long way from 50:50.

49 Mordechai Abir, "The Middle East Challenge to America", *Middle*

East Focus, May 1980, p. 7.
50 Adelman, pp. 250-1.
51 Blair, p. 226; Sally F. Zerker, "Oil: Some Economic and Political Realities", *Middle East Focus*, July 1981, p. 10.
52 Adelman, p. 251.
53 Blair, p. 226.
54 Erickson and Winoker, p. 188.
55 Blair, pp. 54-71. The companies were then known as Standard Oil of New Jersey, Royal Dutch Shell, and the Anglo-Persian Oil Company.
56 Stocking, pp. 381-9.
57 Report of the Twentieth Century Fund Task Force on the International Oil Crisis, *Paying For Energy* (New York: McGraw Hill, 1975), p. 42, table 2.
58 Erickson and Winokur, p. 193.
59 *Ibid.*, op. cit. passim, and p. 194.
60 Landes and Klass, p. 197; Adelman, p. 76, table II-8.
61 *Wall Street Journal*,1 March 1982; *Petroleum Economist*, October 1982, p. 440.
62 M.A. Adelman, "Oil in the Eighties", *Petroleum Economist*, October 1980.
63 Erickson and Winokur, p. 191.
64 Frank R. Wyant, *The United States, OPEC and Multinational Oil* (Lexington, Mass: Lexington Books, 1977).
65 *Ibid.*, p. 62.
66 *Petroleum Economist*, July 1979, p. 271.
67 *Petroleum Economist*, January 1980, p. 2.
68 *Ibid.*
69 *Ibid.*, See also Adelman, "Oil in the Eighties". Adelman says that the Saudis could have quieted the market if they had so desired, but instead they raised production to 10.5 mb/d only from December 1978 to January 20, 1979 at which time they cut to 8.0 mb/d. In February/March they reached 9.5 mb/d, then cut to 8.5 mb/d for three months, rising again to 9.5 mb/d in July. Public statements on moderation were not matched by action.
70 *Ibid.*, and *Petroleum Economist*, February 1980, p. 46.
71 *Petroleum Economist*, January 1980, p. 3.
72 *Petroleum Economist*, December 1980, p. 548.
73 *Petroleum Economist*, April 1982, p. 122. Saudi Arabia, apparently thought a more effective price would be $28 per barrel.
74 *Petroleum Economist*, September 1982, p. 350.
75 *Petroleum Economist*, December 1980, p. 515. See also *Wall Street Journal*, 29 January 1982, p. 1. Nourdine Ait Laoussine, an Algerian official and Geneva-based consultant, maintained that the demand for OPEC oil will remain much below its installed capacity of 35 mb/d for the rest of this century.

[76] *Wall Street Journal*, 24 February 1982.

[77] *Petroleum Economist*, January 1982, p. 2.

[78] *Ibid.* World use fell from 51.8 mb/d in 1979 to 47.3 mb/d in 1981; U.S. fell from 17 mb/d in 1980 to 16 mb/d in 1981 and U.S. imports declined by 15.7%.

[79] See *Petroleum Economist*, September 1982, p. 355; *Wall Street Journal*, 29 January 1982, p. 1.

[80] *Wall Street Journal*, 22 January 1982. Libya and Algeria were by then forcing western countries to take oil as payment, which should have been a warning. The OPEC meeting merely reduced the price of heavier crudes to the level at which they were then selling.

[81] *Petroleum Economist*, March 1982, p. 80; *The Globe and Mail*, 9 February 1982. *Wall Street Journal*, 25 February 1982. Mexico dropped its price for 33° Isthmus by $3.50, Britain's National Oil Corporation reduced its price for 36.5° Forties by $4.25, Iran cut prices in a two week period in February totalling $4 a barrel, and Venezuela offered a $2.50 discount on 1 March.

[82] *Wall Street Journal*, 1 March 1982.

[83] *Wall Street Journal*, 4 March 1982 and 25 February 1982.

[84] *Wall Street Journal*, 8 March 1982; *Petroleum Economist*, April 1982, p. 122.

[85] *The Globe and Mail*, 12 April 1982, p. B12.

[86] *Wall Street Journal*, 5 April 1982.

[87] *Petroleum Economist*, April 1982, p. 122.

[88] *Wall Street Journal*, 9 July 1982.

[89] *Petroleum Economist*, August 1982, p. 315; *The Globe and Mail*, 8 July 1982.

[90] *The Globe and Mail*, 29 November 1982, p. B2.

[91] *Wall Street Journal*, 24 November 1982.

[92] *Wall Street Journal*, 26 November 1982; Riter Drucker's arguments about the waning of OPEC power.

[93] *Petroleum Economist*, September 1982, p. 355.

TERRORISM AND THE DEFENSE OF CIVILIZED VALUES

D.J.C. Carmichael
Department of Political Science
University of Alberta

An especially insidious feature of the politics of the Middle East is the prevalence of terrorism. Rarely does a month pass without some incident branded as "terrorist", often of spectacular brutality. The savagery of such acts affronts us, haunting our hopes for peace with reminders of the politics of bitterness and the frailty of civilized values.

How is the person of civilized conscience to judge and respond to such acts? This question is immensely problematic. In addressing it, therefore, I shall focus upon the justification of terrorism and of counter-terrorist measures in general terms, without specific reference to the movements and events of the Middle East. This is an essential preliminary. Later, the political realities of terrorism in the region will be addressed more specifically in Ross Rudolph's "commentary"and in my own "further reflections". To appreciate these political realities, however, we must begin by understanding the values and issues raised by terrorism in general. These issues are more difficult than they may seem. Indeed, they raise some basic questions about the roots of moral justification in our culture.

I shall present this, in what follows, by way of a problem and a possible solution. The problem is that within the current terms of moral understanding it seems that the worst atrocities of terrorism can be condemned categorically only in terms which impose crippling restrictions upon counter-terrorist measures. If true, this would mean that we are unable to appreciate our most civilized values in terms which permit their effective defense. On this basis I shall then suggest, as a possible solution, that the notion of "civilized values" presupposes the prior moral authority of each community to determine its own standards. It is precisely this authority which is rejected by terrorism's claim to act by right. In this respect, every act of terrorism is categorically incapable of justification, for each such act rejects civilized values *in principle.*

Preliminaries

As the first step in this analysis, I shall assume that all acts of terrorism require justification in terms of civilized values. Further, if these values are truly civilized then the more savage acts of terrorism should be incapable of any form of justification. When schoolchildren are spectacularly murdered by cornered kidnappers, or when innocent and uninvolved citizens are blown apart in the quiet of their worship, the savage brutality of such acts should enrage our deepest instincts. These are acts which should never be tolerated, and which should be incapable of any form of justification.

This is rather an obvious point, and it would be too obvious to be worth mentioning, except that it is often ignored. Discussions of terrorism occasionally trip over deep emotional commitments; and so it is not uncommon to find quite civilized individuals "justifying" the most savage acts when perpetrated in the name of a cause with which they sympathize. If the "justification" is merely that intuitively (or emotionally) one agrees with the cause, then it is not a form of justification at all. This would reduce to saying that "the act is right because I agree with it"; and this is to treat oneself as the exclusive measure of justice in the world. So far from being a form of justification, this is arrogantly to deny that other persons have any claim upon one's conscience. By contrast, properly to justify an act is to show other persons that the act advances civilized values better than alternatives; a reasonable person could act the same way and remain a civilized being.

Correlatively, the values by which we judge any act of terrorism must also be used in choosing, and assessing, counter-terrorist measures. This is crucial. In responding to terrorism, the community defends itself as a civilization. The basic values of the community must, therefore, be respected by the manner of their defense. Otherwise we run the risk of crushing terrorism by means which undermine the community's claim to count as worth defending in the first place.

Again, this rather obvious point is not widely appreciated. The more common view is that terrorism is a terrible evil which must be crushed at all costs, and by any means whatever. In my view, however, this approach is extremely short-sighted: it pursues the short-term goal of crushing terrorism without any attention to the long-term effects of its policy; it is strategically ineffective; it threatens, in many cases, to play into the hands of the terrorists themselves; and it consistently fails to temper its tactics by any concern for what it must defend. My objection, in other words, is not that this approach offends some abstract moral values. The objection, rather, is that civilized values are the practical sinews of any community and potential weapons in its defence. Like all weapons, however, they can be used properly only by those who respect them. And so this means that effective counter-terrorist measures must be guided and restricted by the civilized values they claim to defend.

Contemporary Moral Perspectives

Yet this raises a problem. It may seem rather easy to judge acts of terrorism, and relatively straightforward to "justify" counter-terrorist measures; but it is virtually impossible to do both together, and consistently.

To show this, I shall distinguish two different ways in which any act might be judged. On the one hand, an act might be judged as intrinsically right or wrong, by reference to its inherent moral qualities. Currently, judgements of this type usually focus upon the rights (or legitimate interests) of individuals affected by the act: depending upon whether the act respects or violates these rights, it will be judged as right or wrong "by its nature". On the other hand, the act might instead be judged in terms of its consequences, by the good or evil of its ends and effects. Judgements of this type tend to be "utilitarian": that is, they tend to focus upon the welfare (or happiness) of separate individuals, and they take the maximization of this welfare overall as the basic standard of morality.

In current morality, then, these two perspectives — intrinsic rightness vs. goodness of consequences — tend to be understood more specifically as principles of individual rights and the maximization of welfare. And these principles are potential rivals. The maximization of welfare often requires the violation of individual rights; in such cases, the question is whether to allow the ends to justify the means, or the collective good to prevail over individual rights. The opposite view is to assert the priority of individual rights, and to insist that an act which is morally wrong by its very nature in this respect cannot be justified, whatever its consequences. This rivalry between inherent right and goodness of consequences, or between the rights of separate individuals and the welfare of others, represents the fundamental tension of current moral thought; the principles involved are the basic values of our culture.

Now it is often said that the morality of terrorism depends upon whether the ends can justify the means. But this is too simple. There are problems with each moral perspective.

On the one hand, if we focus upon the rightness of the act (or upon the morality of its means), then every act of terrorism must be condemned as incapable of justification. This is easily shown. Acts of terrorism characteristically inflict violence upon innocent individuals; they often seek by doing so to terrorize other innocents; and they always violate the rights (or legitimate interests) of specific individuals. If one regards these features as inherently wrong, then any such act of terrorism must be judged as wrong by its very nature. And because they are wrong in this way, such acts are incapable of further justification. It cannot then be said in defense of any particular terrorist act that the evils it commits are justified by other considerations (such as the justice of the cause, or the better world it seeks, or even by the possible nobility of the terrorists' intentions in these respects). These considerations are simply irrelevant *if* one adopts a morality of means, for the justification of any act must then be decided exclusively by the inherent rightness or wrongness of the act in itself. Since terrorism violates the lives and rights of the innocent, it follows that every act of terrorism is inherently evil, *period*; and nothing else can ever justify it. To judge any act of terrorism in this way, then, is to condemn every such act as categorically incapable of justification.

But there is a problem. If we adopt this ethic then the features by which we condemn terrorism must be judged wrong under all conditions; and so acts involving these features must also be condemned when committed by the state. Thus, acts which put at risk the lives and rights of the innocent must be considered equally evil, and equally incapable of justification, whether perpetrated by terrorists or by the state in response to terrorists. This imposes rather severe restrictions upon the range of permissible counter-terrorist measures. In particular, such measures must be constrained by an absolute and overriding concern for the safe release of all hostages, for the continuing security of rule of law, and for the rights of all citizens — including those of suspected terrorists. These constraints are extremely restrictive. In most cases, in fact, they would require virtual capitulation to terrorism and invite further attacks. Even so, we cannot ignore these constraints. Since they are implied by the principles used to condemn terrorism, they cannot be violated without committing the same evil as terrorism itself. It seems, therefore, that to condemn terrorism as intrinsically wrong is also to cripple our defenses against it.

In view of the importance of this problem, I shall emphasize it by considering two objections.

First, it may be objected that the community may violate these constraints in the name of collective self-defense. This, however, is a confusion. Strictly speaking, the right of self-defense is limited to defense against immediate assailants: it does not allow measures which injure third parties. The reason for this will be clear. Defensive measures which injure third parties are inconsistent with the principle of respect for the lives and rights of the innocent; but defensive measures against immediate assailants are compatible with the principle precisely because assailants are not innocent in relation to their victims. Thus the right of self-defense is consistent with, but limited by, the constraints cited above. This means that the community and particular individuals within it have the right to defend themselves against terrorist attacks, but they do not have the right to do so by means which put at risk the lives or rights of the innocent. Violations of these constraints cannot be justified by the right of self-defense, for this would contradict the principle on which the right is based.

A second objection is that effective counter-terrorist measures may be justified by the community's need to defend its citizens, and its own integrity, against further terrorist attacks. This objection, however, is inconsistent. Essentially, it appeals to the good consequences of deterring further terrorist attacks. We have seen, however, that if an act is judged inherently wrong, then it cannot be justified by any consequences. Just as the possible consequences of terrorism cannot justify the means it uses, neither can the value of deterring terrorism justify improper means of doing so. It follows, therefore, that we must either reject this way of judging terrorism, or else accept its crippling restrictions upon permissible counter-terrorist measures.

For this reason, let us consider the matter instead from a utilitarian perspective. Initially, at least, this has certain clear advantages, for utilitarianism allows considerably stronger counter-terrorist measures.

This is because utilitarianism judges the evil of terrorism itself in different terms, by its consequences and for the suffering it inflicts. By the same token, counter-terrorist measures are justified solely by their effects in increasing human happiness. And this allows us to justify such measures by reference to their consequences in defending other citizens and the integrity of the community against further terrorist attacks. On this approach, then, counter-terrorist measures may still be justified even where they compromise to some extent the safety of hostages and the rights of others, so long as the losses involved are compensated by corresponding gains. To be sure, the lives and rights of the innocent may be put at risk only to the minimum extent needed for overall welfare maximization; and so counter-terrorist measures must still be guided by a strategic respect for the values they claim to defend. Even so, utilitarianism allows considerably greater latitude and flexibility in the choice of such measures, and so it may seem superior as an ethic on this account.

There are, however, two difficulties with this approach.

In the first place, it must be asked whether utilitarianism does not justify too much, precisely insofar as it allows measures which put at risk the lives and rights of the innocent. In any actual case, for example, utilitarian policy may allow the sacrifice of hostages. Now even if this is necessary to protect the community from further terrorist attacks, the fact remains that this policy essentially justifies the sacrifices of some persons — themselves innocent victims in the first place — for the sake of gains which accrue to *others*. It defends "the community" only in the sense that it sacrifices one part of the community to save the rest. The justice of this policy is questionable. By the same principle, we might also hold the family of any criminal responsible for his acts: 'punishing' the innocent in this analogous way might have some useful deterrent effects, but this deterrence should not be purchased with the lives or liberties of the innocent. The same principle applies in the case of terrorist hostages: if we are not prepared to deter criminals by punishing their families, neither should we deter terrorists by sacrificing their hostages. In each case, therefore, the strong measures and apparent merits of utilitarianism must be opposed if we believe that:

> Each person possesses an inviolability founded on justice that
> even the welfare of society as a whole cannot override.[1]

A correlative difficulty is that utilitarianism justifies vigorous counter-terrorist measures in terms which also allow that terrorism itself might be justified. As we have seen, counter-terrorist measures are justified solely by their effects in maximizing happiness. Now it is possible that certain acts of terrorism — even the most savage atrocities — might be justified precisely in these terms. That is, it might be argued in defense of such acts that, while the suffering they inflict upon their victims is unfortunate, it is also required and compensated by justifying long-term increases in the happiness of others. Presumably, of course, very few such acts could ever meet this standard. The fact remains, however, that some cases might well be justified in this way, and that all cases are potentially justifiable. In every case, moreover, the question of justification depends upon a complex calculation of long-term consequences. Thus no act of terrorism — however savage and brutal — can be dismissed as inherently wrong. Here again, accordingly, it seems that the apparent advantages of utilitarianism in justifying effective counter-terrorist measures come at too high a price; for in its inability to condemn any act of terrorism outright as incapable of justification, utilitarianism seems radically unfit as an ethic for civilized men.

An Alternative Analysis [2]

In short, we seem to have a problem: it seems possible to condemn terrorism as inherently wrong only in terms which cripple our defenses against it; whereas a utilitarian ethic would justify stronger counter-terrorist measures only in terms whose weakness is revealed by the fact that they might allow terrorism to be justified.

If this is a problem, it arises from the abstract individualism which underlies current moral and political understanding. By "individualism" we stress the individual in relation to the community and the state. But there are two dimensions of this individualism which should be distinguished. As a value commitment, "individualism" proclaims the prospective dignity of each person, the importance of rights and liberties in developing this dignity, and the basic right of each person to determine the terms of his or her own existence. In modern political thought, however, these value commitments have typically been based upon a different dimension of individualism, an abstract conception of the person in relation to the community. In this abstract conception, each person is construed as a morally significant being completely in his/her "own right", entirely apart from relations with others; the community, in turn, is conceived as merely the sum of these separate individuals; and, on this basis, any authority of the "community" is held to derive from the more fundamental moral rights of the individual.

In my view, this abstract individualism is a poor basis for our value commitments. Indeed, to conceive any person as an abstract individual, apart from social relations, is to render him a "stupid unimaginative animal", for the person develops into a morally significant and interesting individual only within and through the specific roles and relations of the community.

Now if we take this more social view of the person, it is still possible to prize individual rights and liberties as the requisites of fully developed individuality. But it would also permit a different conception of civilized standards and of communal authority.

The idea, here, is that a group of individuals cannot be considered civilized unless their conduct is regulated by certain standards of inter-personal conduct; and no individual can be counted a member of that civilization unless he accepts its standards as prior limitations upon his rights. If this is true, it implies that the community has the authority to determine these standards, including those which define each individual's rights, and also that this authority of the community is prior to any rights of any individuals within it. This prior authority of the community, therefore, is necessarily presupposed by its claim to count as a civilization. It does not follow, of course, that every community is on that account "civilized": it may be considered relatively "uncivilized" because the standards it adopts are ethically inferior to others. But it will not count as a "civilization" at all unless it has the prior moral authority to decide these standards, whatever they may be. Thus, the notion of "civilized standards" involves two distinct components: one is the ethical quality of the standards, and the other is the prior authority of the community to determine them.

Now terrorism, of course, violates ethical standards and on this account it is evil. But so, too, do criminals. Unlike criminals, however, terrorism claims to violate these standards *by right*. This special feature gives terrorism the public and political significance which purely criminal behaviour lacks. And this political feature also constitutes the special savagery of terrorism. In claiming to violate these standards by right, terrorism implicitly rejects the prior authority of the community to determine them. In turn, this categorically rejects the community's claim to count as a civilization and fundamentally excludes the terrorist from membership in it. Thereby, terrorism places itself in a necessary and belligerent state of nature vis-a-vis all possible civilizations. Through this claim of right, therefore, terrorism rejects civilized standards in principle. On this account, it is inherently savage in the strongest sense possible. Terrorism cannot be justified, then, because in rejecting the community's prior authority it rejects what must be assumed for any process of justification to begin. It is *logically incapable* of justification.

On the other hand, this is not to say that terrorism is devoid of ethical significance. Although terrorism rejects civilized standards in principle, this rejection may be based on quite admirable human motivations and possibly even the loftiest of ideals. Without belabouring the point, suffice it to say that, in certain rare circumstances, terrorism may be the only way to defend the legitimate claims or even the continuing survival of one's children, race, or cultural group. To reject the terrorist option in such circumstances is to acquiesce in the violation of everything a human being

50

might reasonably cherish. Thus, just as we may assess the civilized qualities of any community in the light of higher ethical standards, we may apply the same standards to specific cases of terrorism. In particular, we may consider such questions as the legitimacy of the terrorist's cause, the probability that it can be realized only through terrorist tactics (as opposed to other methods), the amount of evil inflicted by such tactics in comparison to the evils they remove, and the ethical quality of the terrorists' own aims in these respects. Judged by these standards, of course, most cases of terrorism are simply evil. In very rare and severe circumstances, however, a particular case of terrorism might be seen as the only possible means of changing a condition of intolerable injustice. Yet even in these cases, to adopt terrorist tactics is to reject civilized standards in principle and to enter a jungle of moral savagery. The very best that might be said, then, is that individuals in such conditions are forced to choose between their commitments as human beings and their status as civilized men. This is a cruel dilemma — one by no means confined to cases of terrorism — and so we might well sympathize with those whom it confronts. But to sympathize is not to justify. Whatever its motivations, terrorism remains a form of savagery and, as such, it is incapable of justification.

I conclude, then, with two points: that to count as a "civilization" we must oppose terrorism in *all* forms, and that we will count as a civilization worth preserving only by respecting our best values in the manner of their defense.

FOOTNOTES

[1] John Rawls, *A Theory of Justice* (Cambridge, Mass.: The Belknap Press, 1971), p. 3.

[2] This is developed in greater detail in my essay "Of Beasts, Gods and Civilized Men: The Justification of Terrorism and of Counter-Terrorist Measures", forthcoming in *Terrorism: An International Journal.*

COMMENTARY:
CIVILIZATION AND DEFENSE AGAINST TERRORISM

Ross Rudolph
Department of Political Science,
York University

What is distinctively wrong about terrorism? The seemingly obvious answers turn out not to be wholly satisfactory. The fact that terrorists engage in murder does not distinguish them from other criminals, and does not capture the infamy of their actions. The fact that their victims are innocent does not distinguish terrorists from participants in just wars, who regularly, predictably and as a by product of their pursuit of legitimate targets, inflict unintended harm upon non-combatants, and yet I suppose that we would wish to deny to terrorists the label "just warriors." Is it then the intentionality of their failure to discriminate, indeed their positive insistence that in their struggle, there are no innocents? This failure to discriminate similarly characterizes mad bombers and arsonists, yet no one should doubt that terrorists are not lunatics.[1]

This incapacity to generate an unambiguously right answer does not necessarily support the oft-heard complaint of the current disarray of moral and political theory. In part, the difficulty is an example of the familiar experience of the paradoxes which are generated when our familiar categories are extended to their limits.[2] In part, the problem is that in politics we deal with what W.B. Gallie has denominated "essentially contested concepts,"[3] or what Stuart Hampshire has called "essentially disputed concepts."[4] In political discourse, there are no rigid designators. One person's "terrorist" is another's "freedom fighter." This is not just a matter of personal predilection, that words, as Hobbes long ago noted, "have a signification also of the nature, disposition, and interest of the speaker; such as are the names of virtues and vices; for one man calleth wisdom, what another called fear; and one cruelty, what another justice; one prodigality, what another magnanimity; and one gravity, what another stupidity, etc."[5] What accounts for political concepts being essentially contested or disputed is their situation within competing world views, conflicting group ideologies, and different widely held values.

Confronted by such value pluralism and conflict, the political philosopher is left with two tasks, which, if successful, would illuminate our reflective judgements, but in two different ways. On the one hand, the philosopher could offer what we might call high level political-moral advice, the point of which would be to arrive at criteria or guidelines by which political action could be justified or criticized. This could involve several distinct operations: the inference, from commonly held value systems, of principles underlying critical judgements; the adjudication of these principles by independent standards, drawn from intuition, reason, or history; and the application of these standards to controversial actual or hypothetical cases. On the other hand, the political philosopher could analyze the nature of critical political judgement, quite apart from advice of any kind.

In his brief, elegant, and thoughtful paper, Professor Carmichael does all these things, with the possible exception of applying principles to cases. To answer the deceptively difficult question with which we began, Professor Carmichael attempts to cut the Gordian knot by reverting to a notion sometimes canvassed in international law. He declines the definitional gambit by the simple and powerful claim that terrorism violates the standard of civilization that any code must satisfy to qualify as minimally moral. To this it might be objected that there is no univocal standard of civilization. One of the principal hallmarks of contemporary politics is irresoluble value conflict. What could the standards of civilization conceivably be where terrorists born in Japan, trained in Libya, operate in Israel?[6] There simply is no general consensus on appropriate standards by which terrorism could be categorically condemned.

Carmichael's answer to this objection would seem to be that constitutive of civilization, any civilization, is the recognition of the prior moral authority of the community, which renders possible the realization of the rights of individuals. The terrorist, by contrast with the criminal, claims to have acted by right. What is odious about such a claim is not so much its denial to the community of determinative authority, as its arrogating to the terrorist himself that which is denied the community.

This argument has several noteworthy ramifications. The first is its explicit rejection of the abstract individualism, of which much contemporary political thought is the abstract theoretical expression, and political terrorism the concrete active expression. To say this is not to affirm that terrorism is in any sense caused or inspired by defective theory. It is rather that political theories which, explicitly or implicitly, presume individualist premises are debarred from effectively meeting the challenge of terrorism. Professor Carmichael's remarks would seem to situate him in tradition of civic individualism emphasizing the public dimension which goes back, if not to Aristotle, at least to Machiavelli, which formed part of the ideological origins of the American Revolution.[7] Its foremost contemporary chronicler is J.G.A. Pocock,[8] its recent exponents would include in some moods Hannah Arendt[9] and Richard Flathman.[10] The revival of this honourable mode is particularly opportune at a time when philosophical anarchists deny all legitimacy to public authority,[11] and libertarians insist upon absolute constructions of individual rights.[12] How successful is Carmichael in adducing this framework to overcome the deficiencies of abstract individualism in coping with the phenomenon of terrorism?

There are some incidental difficulties. For example, after stipulating that acknowledgement of the moral authority of the community is constitutive or definitive of civilization, the author adds a coordinate principle, namely the ethical quality of the standard which moral authority imposes. Now the adjudication of principles by independent standards is a perfectly legitimate philosophical task, as noted above, but Carmichael has told us nothing of the provenance and warrants of these standards. Without spelling out the status of critical standards, it is not only difficult to accept judgements of ethically superior and inferior communities, but even to allow without further elaboration that the recognition of prior moral authority is the hallmark of civilization.

There are two specific difficulties with the latter equation. The first is that the notion of moral authority is less than transparent. In one sense, authority seems to be incompatible with morality, in a way that it is not with politics or law. The guiding insight here is that, even if the rules to be applied are social and conventional, the locus of moral choice is ineluctably individual. The moral point of view requires a degree of openness, which the public order, political and legal,with its need for mechanisms for definitive resolution of value conflicts, cannot sustain, according to the civic individualist position under review. The natural meaning of "moral authority", however, would seem, as Professor Carmichael says, to involve resort to community-based standards to determine rights, immunities, obligations, duties, and so on. The anomaly here, familiar from critiques of utilitarianism, is that if community standards sanction practices like terrorism, they cannot be gainsaid by resort to "moral authority." This was the point of the relativist critique, cited above. The difficulty of specifying the relevant community in a case of domestic terrorism, like the Red Brigade, is aggravated in the Middle East, where terror is visited by members of one community upon members of another. There is little reason to doubt the sympathy of Palestinians with both the objectives and the methods of the Palestine Liberation Organization, notwithstanding the best hopes of Israel's authorities to eliminate threats and intimidation in those areas occupied since 1967. Nor is the Palestinian attitude *prima facie* morally hypocritical. Support for one's own terrorism is perfectly compatible with universalized support for terrorism on behalf of all others in relevantly similar circumstances.

The second and crucial difficulty with the treatment of civilization as coequal with the recognition of prior community moral authority, and of terrorism as the rejection of that authority, is that this strategy too fails to identify what is distinctively wrong with terrorism. Granting for the moment that a metaethical criterion can be found for the ethical quality of community standards, and that some sense can be made of the notion of moral authority, there are many who have rejected, and continue to call into question, any moral standards that are not imposed by individuals upon themselves, and yet they seem not to be culpable in the way that terrorists are. In different ways philosophical anarchists, iconoclasts, and moral reformers all deny the prior right of communities to set authoritative standards of right, and far from being reprobated, they are lionized.

Allied to the critique of abstract individualism is a perspective on the nature of critical political judgement of some importance, namely the insistence that moral theories which attend exclusively either to intrinsic rightness or goodness of consequences are severely inadequate. Whether or not it is Carmichael's view that they are also mutually incompatible is less clear, if only because he seems in his own voice to adduce civilization both as a standard of intrinsic rightness and wrongness (as in the characterization of terrorism as "simply evil", and "moral savagery"), and of goodness of consequences (as in his dismissal of counter-terrorism at all costs). Ruled out in this way, policy makers, diplomats, soldiers, and individual citizens face two polar extremes. On the one side, it is not open to the political actor to hue to the purely deontological demand that justice be done, though the world perish. Whatever may be the case with moral choices in private relations, political actors operate under the burdensome constraint of calculations of probable effects upon others. Also ruled out, however, are those sliding scale arguments[13] which seek to justify what would otherwise be wrong by the goodness of the consequences, or more accurately by the badness of the consequences likely to result from acting otherwise.

Though Carmichael's discussion illustrates that deontological and consequentialist elements need not necessarily be incompatible, because, as he also shows, the basis of critical judgement is so different in the two cases, all efforts which seek to combine the two perspectives face the ever present possibility that dilemmas will arise in which it is necessary to choose between competing considerations. This is not a fault of the theory, but an accurate reflection of tragic alternatives. A particularly poignant example of such a tragic dilemma is his closing reflection upon those "forced to choose between their commitments as human beings and their status as civilized men." It is to the dilemmas confronting those who engage in counter-terrorism that I now propose to turn.

The subject on which Professor Carmichael has the least to say, which however in the current state of Middle Eastern politics is the most immediately relevant, is the application of the standards of civilization to counter-terrorist measures. What he does say is palpably important, but raises as many questions as it answers.

Professor Carmichael concludes with two points: "that to count as a 'civilization' we must oppose terrorism in *all* forms, and that we will count as a civilization worth preserving only by respecting our best values in the manner of its defense." Consider the two points seriatim. Who is this "we" who must oppose terrorism? Does it embrace decision-makers, those charged with carrying out their directives, as policemen, soldiers, diplomats, officials, and private citizens? Surely it is carrying to heroic lengths the requirements of civilization to demand that the victims of terrorism, for instance the families of kidnap victims or hostages, have responsibilities identical to those of political leaders or officials, or to deny that whatever duties private citizens may have in this regard may be overridden by their countervailing personal relation to the victim. The basic idea here is elementary. There are certain functions, taking into account considerations both of justice and efficiency, which are best left to impersonal, public authorities. Examples might include the collection of funds for collective purposes, raising of fighters for an army, or the imposition of punishment. It is at least arguable that combatting terrorism is another such task. If it is, there are classes of action which when performed by a private individual would be wrong which may be justifiable when performed by a public agent or agency in its official capacity. If someone with an income of $2000 a year trains a gun on someone with an income of $100,000 and makes him hand over his wallet, that is robbery. If the federal government withholds a portion of the second person's income, enforcing its action with the threat of fine and/or imprisonment under armed guard, and gives a much larger sum than the contents of the wallet to the first person in the form of welfare payments, unemployment benefits, free medical care, that is a tax. The first case is an impermissible use of coercion to achieve a worthwhile end, the second the use of legitimate means, impersonally imposed by a public institution.[14] Applying similar reasoning to the case of state counter-terrorism yields a result which flies in the face of much contemporary diplomatic rhetoric, legal opinion, and editorial comment. In the constant alternation of terrorism and counter-terrorism in the Middle East, there is a tendency for a variety of reasons to apply differential standards to the two sides. Terrorism is either justified because of the justice of its cause, or at least excused because terrorists and terrorist organizations are not persons at international law, whereas states are held up to strict constraints on the use or threat of force. If Professor Carmichael is correct that terrorism is categorically wrong and that "we" are in duty bound to oppose it, and if I am correct that the "we" refers especially to states and those charged with carrying out their directives, then very different judgements are yielded.

Even granting that states may, indeed in some cases ought to, do what it would be wrong for an individual to do, when does the defense against terrorists become indistinguishable from the evil it is supposed to remedy?

This brings us to Professor Carmichael's second concluding point, that in discharging the duty of counter-terrorism we must be guided by the values of civilization. This appeal is not unknown in international law literature dealing with the law of war, which is characterized by McDougal and Feliciano as a tension between military necessity and humanitarianism,[15] and by Georg Schwarzenberger as a dialectic relationship between civilization and the necessities of war.[16] The point of both comments is the timely reminder that the conduct of war must not go beyond certain bounds in inflicting harm. We must always be aware that our enemies are human.

Even those generally sympathetic with the objectives of these commentators, who do not reject out of hand such remarks as idle hopes, are forced to acknowledge that, as stated, these principles supply precious little direction to decision makers. One of the foremost authorities on just war theories, James Turner Johnson, for example, acknowledges the need to elaborate the appeals to humanitarianism and civilization, because they only "provide a context for the introduction of value considerations, but they do not provide concrete values,"[17] against the all too concretely posed demands of military necessity. By the same token, Carmichael is not very informative on what the standard of civilization requires by way of counter-terrorism, except to suggest that crushing terrorism at all costs is out.

Though he is cryptic, Professor Carmichael might have said much more and the following comments are meant to draw out the possible implications of his remarks. From what he has said, I suspect that his views are interestingly different from those of writers of the just war tradition.[18] Just war theories generally distinguish *ius ad bellum*, the right to make war, from *ius in bello*, right in war, or the laws of the conduct of war. The first comprises "the ideas of just cause, right authority, right intention, that the war not do more harm than good (proportionality), that it be a last resort, and that its purpose be to achieve peace."[19] The latter embraces two principles, discrimination between combatants and non-combatants, and proportion both as to types of weapon (for example, no nuclear weapons where conventional ones will do) and with regard to non-combatant immunity (for example, no avoidable use of anti-personnel weapons, in areas densely populated with civilians).

Proponents of such theories sometimes infer from them results germane to the current situation in the Middle East. It is sometimes maintained, for instance, applying the *ius ad bellum* standards of proportionality and last resort, that Israel's constant policy since at least 1955 of massive reprisals and resort to war is unjustifiable. As Stanley Hoffman has recently written, "Even when it is a case of self-defense against an armed attack, the old obligation of proportionality of means ought to be observed. An all-out war in response to a raid grossly violates this rule."[20] As to *ius in bello*, it has been eloquently argued that in a struggle fought for the hearts and minds of a population, where fighters, let us say terrorists, are hopelessly comingled with civilians, if the rule of discrimination cannot be observed, perhaps we ought to consider that the fight is not worth waging.[21] Applied to Israel's campaign in Lebanon which began on 6 June 1982 we may say, by parity of reasoning, that an all out war was a disportionate response, the use of a bomb to kill a gnat, and that if the PLO cannot be extricated from its surroundings, then Israel must choose some response to terrorism, such as improved defenses, which spares innocent lives.

If I have understood them correctly, Professor Carmichael's arguments yield a different emphasis. What the just war theorists miss is that opposition to terrorism is not permissive, but mandatory, as sacred and impressive in its way as the requirements of *ius ad bellum*. To put the point slightly differently, counter-terrorist war is a struggle in a just cause, undertaken by a right authority with the right intention, and so on, in a word, a just war. As to the proportionality requirement, the evil combatted is in many ways an ultimate evil, undermining the very bases of democratic values and destabilizing normal life. There are more ways of destroying a society than physically eradicating it. Even if the war is just, however, it must be fought justly. In particular, attention must be paid to the immunity of non-combatants, even in situations where it is difficult to discriminate. According to recently returned eye witnesses,[22] in the southern forty kilometres, Israel's advancing forces followed a uniform plan of forcibly evacuating refugee camps, providing alternate accommodations for the evacuees, separating civilians from suspected terrorists who were then detained, and destroying the camp sites in which terrorists comingled with civilian populations. Just war theorists would tend to focus on the real harm that was done: innocent civilians, already in difficult straits, were displaced, camp sites which were not more legitimate targets than cities, were destroyed, terrorists were mistreated, and so on. It is possible, however, to maintain that Israel scrupulously sought an alternative to combatting terrorists with one arm tied behind its back and, within the limits of civilization and human fallibility, succeeded.

Several cautions are in order about the foregoing remarks. I do not mean to father upon Professor Carmichael more than he intended, though I believe my construction is consistent with what he says. Secondly, while aspects of Israel's action in Lebanon are justifiable from a certain perspective, not all claims made on their behalf are equally plausible. In particular, apologia which appeal to military necessity or a putative analogy between Israel's action in West Beirut and Israel's policy in case of hostage-taking strike me as sophistical. Finally, and this cannot always be safely presumed, if we are correctly informed about the campaign in West Beirut, numbers of casualties and weapons used, such as phosphorus and cluster bombs, levels of bombardment, then much of the conduct of the war seems beyond the pale, no matter whether the standards are those of just war or civilization.

Professor Carmichael alluded to the tragic alternatives facing terrorists in extreme cases. Let me close by drawing attention to the equally inescapable dilemma of the counter-terrorist. Though never forced to choose between doing nothing and committing atrocities, counter-terrorists are regularly confronted by a choice from among scarce alternatives, all of which would be wrong. Indeed one of the most damnable things that can be said about terrorists, though not even that is an adequate response to our innocent-looking opening question, is that they force their victims into that untenable position. Before we render a conclusive verdict on any counter-terrorist action, we ought to ponder Thomas Nagel's sobering reflection, "Given the limitations on human action, it is naive to suppose that there is a solution to every moral problem with which the world can face us. We have always known that the world is a

58

bad place. It appears that it may be an evil place as well."[23]

FOOTNOTES

[1] See Simcha Jacobovici, "The Ideology of Terror," *Middle East Focus* Vol. 4 No. 3 (September, 1981).

[2] I owe this point to a discussion with Dr. John Shafer.

[3] W.B. Gallie, "Essentially Contested Concepts," Proceedings of the *Aristotelian Society*, Vol. 56 (1955-56). For an example of this mode of analysis, see Gallie's "Liberal Morality and Socialist Morality," in Peter Laslett (ed.), *Philosophy, Politics, and Society, First Series* (Oxford: Basil Blackwell, 1963).

[4] Stuart Hampshire, *Thought and Action* (New York: Viking, 1959).

[5] Thomas Hobbes, *Leviathan*, Chap. 4.

[6] A question along these lines was posed to Professor Carmichael following the oral presentation of his paper, by Professor A. Leslie, University of Toronto.

[7] Bernard Bailyn, *The Ideological Origins of the American Revloution* (Cambridge: Belknap Press of Harvard University Press, 1967).

[8] J.G.A. Pocock, *The Machiavellian Moment* (Princeton: Princeton University Press, 1975).

[9] Hannah Arendt, *The Human Condition* (Chicago: The University of Chicago Press, 1958).

[10] Richard Flathman, *The Practice of Rights* (Cambridge: Cambridge University Press, 1976), and *The Practice of Political Authority* (Chicago: The University of Chicago Press, 1980).

[11] Robert Paul Wolff, *In Defence of Anarchism* (New York: Harper and Row, 1970).

[12] Robert Nozick, *Anarchy, State, and Utopia* (New York: Basic Books, 1974).

[13] For a subtle and complex critique of sliding scale arguments, see Michael Walzer, *Just and Unjust Wars* (New York: Basic Books, 1977), Part Four.

[14] The example is shamelessly cribbed from Thomas Nagel, "Ruthlessness in Public Life," collected in Thomas Nagel, *Mortal Questions* (Cambridge: Cambridge University Press, 1979), p. 88.

[15] See Myres McDougal and Florentino Feliciano, *Law and Minimum World Public Order* (New Haven: Yale University Press, 1961), pp. 72-76.

[16] See Georg Schwarzenberger, *A Manual of International Law*, 5th ed. (London: Steven and Sons, 1967), pp. 197-199.

[17] James Turner Johnson, *Just War Tradition and the Restraint of War* (Princeton: Princeton University Press, 1981), p. 94. Emphasis in the original.

18 It is hopelessly oversimple to suggest that there is only one universal tradition of a single just war theory, and that all its advocates come down on the same side on all issues. In what follows, I summarily canvass some characteristic themes. For subtle surveys of the variety of just war theories, in addition to the Walzer and Johnson already cited, see also James Turner Johnson, *Ideology, Thason, and the Limitation of War: Religious and Secular Concepts, 1200-1740* (Princeton: Princeton University Press, 1975), and the references in all three.

19 Johnson, *Just War Tradition*, p. xxii.

20 Stanley Hoffmann, *Duties Beyond Borders* (Syracuse: Syracuse University Press, 1981), p. 60.

21 On guerrilla war in general, and Vietnam in particular, see Walzer, *Just and Unjust Ways*, Chapter 11.

22 I am indebted for the following intelligence to members of the CPPME study group recently returned from Lebanon, Professors David Demson and Henry Weinberg, both of the University of Toronto and Professor Louis Greenspan of McMaster University, who reported their findings to members of the University of Toronto and York University chapters of the organization. These remarks were completed before the entry of Israel's forces into East Beirut and before the tragic events in the Shatila and Sabra refugee camps.

23 Thomas Nagel, "War and Massacre," in *Mortal Questions*.

FURTHER REFLECTIONS ON
"TERRORISM AND THE DEFENSE OF CIVILIZED VALUES"
— THE PLO VS. ISRAEL

D.J.C. Carmichael
Department of Political Science
University of Alberta

I cannot pretend at this point to do justice to all of the criticisms which are raised by Ross Rudolph's commentary on my analysis. Indeed, Professor Rudolph's generous but effective criticisms constitute an original essay on the subject in their own right. Instead of replying individually to each of the points he makes, accordingly, I shall try rather to emulate the spirit of his own approach by developing my analysis further, and with reference to more specifically political issues. Three such issues might be raised as problems with my account of the 'prior moral authority of each community': viz,

(1) it seems excessively authoritarian;
(2) it is unclear about what counts as "the community" and about how "communal authority" is to be identified; and
(3) it fails to address directly the political realities of terrorism in the Middle East.

These problems[1] are given practical effect by the following objection:

It is generally not true to say that terrorists reject the prior moral authority of the community. Instead, they hold different views about what counts as the *legitimate* community and about who may properly speak for it. Thus the PLO do not reject communal authority or civilized standards *per se*. On the contrary, any member of the PLO will insist that the proper community to which he belongs is Palestinian, that it is represented by the PLO, and therefore that terrorist acts against Israelis are simply affirmations of the *true* "authority" of the only legitimate "community" for that territory.

Can this objection be answered? There are many who will say that it "depends upon one's point of view", i.e., upon whether one supports the PLO or Israel. But this is too simple. What is at issue is whether one *should* support either the PLO or Israel; and this issue is raised both as a profound question of political right and also as a central problem of peace in the Middle East. The issue is too important, therefore, to be "answered" simply by taking sides.

Yet objective analysis here is exceptionally difficult. The issue is complex, divisive, embittered by protracted struggle, and obscured by the ideological pretensions of the contending parties. As a result, much of what passes for "political analysis" is barely disguised academic proselytism. This is perhaps inevitable in the circumstances. But it means that the issue — the legitimacy of rival communities — must ultimately be confronted in basic terms, apart from the claims made by the contending parties, as a question about the nature and legitimacy of political authority in general.

To do so I shall begin with the most fundamental question possible — "how can we ever justify anything at all?" — and then deduce some axioms of political right which may be applied to problems of peace and authority in the Middle East. For the sake of brevity, I will focus upon central propositions and ignore (except where absolutely relevant) many of the qualifications and objections which would be part of a more comprehensive account. Within these limits, what follows is a *strict deduction*: problems of peace and authority will be answered by deriving conclusions which are objectively and demonstrably true.

The Argument

I begin with the question, "How can we ever justify anything at all?"

We all have fundamental beliefs about how we — and others — ought to behave. These beliefs function as competing manners, moralities, and social codes. And they emanate from a variety of sources; e.g., from tradition, religion (including revelation), and the light of natural intelligence. Whatever its source, however, to use any belief as a standard of social behaviour is to impose it, through law or a social code, upon others. And this means that some individual must claim the authority to proclaim the standard as the correct one to use, and to interpret its requirements for the behaviour of others. As a consequence, all issues of social legitimacy and justification eventually devolve upon two basic questions: (1) which standards ought to be used? and (2) who has the right to decide this?

Of these two questions, the second ("whose right?") is decisive. This may be shown as follows.

Assume[2] that all persons are roughly equal, in the sense that each may be presumed capable (in the absence of clear proof to the contrary) of deciding for himself how best to live his life. No one may be presumed to be by nature a slave, so incapable of governing himself as to warrant his being ruled by others; nor may anyone presume to rule others as slaves by the right of his own natural superiority. Thus each person has by nature the equal right to govern himself, or "to live his own life"; and this right persists until he lays it down. The person may be ruled, therefore, only through his own assent. Further, this natural right of governing oneself must include the right to decide the standards by which to guide and judge one's conduct. And this means that no belief, standard, or rule may be imposed upon any individual against his will, however correct and pressing the

62

standard might seem to be. Hence, if we assume that persons are roughly equal (in the sense that no one may be presumed a natural slave), then it follows that any question over which standards are best is one which each individual has the right to answer for himself; and no individual has the right to impose his answer upon anyone else.

It should be noted that this "rough equality" is only presumed until proven otherwise. Children, for example, and the severely retarded are ruled by others in their best interests because they are not fully capable of governing themselves. In such cases, however, the person's alleged incapacity can be proven. This is crucial. There are those — "true believers" — who notoriously treat disagreement with their views as proof in itself that their opponents are mentally or morally incapable of appreciating the truth. On this basis, "true believers" have sought throughout history to impose their views by force, and in the name of the "best interests" of their unwilling victims. In effect the "true believer" treats his opponents as slaves, that is, as beings who are incapable of governing themselves in important matters and who must, therefore, be ruled *by him* "in their best interests." And the sole pretext for this procedure is the fact that his opponents disagree with him[3] on some issue which *he* considers vital. By this pretext, each person on the face of the planet might claim to enslave all others. Civil society would be impossible on this basis. The only alternative is to presume that each person is generally capable of governing himself, and to insist that this presumption can be relaxed in particular cases only through strict and independent forms of proof.

The problem is that some standards may seem to be so true that they cannot reasonably be doubted; and so the importance of these standards may seem to justify imposing them upon others. But who decides the truth and importance of any standard? As we have seen, this can be the right of any individual only if it is also the right of each separate individual; to deny this right in the case of any person by imposing standards upon him is to treat him as a slave, as if he were incapable of governing his own life. And this cannot be justified.

But suppose it is said: "I recognize your right of governing yourself in general, but not in this one respect where the importance of the issue justifies coercion in your best interests." The answer will be plain. If I can decide exceptions to your right, then I might quite consistently reject your right in every single case. By claiming the right to determine exceptions, I am effectively claiming to decide where your right does, and does not, apply; and this is to decide where you are, and are not, capable of governing yourself. To claim the right to make exceptions, therefore, is to deny that you are capable of governing yourself; this rejects your right of governing yourself completely, and in principle. Thus any claim to recognize a right "except in certain cases" is absolute sham: it does not recognize the right at all. To recognize any individual's right of governing himself is to acknowledge his right to decide where, and when, it may be exercised.

In short, each person must be presumed by nature to have a right of governing himself, or to live his own life as he judges best. This right is basic: it cannot legitimately be limited either by abstract moral standards or by anyone else's right. Until the individual lays aside this right, therefore, it will justify everything he does.

How extensive is this right? Since each person may decide where and when his right may be exercised, and since there are no other moral considerations by which it may legitimately be restricted, then it follows that each person's right is unlimited. There is nothing an individual cannot claim in the name of his right of nature, even if this appears evil or absurd to the rest of us. The individual may with "full right" seek to kill or to enslave any other person, or to seize his possessions; and each individual may assert this same right over all men. In respect of his right of nature, therefore, each person is lord of the entire cosmos, and sovereign (de jure) over all creation: he has an unlimited right to all things.

And yet this is absurd. For if my unlimited right allows me to kill you, then you have the same right to kill me; and all other men have the same right to kill each of us. The result is the paradox stressed by Hobbes: if everyone has a right to all things, then no one will have any duties to respect anyone else's right, and each person's right will be nullified by the conflicting rights of everyone else. If all men have a right to all things, accordingly, no one can have an effective right to anything. By the same token, this right justifies everything, but nothing: it allows each man to act in all ways with perfect right, but it means that no restrictions upon any person's right or conduct could ever be justified. Thus no form of socio-political authority could ever be established. In short, "right", "authority", and "justification" are all rendered meaningless.

At this point it might be objected that these problems show that it is absurd to treat natural right as unlimited: properly understood, the right of nature must be limited to areas which are morally justifiable. This objection is tempting, but deeply mistaken. For *who decides* upon these limits of natural right? Notice, here, that each person cannot be presumed to do this for himself, for this is equivalent to unlimited right. The objection requires, therefore, that some individual must claim the authority to determine the limits of everyone else's right, even where these others disagree. To assert such limits, then, is in effect to claim the authority to rule all others, and on the grounds that they are incapable of governing themselves. But this claim, as we have seen, means that such men could not have the right of nature in the first place. To restrict any person's natural right is to deny it in principle, for the idea of a limited right of nature is a contradiction: it must be recognized in principle, as unlimited, or else not at all.

An important conclusion follows. As we have seen, each person must be presumed to have the right of governing himself; the recognition of this right, indeed, is a condition of civilized existence. Yet this right must be recognized as unlimited, in a way which would undermine effective right, authority, and civilized life. If civilized existence is possible, then, it follows that each person must be presumed to have laid aside his unlimited right. This is the *sine qua non* of civil society. Each person must abandon the pretense of being sole lord of the cosmos and seek, with others, to underwrite some form of collective authority. This requires that each person lay aside the empty sovereignty of unlimited right, and that he transfer this right to the community. Thereafter the community is authorized to act with, and by, the right of each of its citizens.

Moreover, each citizen must be presumed to act in this way on an equal basis. There would be no reason for anyone to lay down his unlimited right unless all others did so as well, for otherwise he would become their slave. And we have seen that by nature no one may be presumed a slave. Nor, by the same token, may any person claim to be superior, or to rule others by his superior right. In this sense, the possibility of civil society assumes not only that each person lay aside his natural right, but also that each person do so along with others on an equal basis. This recognition of equality is crucial. For there may be some rights which no one could ever be assumed to lay aside (e.g., as Hobbes[4] suggests, the right of self-preservation). We need not discuss here what these rights might be; the point is that each person would naturally be concerned to protect the rights of greatest importance to himself, and to oppose this procedure on the part of everyone else. But this would again violate the equality condition; it would also render civil society impossible. The existence of civil authority, therefore, assumes the transfer to the community of each person's unlimited right, a transfer through which each person acknowledges all others as beings whose rights and status are equal to his own.

Of course no one, in our community at least, has ever gone through this "social contract." What matters, however, is whether men act *as if* they had done so, in a way which establishes effective civil authority. And this is simply effected insofar as each person acknowledges — in conscience and in conduct — the equal right of his fellows and the prior moral authority of his community. Any person who meets this condition as a matter of daily practice is, thereby, a member of the community, subject to its authority, and attired in its civility. Any individual who rejects this condition — by refusing to acknowledge either the rights of his fellows or the authority of his community — casts himself out of the community into the lonely sovereignty of unmitigated right.

Let us summarize, now, before proceeding further. I have assumed that no person may presume by the right of his natural superiority to rule others as his slaves. On this basis, the possibility of civil society entails: (1) that each person possesses by nature an initially unlimited right, as lord of the entire cosmos; (2) that each person must lay aside this right and transfer it to the community, acknowledging thereby the community's prior moral authority to determine his legal rights and standards of behaviour; and (3) that through this acknowledgement, each person must recognize the equal rights and status of all others. These three propositions have been deduced, rather strictly, as logically necessary conditions for the possibility of civil society and authority. Let us now examine their political implications.

"Authoritarianism"

Consider, first, the question of authoritarianism. In my earlier account of the savagery of terrorism I asserted, rather brazenly and without justification, that the authority of each community to determine its own standards must be recognized by its members as prior to their own rights. Stated so brazenly, this conception might appear objectionably authoritarian. But the conception has now been given much stronger support: it has been deduced rather strictly, as a condition of civilized existence. The "prior moral authority of the community" must therefore be accepted as true, however objectionable it might appear.

However, the terms of its derivation show that this conception is not as "authoritarian" as it might appear. In particular, it does not invest the community or state with moral significance "in its own right", as an entity existing apart from its members. On the contrary, the community "exists" only as the sum of its members in their socially developed roles and relations. Considered apart from these individuals, "the community" has no reality whatever. And any authority of the community derives from the natural right of these individuals, insofar as each individual may be presumed to have laid aside this` right and to have transferred it to the community. Thus the authority of the community is simply the collective right of its several members. Further, the transfer of right which establishes this communal authority is neither perpetual nor prospectively binding; it is effected only through the ongoing allegiance of the citizen. Each citizen remains free at any time to withdraw this allegiance and to reclaim the lonely sovereignty of his unlimited right. And each citizen might well be pressed to do so, as I have suggested, if the community's authority violates his commitments as a human being. The authority of the community rests upon the right of its members, and its civilized character requires their continuing vigilance.

There is nothing "authoritarian" about this conception. The idea is simply that, since civilized life is impossible if each person retains unlimited natural right, then this right must be laid aside at the gates of any community. The right may be reclaimed at any time, but only by stepping outside the community. Within the community, it is a condition of continuing membership that each person acknowledge the community's authority to determine the standards of appropriate behaviour and the extent of civil rights. What makes any community "authoritarian" is not *whether* it possesses this authority, but rather *which* specific standards it adopts; viz, whether these standards do, or do not, provide extensive rights and liberties as the means of making room for the full and free development of the individual personality. This issue must eventually depend upon what, in view of actual human capacities and resources, makes for the best life; and this calls more for prudent judgement than for abstract right. Where communities are "authoritarian", therefore, it is because of the restrictive standards they impose, and not because of the authority by which they do so. We would do better to contest these standards than the right by which they are enacted.

The Relevant Community

How, then, can we identify precisely which community possesses this "prior moral authority" in relation to any set of individuals?

In theory, the answer is straightforward. Since the community's authority exists only insofar as the individual has transferred to it his natural right, it follows that any 'X' will count as "the community" (or as its authoritative voice) in relation to the individual only insofar as the individual himself assents to this. No other answer is possible. To determine the proper community (or state) in any case, then, we need simply identify the groups and agency to which individuals typically give their allegiance.

In practice, this may be more complicated. Political allegiances may be divided, or uncertain, or even non-existent. In such cases, no group may legitimately hold authority over the individual. This authority will, of course, be claimed by specific groups, using a variety of time-worn pretexts (effective control, territoriality, the public interest, and the 'true' will of the individual). But these claims are simply bunk: apart from the express allegiance of the individual, no group can legitimately wield authority over him.

The situation is different if the individual lives as an "outsider" in the midst of an ongoing community. Here, because the community is not accepted by the outsider, it holds no authority over him: the outsider retains unlimited right in a "state of nature" vis-a-vis the community and each of its members. But if the community is supported by any others, then it may legitimately act against the outsider in the name of the unlimited right which its members have transferred to it. Consequently, even though the community does not hold proper "authority" over such outsiders, it has unlimited right against them and may act on this right with complete justification.

What happens if two rival communities cohabit the same territory? Each holds authority over its own members, but none at all over the members of the other. If the two communities refuse to recognize one another as legitimate, then each will regard the other (and its members) as "outsiders." As a result, the two communities (and all their members) will be in a state of nature in relation to one another, and so the members of each community will have complete right against all the members of the other. In this clash of unlimited right, as we have seen, all the comforts and standards of civilization vanish: each side may act with perfect justification in *any* way against the other, and each side is as fully right in all respects as the other.

Only two outcomes are possible. One community may brutalize the other into conceding its supremacy; this 'solves' the problem of rival communities by forcibly eliminating one of them (probably along with many of its individual members). The only alternative is for each community to limit its claims of natural right in relation to the other. This is the essential condition of civilized relations between them, just as it is between individuals. But this civility requires that each community (along with its members) acknowledge the equal rights and status of the other. This entails that all persons must be conceded the right to constitute the community of their choice. Any failure to respect this equality of right is to reject in principle the possibility of civilized existence.

Similar considerations apply to the relations between separate states. The possibility of civilized relations between them assumes, as an absolute condition, that each recognize the right of the other to exist; and this must be anchored in a deeper recognition — by the members of each community — of the equal right of all other persons to form their own communities. In the final analysis, this right is the foundation of any state's legitimacy and the basis of its recognition by others. Whatever the lawyers and politicians may say, therefore, no state owes a duty of recognition directly to any other; rather, each state (and its citizens) must acknowledge the equal right of all other *persons* to form the communities of their own choice, even if this means recognizing rival communities on the same soil. Any state which denies this equal right of self-determination to any set of persons thereby rejects the possibility of civilized relations with them and undermines the claims of its own legitimacy as a civilized community.

This is complicated, of course, wherever rival communities must be recognized as sharing the same land. In particular, each community will naturally seek to establish sole title to the land; this, eventually, would secure its exclusive sovereignty. But such claims may be dismissed as incapable of foundation. Since all persons have unlimited natural right until they lay it down, and since this right overwhelms all other moral considerations, then the members of each community may claim exclusive ownership of the land by natural right, and this conflict logically cannot be decided by any standard of abstract morality. Each community may claim the land by the same justification as the other: the only title possible is the clash of unlimited right. Thus each community must either exterminate its rival, or acknowledge its equal right. If a community acknowledges the other with equal right then the land — and jurisdiction over it — must be shared. Mutual recognition, therefore, is a necessary condition of effective

68

ownership.

In the absence of such an accommodation the rival communities will confront one another antagonistically; and they will naturally seek alliances and support in their conflict from other states. But all other states must beware of taking sides. Strictly speaking, every other state must respect the right of self-determination for all peoples; and so every state must recognize the legitimacy of *each* of the rival communities. This will inevitably create difficulties, not least because the rival communities will shop for exclusive recognition by retailing stories of its special legitimacy: each will claim exclusive title to the land through the right of first possession, or of effective control, or of special suffering. But all of these claims are irrelevant. For it follows from our argument that (1) each community possesses, through its members, an unlimited natural right; (2) this right, on the part of each community, logically excludes all other moral considerations; and (3) this right, in the form of the right of self-determination, cannot be denied by any other state without automatically undermining its own legitimacy. Consequently, each outside state must recognize the legitimacy of both rival communities; there is absolutely no moral basis on which this legitimacy may be rejected. No cause, however compelling, nor any oppression, however severe, can ever justify one community in refusing to recognize the other.

But why, it may be asked, cannot a state claim in the name of its sovereignty to recognize one of two rivals as the legitimate authority over another territory? Legally, of course, any state may do so. But the legal right, in this case, is morally worthless. If we assume that both of the rival contenders are genuine communities in the sense that they are supported by actual individuals, then it will follow that an outside state can recognize the legitimacy of one side to the exclusion of the other only by denying — wholesale and in principle — the right of self-determination for all members of the excluded community. This would be objectionable for two reasons. First, the outside state's authority within its own borders derives from the transferred right of its citizens; this assumes that the citizens have some right which they may transfer; hence the authority of the state is grounded in the principle of self-determination as the right of its own citizens. To deny this right in the case of any other community is, therefore, to reject the principle of its own legitimacy! Morally, there *cannot* be any right to deny the legitimacy of another community. To claim this right, moreover, is to reject that condition of equality which is the basis of civilized relations among all communities. That is, to reject the legitimacy of any other community is to assert the unlimited right of nature; and this right implicitly puts the state at war with all communities. In short, the internal authority and external legitimacy of any state alike require that it recognize and respect the principle of self-determination on the part of all communities.

Terrorism and The Middle East

Let us now return to the problem with which we began. Earlier, I argued that all acts of terrorism are inherently savage: by rejecting the prior moral authority of each community to determine its own standards, such acts reject the possibility of civilized standards in principle. But the question is whether this is true of PLO terrorism against Israel. For any supporter of the PLO will naturally insist that it is the authoritative voice of a genuine community (the Palestinians); if so, then PLO acts against Israelis would affirm the 'true' authority of the only 'legitimate' community.

On the other hand, the PLO denies the right of the state of Israel to exist in any form. This denial is sweeping and categorical. The PLO claims exclusive sovereignty over the entire territory now occupied as "Israel", and it denies the right of individual Israelis to constitute a community on this domain. Thus the PLO's claims to represent a genuine community are premised from the outset upon a rejection — wholesale and in principle — of any right to self-determination on the part of individual Israelis.

This is crucial: by rejecting this right, the PLO nullifies its own legitimacy. As we have already seen, this right of self-determination is absolutely basic: it cannot be denied in the name of any other principle, however important. Consequently we may assume (for the sake of argument) the truth of every single claim made by the PLO in support of its cause; e.g., that the Palestinians occupied the land first, and longest, that they were wrongfully displaced, and that their record of oppression and suffering is more grievous than that of any other people. These claims might all be true; but they are irrelevant. No cause, however compelling, could ever justify a refusal to recognize the right of self-determination, for this right is the foundation of all authority and justification. In denying this right to individual Israelis, therefore, the PLO rejects the principle of its own legitimacy. In doing so, moreover, the PLO refuses — in the name of unlimited right — to acknowledge that condition of equality which is the foundation of all civilized relations.

To be clear, here, this is not to say that the PLO must recognize Israel's claims to exclusive jurisdiction over the land, nor any other claims which are incompatible with the Palestinians' own existence as a community. Indeed, it is not necessary even that the PLO agree to live at peace with Israel. The *sole* requirement is that the Palestinians (through the PLO) acknowledge individual Israelis as persons of equal right and status, and thence as beings who (individually and collectively) have the same rights of self-determination. This one requirement is essential. Until Palestinians accept it, they cannot be counted a "civilized community".

This is the answer to the question raised earlier. It is true that any PLO member recognizes the prior moral authority of his own community. But this moral authority is based upon a principle which (1) denies itself and (2) rejects the conditions of civilized relations among communities. To accept

70

the 'authority' of the PLO on this basis is to reject the principle of civilized society.

But this, alas, is only half the truth. For what has been said so far about the PLO might also be said about the state of Israel. Indeed, in their "dealings" with one another the PLO and the state of Israel (along with their respective communities) have been rather mirror images of one another. Currently, the government of Israel is opposed — implacably and in principle — to any recognition of the PLO or the Palestinians. Within limits, this is appropriate: one cannot recognize another community if it is officially dedicated to one's own extermination. But these limits are far exceeded by Israel's policy. The Begin government seems opposed absolutely to any form of accommodation with the Palestinians; it specifically refuses to share land and jurisdiction with them; and it seems determined not to recognize the PLO under any conditions. In all these respects, Israel denies Palestinians the right, individually and collectively, of self-determination. And so we must say of Israel what we said of the PLO: by acting on this basis, it undermines its own legitimacy as a community and its own claims to count as a civilization.

For those of us outside the region, an important conclusion follows. It is inevitable and probably desirable that, in the short run, we will support one side of the conflict more than the other. In the long run, however, peace and justice alike require that the rival communities recognize one another as legitimate. On this account, any sympathy for either side should be premised upon the legitimacy of both communities, and their mutual recognition should be made an essential condition for our continued support.

FOOTNOTES

[1] These problems were raised by Ross Rudolph's commentary, and also by participants at the CPPME conference at which the "Terrorism" paper was originally read.

[2] Of course, this begs the question against classic natural law perspectives.

[3] I do not want this to appear too easy. What would we say, e.g., of an individual who engages in child abuse because he sees nothing wrong with it? It would be tempting to treat such a view as proof, *eo ipso*, of moral incapacity.

[4] The Hobbesian basis of this entire account will by now be clear. Peculiarly, this is an interest I share with Ross Rudolph; and it was discussion with him on this aspect of Hobbes which originally prompted this analysis.

POLITICAL IMPLICATIONS OF FUNDAMENTALIST ISLAM

Saleem Qureshi
Associate Dean of Arts and Professor of Political Science
The University of Alberta

Islamic fundamentalism leapt onto the centre stage of world politics with the exile of Shah Mohammad Raza Pahlavi and the emergence of Ayatollah Ruhollah Khomeini as the embodiment of the Iranian Revolution and the sole guide of Iranian destiny. The capture of the Grand Mosque in Mecca, Saudi Arabia, by what were described as fundamentalist fanatics, reminded the world that the phenomenon was neither isolated nor confined to a single nation. If any further confirmation was needed, it was provided by the assassination of President Sadat by self-proclaimed protagonists of Islam.

This wave of religious resurgence or, more appropriately, political militancy in the name of religion that seems so pervasive is by no means confined only to Islamic states. Even secular Turkey has not been able to escape the fury of religious passions. And in Jewish Israel, religious militancy has shown its power in matters ranging from Sabbath observance to the domestic and diplomatic policies of the government. Militant clerics of Iran have their counterparts in militant rabbis in and out of Israel. Thus religious-political militancy is not confined to one kind of society or political structure or religion but is widespread throughout the Middle East. This chapter, however, is not concerned with the entire phenomenon of religious fundamentalism but only with fundamentalist Islam and its political implications. We will therefore examine the nature of this religiously inspired political militancy in Muslim lands, relating the phenomenon both historically and spatially by exploring parallel movements in the Islamic world. We will inquire into the motivations of the activists, the causes of the development of political militancy, and attempt an analysis of its political implications.

Islamic Fundamentalism

A term commonly used, when dealing with the political militancy of the Muslim religionists, is Islamic fundamentalism. Fundamentalism suggests a return to the roots, a rejection of influences that have crept in from the outside. Montgomery Watt, in explaining Islam, describes fundamentalism as essentially isolationism. In his view it is:

a tendency... to shut oneself off from the dominant intellectual culture of the day because it [is] difficult to harmonize various scientific discoveries with the traditional understanding of the [religious texts], or rather with the traditional understanding of the epistemological status of the [scriptural] record...[1].

72

This view of fundamentalism is supported by the rhetoric of the Islamic militants who in general have emphasized a rejection of things western and a return to the pristine or the primitive purity of the Islamic society of seventh century Arabia. But in reality there can be no going back, whether in Shiite Iran, Sunni Saudi Arabia or socialist Libya — three of the most vocally Islamicist regimes of the day. Modern technology has been eagerly sought and modern implements extensively used. The phenomenon of fundamentalism, moreover, is not simple and uni-dimensional. It has a revolutionary component, as Alfred Hottinger has observed in the case of Egypt. If we disregard the rhetoric of Egyptian fundamentalists about a return to purity and probe their objectives, we find them to be revolutionaries, for their ideology promises a fundamental change once Islam is established in accordance with the Divine Order. The strength of the ideology lies in its combination of revolutionary appeal to overthrow the incumbent 'repressive' regime and the promise of return to the comfort of tradition. The protagonists of this ideology are the deprived and the underprivileged who hope to be able to rule a future Muslim state. Because the deprived and the underprivileged generally are unable to deal successfully with the existing world, they often see forcible change as the only solution. In addition to their own misery, they see a shocking amount of injustice, wrong doing, and corruption among political leaders and conclude that the overthrow of corrupt leadership is justified even through violence.[2] Consequently, in terms of what they have actually done[3] and what they plan to do, the Islamic militants seem more revolutionary than fundamentalist. Islamic fundamentalism is thus revolutionary at the same time as it is fundamentalist.

The Search for an Islamic Order

This current of revolutionary fundamentalism is not new in the world of Islam. The search for a better life, a life in accordance with the Divine Order, has motivated religious thinkers and reformers at various times and places whether they demanded legal and theological or political and social reform, and whether the reformer was a *faqid* (an expert in jurisprudence), a *mujadid* (a reformer), or a *mahdi* (a messianic leader). The early jurisprudents or *faqids* codified Islamic law in protest against the laxity and arrogance of the Umayyads. Political dissent, even dissent arising out of social causes, often took on a religious character in the same manner as religious dissent has on occasion assumed a political cast. The vision of a *mujadid* to reform or of a *mahdi* to restore what has been lost and to recreate what once existed has always been present in Muslim culture. Since the ideal is rarely realized, Muslims over the centuries have tolerated all kinds of rulers, sometimes in the name of the unity of the *Ummah* and sometimes in preference to chaos, but the search for a truly Islamic order has been ever present as a cherished ideal. The vision has on many occasions taken the form of a general longing for change when Muslims considered themselves to be under the political influence or control of non-Muslims or felt their religion threatened by the imposition of non-Muslim practices, even when these were imposed by Muslim rulers. The imposition of secular practices occurred only in the context of the rise of the West, particularly since the eighteenth century. However, this craving for deliverence is not exclusively Islamic since religion has been the refuge of the discontented in other faiths as well.

The concept of a *messiah* or a *mahdi*, the restorer or the deliverer, exists in all three revealed religions that originated in the Middle East but while the expectation of deliverence may exist at all times, it requires a particular context of time and place as well as the personality of the claimant to seriously challenge the existing order. A deeply-felt protest must exist among the population. The *mahdi* articulates this protest and offers himself as the deliverer, thus establishing a political bond with the people. If he succeeds in organizing a political movement of protest, his leadership may threaten and displace the existing regime. Since the personality of the *mahdi* is central to the movement, his personal charisma carries the movement forward even without the support of a detailed religious and social programme. This phenomenon of the *messiah* or the *mahdi* has usually occurred in Sunni or majoritarian Islam. In Shii ideology, the deliverer is not the *mahdi* but the hidden *imam*, a descendant of the Prophet's daughter, who is supposed to have disappeared in the ninth century and, according to Shii belief, will reappear to restore Islam to its glory.

Among the more famous protest movements during the past three centuries have been the Wahabiya in the Arabian peninsula, the Sanusiya in present day Libya, and the Mahdi in the Sudan. The founders of all three, namely Abd al Wahab, Muhammad al Sanusi, and Mohammad Ahmad, protested against prevailing conditions, infused theology into political action, organized dissent, and ultimately founded new political orders. Saudi Arabia is the living epitaph to Abd al Wahab, the Sanusiya thrives in Libya, and Mahdism is far from dead in the Sudan. In nineteenth century India, Syed Ahmad waged a holy war against the Sikhs and the British to deliver Muslims from the bondage of the unfaithful. Earlier, men such as Ubayd Allah al-Mahdi and Ibn Tumarat, claiming to be *mahdis*, led reform movements and founded states.[4] More recently, Ayatollah Khomeini has successfully turned political dissent against the Shah in Iran into a religious ideology of '*vilayat-i-Faqih*' and established a theocracy in which he embodies the 'Hidden Imam'. Both in Syria and Egypt bloody attempts have been made to bring down governments which did not espouse the establishment of a sacerdotal order and endeavoured to be non-denominational.

The Political Culture of Islam

The history of Islam does establish that fundamentalism or a search for an Islamic Order has invariably been a part of the attempt of Muslims to cope with the stresses of life. In order to understand the Muslim way of life it is useful to examine the political culture of Islam to determine how Islamic theology prepares or socializes Muslims to seek and accept fundamentalism.

In his *Religion and Political Development*, Donald Smith analyzes four world religions: Hinduism, Buddhism, Islam and Catholicism.[5] Smith argues that Islam is a historical religion: it relies on a "book" which contains the basic dogma and provides a framework for society. Further, in contrast to church religions, Islam is an organic religion with no institutional structures. And, finally, Islam is an egalitarian religion: its theology emphasizes equality.

As an historical religion Islam is fundamentally concerned with truth as revealed in the 'book' and this "truth revealed objectively in history is the same for everyone and therefore absolute."[6] This absolutism regarding truth is not especially conducive to tolerance of contrary opinion in spite of the Quranic injunction against compulsion in religion. In practice this absolutism has tended to reinforce a rigid and dogmatic view of life, an ideologically authoritative enunciation of political objectives, and an anti-pragmatic approach leaving little room for differences of opinion even on temporal and mundane matters. In sum, Islam has cultivated a political culture often conducive to the acceptance of authoritarian leaders by the masses. Empirical observation reveals further that Muslims prefer strong leaders to those who hold notions of diffuse authority and readily follow those who enunciate clear political goals and have the ability to command rather than to lead.

Smith also suggests that church religions are more supportive of secularization whereas organic religions are more resistant. Secularization can be strengthened if role differentiation is acknowledged but Islam does not recognize any such dichotomy. Among the more than 40 Muslim states only one, Turkey, has adopted secularism as its official creed, and even in Turkey the strength of Islamic forces is a constant challenge to secular power. And, over the past few decades, increasing numbers of Muslim states have found it prudent to adopt Islam as the state religion and designate themselves as Islamic states.

Since Islam is an egalitarian not a hierarchical religion, this egalitarianism should support political participation. Theoretical and historical evidence is supportive of political participation but in the absence of a developed political infrastructure, mass political participation has often meant street mobs and demagoguery. Mullahs in the mosques, preaching against alleged violation of Islamic norms, have spurred congregations of the faithful to irrational or violent action. Political participation has,

75

therefore, tended to be anomic, negative, violent, and often resulted in 'mobocracy', invariably ending in dictatorship. Evidence from contemporary Muslim politics supports the conclusion that dictatorships, even military dictatorships, have little to fear if they succeed in cloaking themselves in Islamic legitimacy.[7]

Twentieth Century Developments in the World of Islam

The historical evidence and the political culture of Islam suggest that Muslim countries, as they became independent, should have adopted Islam or transformed themselves into Islamic polities. However, such has not been the case, at least not until the late 1970s. Even a country like Pakistan which was created in the name of Islam did no more than pay lip service to religion. By and large, in almost all Muslim countries, politics remained what it had been before, the preserve of the secularists. Even in Saudi Arabia, politics moved in the familiar grooves, even though these grooves were not properly secular; Saudi Arabian politics remains tribal within a desert democracy ruled by a king who maintains a traditional alliance with the *ulama*.

The political development literature, created mainly by western scholars, emphasized inevitable progress, whether through socialism or liberal democracy, from a confessional and ideologically dominated society to a pragmatic and progressively secularist society. These scholars, largely American, argued that increases in education, urbanization, and industrialization — indices to the growth of secularism — would have the same effect on Muslims as they have had in the west. As we shall see, the expansion of education, far from having a secularizing effect, has created greater awareness among Muslims of their origins and past even among those segments of society who, prior to their education, were ignorant and therefore indifferent to their past.

Factors Contributing to Fundamentalist Resurgence

What then does account for this latest wave of Islamic fundamentalism? No unilinear process nor single factor can explain this latest revival. Rather, a multiplicity of diverse factors, encompassing a wide range of socio-political, economic, and even psychological dimensions, has led to this most recent wave of fundamentalism.[8] The extension of education, especially secondary and higher education, to the lower, middle, and working classes, instead of accelerating secular and westernizing tendencies, has tended to strengthen traditional values. The newly educated have become more articulate in their defense of Islam. Their education has given them access to their history and the achievements and glories of the past have generated a new pride and self-confident identification with their religion and culture. As a consequence, Islamic ideology is more widely and openly accepted and preached. One need look only to the change in the manners, clothing, veiling, and segregation of women to measure its impact. Educational institutions, new communications technology, and organizational skills have provided the facilities and tools for better propaganda and preaching. The effective organization of political parties and movements followed quickly.

National liberation movements and independence struggles in former colonies and anti-imperialist movements against economic colonialism inculcated a consciousness of the exploitation of the masses and raised hopes that independence and liberation would bring great benefits. The industrialization and economic reforms that have been instituted, however, have tended to make the rich richer and the poor poorer, if not in absolute terms then in relative terms. In the oil producing countries, the windfall profits and great wealth benefitted principally the small ruling elite and its allies and even where some wealth has filtered down to the lower levels the gap between the new rich and the new poor has become glaring. The conspicuous consumption and flashy life styles of the upper classes have not only engendered resentment but are considered anti-Islamic. Additionally, in their behaviour, the westernized elites resembled and reminded the poorer classes of the imperialists: haughty, aloof, and domineering. In contrast the Islamists, the clerics, were accessible and available to help and provide solace. The services that clerics provide to the lower classes cover a wide range: blessed water or herbs for ailments, amulets for misfortune, a ready ear if they could offer nothing else, prayers, religious education, and instruction in writing and reading for the illiterate. Thus, not only have numerous bonds been forged between the clerics and the masses but the clerics appear as part of the flock whereas the westernized leaders look like the wolf. It is understandable, consequently, that the egalitarian ideology of Islam looks attractive to the have-nots, and it is natural that Islamic egalitarianism is pressed into the service of the many against the few, especially when the lifestyle of the *nouveau riche* smacks visibly of blind imitation of the west. The self-sacrificing puritanism, charity and sharing of Omar and Ali are obviously more appealing than the logic of economic development plans which requires the poor to make increased sacrifices today in return for a promise of abundance in the future. This is especially so when the entrepreneurs and business magnates live in comfort if not luxury.

Economic development plans, industrial projects, mineral exploration, business and governmental expansion, have all resulted in the uprooting and displacement of large numbers from the countryside to the city. The uprooted are often those psychologically least able to cope with the unknown and the strange, and the dislocation often results in alienation and loss of identity. As a consequence, such people are eager to clutch at the familiar, in culture or religion. Clerics have very often been the main psychological support of the alienated.

The western institutions that Muslim countries have adopted have had no support in the political cultures of those societies.[9] The regimes became autocratic, arbitrary, and corrupt. In contrast Islamic puritanism and the mythology of the *Khalifat-i-Rashida*, the righteous caliphate, serve as the symbols for the new political order to follow the victory of religious forces against corrupt, alien, and secular regimes.

While, by and large, the current wave of fundamentalism seems to be the product of an emotional, strong, and negative reaction to westernization, one major event that has considerably reinforced the anti-western feeling has been the creation of Israel. The creation of Israel by a United Nations clearly controlled by the western and colonial powers, against the very strong but ineffective opposition not only of the Arabs but of the third world and non-aligned states; Israel's recognition by the U.S.A. immediately after its declaration of independence; for the most part the unreserved political, military, and economic support of Israel by the U.S.A. and Western Europe; all these have strengthened the view of the fundamentalists that the Christian west remains implacably hostile to Islam and Muslim aspirations of independence and equality. The fundamentalists who believe Palestine to be part of the Islamic world for the last fourteen hundred years attribute its alienation directly to Britain and the United States. The repeated victories of Israel, the military defeat of the Arabs, and Israel's bombardment of Baghdad and Lebanon with arms supplied by the United States, have strengthened the fundamentalist belief in the calumny of the west.

All these factors worked together to fuel the Islamic revival or Islamic fundamentalism. Both lower-middle and working class Muslims have become more open and articulate in their Islamic identity and the upper classes, which in the past had generally shown a preference for a western life style are now familiar and at home with Islamic theology and are no longer defensive or reticent about being Muslim. This phenomenon is not confined only to Muslim countries but is evident among Muslim immigrants in North America and Western Europe. In short, this Islamic revival is neither a passing phase nor the fancy of the poor, the ignorant, or the bigot. It is pervasive, it has stirred deep feelings, and it has established a bond of identity among Muslims across many countries. For evidence, we need look no farther than the wave of anti-American demonstrations which spread throughout the Islamic world when Khomeini accused the American government of responsibility for the takeover of the Grand Mosque in Mecca in November 1979.

Implications

There are both broad-ranging and specific political implications of this revived Islamic fundamentalism. Generally, this renewal of Islamic fervor has led to: (a) greater self-confidence among Muslims regarding their

Muslim identity; (b) increased militancy and aggressiveness which manifests itself largely in anti-western behaviour but also in opposition to domination of Muslims by non-Muslims especially where Muslims are in the majority in the region; (c) an isolationist tendency which comes from a renewed pride in Islam and focuses attention principally on the Muslim world mainly through proselytization among Muslims — with the ostensible purport of bringing them back to the 'correct path' —; (d) the purification of Islam by eliminating foreign accretions; and (e) an effort to 'correct' the history of Muslims which has been 'distorted' by non-believers.

In terms of political implications, this current wave of fundamentalism has consequences both for domestic power structures and for interstate relations. One might expect that since each new wave of fundamentalism meets a different set of actors and a changed domestic and external environment, there would be a new or a different objective, a different formulation for a different generation of fundamentalists. On the other hand, since fundamentalism is rooted in Islam, generated by similar religious impulses, infused with religious rhetoric and symbolism, could the manifestation and thrust of any variant of Islamic fundamentalism be substantially different? Looking at the experience of the past it is difficult to discern any substantive difference. There seems to be a historic continuity in the flow of fundamentalism.

The historic continuity can be seen in the symbiosis between religious ideology and political protest. Political dissent continues to be presented in the form of religious ideology — the assassination of President Sadat is an obvious example — and religious dissent takes the form of political rebellion — the Iranian revolution and the occupation of the mosque in Mecca are cases in point. Since Islam does not recognize the dichotomy of religion and politics, the use of religion for political ends or the capture of political power for religious objectives is legitimate and accords with Islamic principles. Consequently, religious organizations like the *Ikhwan al Muslimin* and *al Takfir wal Hijra* of Egypt, the *Jama' at-i-Islami* of Pakistan and even informal groups such as the clerics in Iran can and will be able to operate as political parties just as easily as they perform charitable services, preaching politics in religious terms and utilizing the mosques and sermons to stir the faithful to political action.

In this respect there is a remarkable consistency and continuity in the Muslim world. Indeed, one could argue that the values, socialization, and political culture of the Muslims have not undergone any noticeable transformation in spite of western political, economic and military domination, technological superiority, and the teaching of western philosophy and morals. That is to say, the inner core of the consciousness of the Muslim has remained unchanged and western dominance has had no visible impact on the core elements which constitute the identity of a

79

Muslim. This despite the centuries long confrontation between Islam and the west, first in armed conflict with Europe and also in theological competition with Christianity.

This confrontation has not always played itself out, however, on the same stage. For almost one thousand years of this confrontation, Islam was either dominant or equal to its western adversaries, neither defeated nor subjugated. When Islam was powerful it mattered little what the west did; political or religious dissent consequently made no reference to the relationship with the west. As a result the movements arising out of religious or political dissent remained regional and confined. Also, means of communication were limited and what happened in one part of the Islamic world only very slowly came to the notice of the rest. But since the eighteenth century, Islam has been on the decline and the west on the rise and Islam has confronted the west from a position of weakness and defeat. Islam has lost the initiative and has been forced to react to the west. Since this western dominance and Islamic reaction have remained constant over the past three centuries, they alone cannot explain revived Islamic identity and commitment.

Two new developments, however, in the recent past can explain the vehemence of contemporary fundamentalism: the westernization of the Muslims and the establishment of Israel. Westernization of the Muslims has added insult to injury, for Islamic militants argue that westernization has destroyed the unity of Muslims, subverted and undermined the community, and transformed the westernized into agents and stooges of western domination: the Shah of Iran and President Sadat are the prime exemplars. Similarly, they view the creation of Israel as an affront to Islam, an implanted western community inside the realm of Islam that alienated lands belonging to Muslims for more than fourteen centuries. These developments have gathered force in the past half century and with the expansion of rapid and instant communication what happens in one Muslim country does not remain hidden from Muslims in another. As such, this assessment of a great and profound injustice perpetrated by the west on the Muslim world through the subversion of the community and the creation of Israel is widely shared and has given universality to contemporary dissent and militancy to the fundamentalism of today.

The implications of this fundamentalism seem awesome. Countries like Egypt and Saudi Arabia are likely to be the prime targets: Egypt because of its peace treaty with Israel and Saudi Arabia because of the inevitable clash between tradition and modernity. In Egypt the *Ikhwan al Muslimin* and *al Takfir wal Hijra* will continue to press the new government of President Mubarak to implement an Islamic order and to adopt a more aggressive policy on behalf of the Palestinians. There is no inherent component in fundamentalist thought which deals directly with the Palestinian cause. Rather, since Israel's territory was under Muslim jurisdiction for fourteen hundred years and contains holy Islamic shrines, Islamic militants insist that the territory must revert to Muslim control and sovereignty. Arab control of Palestine meets this condition.

The impact of fundamentalist pressure on President Mubarak is evident in his reluctance to follow in his predecesor's footsteps and go to Jerusalem and in a subtle policy shift toward accommodation with the PLO, a shift which has been loudly criticized in Israel. The growing impact of fundamentalism will certainly not allow Mubarak to deal with Israel as freely as did Sadat and may well force Egypt back into Arab politics. If President Mubarak does not reorient Egyptian policy toward the Muslim world, a new round of political turmoil and violence is likely.

Sadat's personal piety and public religious observance did not make him acceptable to the fundamentalists. Rather, his opponents criticized him as an arch traitor for opening Egypt to American influence and concluding a peace treaty with Israel. Sadat was assassinated not because he was personally deficient in religious observance but because he was labelled an agent of the west. It appears that the fundamentalists may be willing to tolerate less than complete personal religious observance by their political leaders but they will not brook the westernization of their society. It was precisely the westernization of Iranian society, along with the Shah's policies toward Israel, which paved the way for the revolution of the Ayatollahs.

In Saudi Arabia the sudden influx of money, the arrival of thousands of technicians and advisors, and the expansion of education and channels of communication, has brought the west into the desert kingdom very dramatically and without any social and psychological preparation. At the same time, very harsh and restrictive measures to keep society in change-less time have generated internal pressures. The takeover of the Grand Mosque in Mecca clearly indicates that socio-political dissent has been given a religious cast and ideology. That ideology is fundamentalist and militant for it regards even the highly conservative and Wahabi house of Saud as insufficiently Islamic. Although the Saudi rulers project an image of religious piety and conservatism, their political and economic policies have created military dependence on the United States and have brought in large numbers of westerners. Fundamentalists consider the close alliance with the U.S. as the principal restriction on Saudi Arabia's policy choices. Sensitive to anti-western feelings within the country, Saudi Arabia has rejected proposed American military bases or the stationing of American forces on Saudi soil. It is caught in the crossfire of creeping modernization, resentment against harsh restrictions, and hostility to expanding American domination. It may not be long before Saudi Arabia faces an even more extreme challenge than did Iran.

Egypt and Saudi Arabia are centrally important within the Arab world, Egypt because of its population and military power and Saudi Arabia because of its guardianship of the Islamic holy places and its enormous petrodollar reserves. Other countries of the Middle East, such as Turkey,

Syria, and Iraq, however, are equally vulnerable to fundamentalist resurgence and consequently are as prone to instability. The ideological forces unleashed by Iran are likely to be felt in almost all countries of the Middle East.

The Middle Eastern country that seems to be most susceptible to fundamentalist militancy and political instability is Syria. The ruling elite are Alawis, a Shiite minority who constitute no more than 11 % of the population. The Muslim Brotherhood, operating within Syria, champions Islamic fundamentalism, though it is not alone in opposing the regime. Opposition centres on the secularism of the Assad regime and the socialism of the Baath Party. In contrast, the Muslim Brotherhood advocates Islam as a state religion and the establishment of the *sharia* as state law. Although sporadic violence has been endemic and the level of murders and bombings high, in early February of 1982, after having amassed a large quantity of arms, the Brotherhood decided to challenge the Assad regime openly in Hama. Although the confrontation ended in a stand-off,[10] the stalemate was a victory for the fundamentalists and a defeat for the regime. The inability of the government to stamp out fundamentalist forces was visible for all to see. The government has been able to rely upon the support of the military only by arresting and executing, just prior to the uprising, many senior officers suspected of questionable loyalty, and by involving most of the officer corps in counter-terrorism against the Brotherhood. More generally, the army supports a secular regime; secularism in Middle Eastern armies has a long history, going back to the days of Ibrahim Pasha, the son of Mohammad Ali of Egypt. It is especially surprising, therefore, that the fundamentalists were able to bring such large quantities of arms into Syria. That they were able to do so testifies to their organizational strength, financial resources, general support, and the inroads they have made within the Syrian army itself. Their capacity to penetrate the ranks of the army was facilitated by an attempted coup against the regime on January 19, 1982. After the coup, large numbers of officers, almost all of them Sunni, were arrested and many executed. It appears that as the regime alienates many among the Sunnis, especially the officer corps, the Brotherhood builds support within the army.

The stand-off suggests that neither side has been able to achieve its objectives and therefore will try again. Recent Syrian policies do not make confrontation less likely. Support of Iran, a Shii country against Sunni Iraq, inaction on behalf of the PLO when they faced Israel's armour, and the general humiliation of Muslims in Lebanon make the regime vulnerable and susceptible to further attacks by the fundamentalists. Relying upon the growing unpopularity of the regime as a result of its less than heroic stand against Israel and the widespread fury over the loss of urban life and the destruction of many mosques in Hama, fundamentalist forces are likely to interpret the stalemate as a political success and continue their campaign of attrition against the Assad government.

Turkey, the only avowedly secular state among the Muslim states, has long been beset with ideological conflict between left and right which exploded into political assassinations. After the politico-religious clashes of December 1978 in the city of Karaman between the Shii and Sunni Muslims in which dozens of Shiites of the Alawi sect were massacred,[11] the government proclaimed a 'state of siege'. In Turkey the main conflict is ideological, not religious, and its main causes are economic. Large segments of the disadvantaged, led by a vocal elite, attribute economic stagnation to western capitalism, criticize secularism and western influences, and look to Islam for political salvation. Necmettin Erbakan vocalizes the disaffection of the disenchanted in the political arena. As the leader of Turkey's ultra Islamic National Salvation Party he has advocated an Islamic currency unit, an Islamic defense community, and the commitment of Turkish units as part of an international Islamic expeditionary force to Afghanistan. He has demanded recognition of the *sharia* as state law and the reintroduction of the Arabic alphabet.[12] While Turkey's army remains deeply nationalist and committed to Ataturk's secularism, many army officers privately are pious. Whether they will be able to resist the wave of Islamic fundamentalism is questionable.

The forces of fundamentalism are likely to be fueled both by the ongoing Islamic revolution in Iran and by the current Israeli-Palestinian conflict in Lebanon and the dispersal of Palestinian fighters to other Arab countries.

The Iranian revolution and its "dazzling" successes — the ouster of the Shah, his humiliating travels from one refuge to another, the seizure of the American embassy, the capture of American hostages, the successful defense against Iraq's invasion of Iranian territory, and the military offensive against Iraq — all these signalled to many within the Muslim world that Islamic fundamentalism is an idea whose time has come. Muslims could easily understand that God was helping those who had reposed their trust in Him and then begun to help themselves. Evidence of God's help was clear: one need look no further than the overthrow of the peacock throne, the humiliation of the United States, and the international prominence of Iran.

The Iranian revolution is a Shii revolution, but it is presented as an Islamic revolution and therefore touches the feelings of Muslims around the world regardless of their sectarian affiliation. Although Sunni Muslims may not be especially eager to follow the lead of Khomeini, they may still be enthused by the vision of an Islamic revolution. For Shii Muslims, Khomeini is the redeemer and the restorer and, indeed, some acknowledge him as the Imam. Already, the Shii populations of Kuwait, Bahrein, and Saudi Arabia have risen in opposition in response to the message coming from Qom, and it is not surprising that regimes along the Gulf feel threatened. If Iranian armour does prevail in Iraq, the government of Saddam Hussein will likely be replaced by a Shii-led regime. If Hafez al Assad survives in Syria, Iran could form a powerful alliance with Syria and

Iraq. This Shii/Iranian hegemony in a crucial region of the Middle East would threaten the stability of the kingdoms and sheikhdoms of the Arabian peninsula. Israel, the target of Iranian threats to march to Jerusalem, and the United States, anxious to stabilize the supply of oil, would view such an alliance with great disquiet. Finally, an Iranian victory over Iraq and continuing conflict between the Muslim Brotherhood and the Alawite government in Syria could explode in a sectarian war between Shiis and Sunnis.[13] Religious fundamentalism generates fanaticism and directs its fury against unbelievers, and usually the first to suffer are the minorities. If religious zeal intensifies, it is not at all unlikely that Shii would take arms against Sunni. Already Muslims are fighting Muslims in Iraq and they have done so in Syria and Turkey.

The other development which threatens the stability of the region is Israel's successful invasion of Lebanon and the expulsion of the PLO. Throughout Israel's bombardment of the Palestinians, not a single Arab leader, not Qaddafi of Libya nor Fahd of Saudi Arabia, offered aid to the Palestinians.[14] As Lebanese Prime Minister Wazzan felt compelled to remark, the silence of the Arab world was stunning. If Israel does succeed in ejecting the remainder of the Palestinian forces from Lebanon, they will most likely be dispersed throughout the Arab world. Their bitterness, their disappointment, their antagonism toward the Arab leaders who stood by, may well lead to activism, political radicalization, and ultimately threats to the survival of conservative regimes. Even more threatening and with greater potential for instability in the Middle East is the identification of the fundamentalists with the Palestinian cause. The Muslim Brotherhood and its affiliates reject Sadat's peace treaty with Israel, and *Al Dawa* of Egypt has ruled that "no peace treaty signed with the Jews is worth even the paper on which it is written."[15] Since the Camp David meeting, fundamentalists have called for a holy war against Israel. The current humiliation of the Arabs and the defeat and expulsion of the Palestinians from Lebanon may divide the Arab and the Islamic world between radicals, who are making common cause with the Palestinians, and the moderate regimes. The radicals are likely to focus their anger not against the Arab masses but against the 'moderate regimes' who were not sufficiently Islamic to champion the Palestinian cause. As Dr. Fathi Arafat, brother of PLO Chairman Yasser Arafat, said: "It is time to not only liberate Israel but also the Arabs [from their regimes because the Arab leaders had not taken time off] from their wealth and women."[16]

In the Israel-Palestinian conflict, Islamic fundamentalists are pursuing a narrow and sectarian strategy, regardless of its consequences. Now that the Palestinian movement has lost its military capability and base of operations against Israel, it has become more dependent upon Arab leaders since it has no independent military option. It has little alternative, at least for the moment, but to try to gain political strength and respectability to pursue its objectives through diplomacy instead of war.

Fundamentalists, seizing a moment of weakness, are demanding the Islamization of the Palestinian movement. While the support the fundamentalists can offer is at best limited, the Islamization of the Palestinian movement would certainly destroy its only and real constituency — the Palestinians, both Muslim and Christian. From the earliest days, Palestinian Christians have been an integral part of the Palestinian movement. Moreover, a key plank in the platform of the PLO is the commitment to a secular state. Islamization, as Shafik Hout recently explained, "...will lead to more disputes. For instance, who can speak on behalf of Islam: Khomeini, [Saudi Arabia's Sheik Abdul Aziz bin] Baz or the Moslem Brotherhood [in Egypt and Syria]?"[17]

Conclusions

While Islamic fundamentalism appears to be riding the crest of a wave and indeed, in the short run, may engulf a major part of the Muslim Middle East, will it be able to find an answer to the Palestinian problem or resolve the conflict between tradition and modernity, religion and secularism, conspicuous consumption and deprivation? At the moment, like a new toy, it retains its appeal to the underprivileged, the deprived, and the alienated. Yet it has not produced a single schema, blueprint or plan for the solution of the grave economic or political problems besetting the Muslim world. It rests largely on negative reaction to the western world — the world of technology — and on a vision and a hope that establishment of an Islamic state and society would cure the ills of the modern world. But would it? Even to raise such questions is either heresy or treason or both among Muslims and so far few have dared to examine critically the promise of fundamentalism.

It is ironic that among all the people of the world it is Muslims who seem bent upon turning back the clock. While the advanced west is exploring space and the developing world is struggling to solve the problems of development, Muslims seek the rule of the *mullahs*. Theocracy is, of course, not unknown, but it flourished in medieval times when the world was steeped in superstition and fear was the dominant emotion. Much has happened since then, but the conclusions Muslims derive from their own and world history are at considerable variance from other analyses. There is not much that the rest of the world can do about the regression to fundamentalism as long as the Muslims will or can not do anything themselves. Islamic fundamentalism will retain considerable appeal for the Muslims and, like other movements, is not likely to dissipate until in practice and over a considerable period of time it fails to provide meaningful and practical answers to the problems which originally made it so attractive.

FOOTNOTES

1   W. Montgomery Watt, *What is Islam* (London: Longman's Librarie du Liban, 1968), p. 197.

2   See A. Hottinger, "Power and Impotence of the Egyptian Fundamentalists", *Neue Zurcher Zeitung*, Oct. 11, 1981.

3   The seizure of the Grand Mosque, the assassination of President Sadat, the overthrow of the Shah of Iran.

4   Derek Hopwood, "A Pattern of Revival Movements in Islam", *Islamic Quarterly*, Vol. XV, Nos. 3-4, Jul.-Dec. 1971, pp. 149-158.

5   Donald E. Smith, *Religion and Political Development* (Boston: Little, Brown, 1970).

6   *Ibid.*, p. 249.

7   Saleem Qureshi, "Military in the Polity of Islam; Religion as a Basis for Civil-Military Interaction", *International Political Science Review*, Vol. II, No. 3, 1981, pp. 281-2.

8   See Nikki R. Keddie, "Iran: Change in Islam, Islam and Change", *International Journal of Middle East Studies*, 11 (1980).

9   For the political culture of the Muslim Middle Easterner see Hisham Sharabi, "Family and Cultural Development in Arab Society", *The Jerusalem Quarterly*, No. 2, Winter 1977, pp. 60-72.

10   *The Economist*, Feb. 27, 1982.

11   *The Manchester Guardian Weekly*, July 15, 1979.

12   *Ibid.*, Sept. 28, 1980.

13   A. Hottinger, "Syria: On the Verge of Civil War?", *Swiss Review of World Affairs*, Vol. XXXII, No. 4, Jul. 1982.

14   Shafik Hout reported in an interview that not one Arab leader, among the many assembled in Mecca, was willing to pledge to fight Israel. See *The Globe and Mail*, Oct. 27, 1982.

15   *The Manchester Guardian Weekly*, Apr. 1, 1979.

16   *Ibid.*

17   *Ibid.*

PART II
EXTERNAL POWERS

ACCOMMODATION OR AGGRESSION?: AN EXAMINATION OF SOME OF THE FACTORS SHAPING SOVIET FOREIGN POLICY IN THE 1980s

Paul Marantz
Department of Political Science
University of British Columbia

In recent years, the Soviet Union has frequently been portrayed as a country in deep trouble. Economic difficulties, uncertainties concerning the health of its senior leaders, and growing nationality tensions have captured the headlines. Based upon this image of the Soviet Union, a number of dramatic — and often conflicting — scenarios have been put forth. Some suggest that the Soviet Union will advance into the Middle East and Persian Gulf due to its thirst for oil and its desire to insulate the restive Muslim population of Soviet Central Asia from unwanted foreign influences. The Soviet leadership will be tempted to provoke foreign crises so as to arouse patriotic fervor and defuse the discontent caused by a stagnating standard of living. Conversely, it has also been argued that the Soviet Union's difficulties are so profound that it will be forced to turn inward and seek a respite from foreign involvement. Soviet inaction during the 1982 Lebanese crisis has been cited to support this rather different view. In other words, some observers argue that internal Soviet weakness will be an important factor leading to crises, confrontations, and acute danger for the non-Communist world, whereas others believe that it provides a golden opportunity for the west to stand firm and obtain concessions from its debilitated opponent.

How weak is the Soviet Union? In what ways are internal forces likely to shape Soviet foreign policy in the years to come? This paper examines these questions to provide a firmer foundation for understanding some of the factors that influence Soviet policy toward the Middle East and east-west confrontations more generally. Specifically, we will discuss four of the domestic problems that figure prominently in western discussions of Soviet foreign policy: Soviet petroleum shortages, the growing Muslim population, the decline in the growth of the Soviet economy, and the post-Brezhnev succession struggle. Our basic conclusion is that while the Soviet system is clearly under a degree of stress and strain from these developments, the difficulties are not nearly as severe as is often assumed. The Soviet leadership still has a great deal of room to maneuver, and a variety of options are available to them for dealing with these troublesome — but hardly fatal — problems.

Soviet inaction in Lebanon is certainly striking, and its implications need to be pondered. But to generalize from this single case to the pattern of future Soviet policy would be as much in error as to anticipate a series of armed incursions based upon the unique circumstances that provoked the 1979 invasion of Afghanistan. At this point in time, future trends are especially difficult to anticipate. There are simply too many uncertainties and imponderables. What is needed is prudent caution, preparation for a wide range of possible alternatives, and an imaginative search for effective means of constructively influencing the choices that the future leaders of the Soviet Union will make.

Oil

In April 1977, the U.S. Central Intelligence Agency issued a gloomy report on the state of the Soviet petroleum industry. It predicted that Soviet oil production would peak within a few years, perhaps as early as 1978. Production would then begin to decline at a rate which would "almost certainly be sharp."[1] The C.I.A. projected that by 1985, the Soviet Union, which had been a net exporter of large quantities of oil, would find itself short by perhaps as much as 3.5 to 4.5 million barrels a day.

This situation would create a profound crisis since the Soviet Union would be unable to pay for imports on this scale. The Soviet Union had been relying upon oil exports to generate roughly 50% of its much-needed foreign exchange. The loss of this hard currency income would in itself be a severe blow. There was simply no way that the Soviet Union could find new sources of revenue to enable it to import rather than export oil. Thus the C.I.A. report fueled fears that the Soviet Union, in desperate need of new sources of energy, might attempt to seize control of the Persian Gulf.

Two years later, the Soviet Union's unexpected thrust southward into Afghanistan seemed to confirm the C.I.A.'s dire predictions. Although Afghanistan has no significant oil reserves of its own, the occupation of that country extended the Soviet Union's border with oil-rich Iran and put Soviet planes within striking distance of the Persian Gulf, the world's single most important source of energy. Energy experts were called to testify in closed hearings before the U.S. Senate. According to an official present at those hearings: "The message was pretty ominous. We were told that the Russian bear has an appetite [for oil] and that that appetite could drive him south."[2] Front-page headlines announced: "U.S. Aides Say Soviet May Look to Persian Gulf for Oil in 1980's."[3] Fear of an energy war in the Middle East helped push the price of gold to record levels.

Now, with the benefit of a few years' additional perspective, we have a better understanding of the factors motivating the Soviet invasion of Afghanistan. It would appear that the thirst for oil was *not* a major factor influencing Soviet conduct. Far more important was the determination of the Soviet leadership to move decisively to prevent the imminent collapse of the Communist government in Kabul. The Kremlin's rulers were unwilling to see a hostile, anti-Communist regime establish itself on the Soviet Union's border, and they were determined not to appear to others to permit the overthrow of a regime allied to the Soviet Union. In essence, Soviet stategic concerns about Afghanistan were not too different from the anxieties presently felt in Washington over the possibility that El Salvador might follow the Cuban path. It was these strategic fears, rather than the seizure of Persian Gulf oil wells, that was at the root of Soviet policy.[4]

Evidence of the last few years also provides the basis for an evaluation of the C.I.A.'s analysis of an impending Soviet oil crisis. Although the C.I.A.'s dramatic predictions captured the headlines, even at the time they were questioned by a number of economists.[5] The debate raged for some years as different experts made their own assessments of the Soviet energy future. However, now that "the future" of the early 1980s has arrived and Soviet oil production has not declined, the C.I.A. has been forced to revise its previous estimates and acknowledge that the Soviet Union will be able to meet its energy needs throughout the 1980s without having to import oil.[6]

What did happen is that instead of plunging, Soviet oil production has plateaued. No longer is it increasing rapidly, as it did in the 1960s and early 1970s (when annual increases of 7-8% were common), but neither is it declining. Production for 1980 was approximately 10% higher than it had been in 1977 at the time the C.I.A. was predicting an imminent drop.[7] The official Soviet Five-Year Plan for 1981-1985 projects a modest 0.6-1.4% annual increase in oil production, and thus far it is on target. Production in 1981 increased to 609 million tons from 603 the previous year, a 1% increase.[8]

Perhaps even more important is the fact that the Soviet Union is now in a position to compensate with other sources of energy for any future short-fall in the petroleum sector. It has embarked upon an ambitious program — unencumbered by any anti-nuclear lobby in that country — to use atomic power to generate electricity.[9] In addition, while oil production is leveling off, the production of natural gas continues to increase at an impressive rate. The 1981-1985 Plan envisages a 6-8% annual rate of increase, and this target was achieved in 1981.[10] By the end of the 1980s, the Soviet Union may be earning in the order of $4-8 billion through the sale of natural gas to Western Europe, a sum which should be quite adequate to compensate for any loss of earnings due to cutbacks in its export of oil. In fact, in many quarters — most notably Washington — the dominant strategic worry is no longer Soviet dependence on Persian Gulf oil, but West European dependence upon Soviet natural gas![11] Thus there seems little reason to fear that a thirst for oil will drive the Soviet Union southward.

Nonetheless, this certainly does not mean that the Soviet leadership is unmindful of the vast oil wealth of the Persian Gulf. Oil politics are as important in Soviet calculations as they are in the minds of western leaders. If the Soviet Union can find ways of attaining Middle Eastern oil on favorable terms, it would be delighted to do so. Depending upon the opportunities that arise, this might be done by exerting pressure on vulnerable states to conclude trade agreements on terms favoring the Soviet Union (e.g., barter agreements exchanging Soviet goods for oil) or it might involve assisting the activities of pro-Soviet forces in the area such as the Tudeh Party of Iran.

Moreover, even if the Soviet Union is unable to gain direct control over the oil of this region, if it can create a situation where Japan and Western Europe must take into account a potential Soviet ability to restrict other countries' access to this oil, then it may reap handsome political dividends and be in a position to exacerbate fissures within the western alliance. Control over Mideast oil — or even the creation of an image of potential control — could have a decisive influence on international politics and hence must be taken into account by western policy-makers. However, a prudent appreciation of what the Soviet Union might hope to gain through the shrewd manipulation of political forces is very different from an alarmist assertion that the Soviet Union is compelled by an approaching energy crisis to gamble upon the direct application of its military power. If the Soviet Union would like to see the break up of Iran, the seizure of Iranian oil fields is but one of the factors involved.

The Muslim Problem

The Soviet invasion of Afghanistan, coming as it did hard on the heels of the totally unexpected toppling of the Shah of Iran by the followers of the Ayatollah Khomeini, focused attention on the Soviet Union's growing Muslim population and on what were said to be the Soviet leadership's anxieties over the possibility that Islamic fundamentalism might spread to the Soviet Union. In its most graphic — not to say lurid — form, the problem has often been presented as follows: the Muslim population of the Soviet Union is now more than 43,000,000, which means that there are more Muslims in the Soviet Union than in such countries as Iran, Egypt, or Iraq. The growth rate for the Muslim population of the Soviet Union is more than three times that of non-Muslims. Already one out of every six Soviet citizens is of Muslim origin, and within less than 20 years, by the year 2000, the proportion could be one in four. People of Russian nationality now comprise more than half the Soviet population (52.4% according to the 1979 census), but sometime during the next two decades they will cease to enjoy this position. By the year 2000, 52-54% of the population will be made up of non-Russian peoples.[12]

It is argued that the Soviet regime faces severe problems due to the confluence of adverse demographic trends, the strains engendered by the rapid modernization of the Muslim regions of the Soviet Union, and the infectious example of Islamic fundamentalism across the border in Iran. Such concerns, the argument runs, were at work in the Soviet Union's intervention in Afghanistan and may well shape future policies toward Iran and the Middle East.

I would argue that this interpretation very much overstates the magnitude of the problem. It is certainly true that the Muslim population is increasing very rapidly, and the largely Russian leaders of the Soviet Union are concerned about this. [13] However, it would appear that the various means at their disposal — including such potent instruments as coercion, control over all communication media, and the selective channeling of economic rewards and career advancement — are more than adequate to deal with present or future problems.

While there have been reports of unrest in Central Asia, the problems there are a good deal less acute than those encountered in the Ukraine or the Baltic republics. [14] The appeal of Islamic fundamentalism to the people of Central Asia is limited not just by the ubiquitous controls exercised by the regime, but by past efforts aimed at increasing the standard of living and discouraging religious beliefs. These policies have achieved much success. Islamic consciousness among the people of the region has been attenuated, and they feel much pride in their educational, economic, and scientific attainments. Local elites have been brought into being which benefit from, and have a stake in, the status quo. In each of the Central Asian republics, there is a large number of Russians to monitor and check on nationalistic tendencies. It is these factors that provide the basis for the Soviet leadership's confidence in its ability to manage the situation effectively. [15]

It may make dramatic newspaper copy to say that non-Russians will soon be a majority of the Soviet population. But in reality, a shift in the non-Russian population from 47.6% in 1979 to 54% in the year 2000 is of negligible political significance. Free elections, in which ethnic voting blocs can make their weight felt, are not a conspicuous part of the Soviet political scene. Power is exercised through the Communist Party which is tightly controlled by its two top institutions, the Politburo and the Secretariat. These in turn are firmly and quite disproportionately dominated by Russians.

Prior to Brezhnev's death on November 10, 1982, 9 of the 13 full members of the Politburo were Russian (i.e., 69%). At the present time, 7 out of 12 Politburo members are Russian, and only one is from Central Asia (Kunaev who is a Kazakh). The situation in the Secretariat, the nerve center of the Soviet political system, is even more imbalanced since at least 7 out of 9 Secretaries are Russian. (One, Zimyanin is Belorussian, and the nationality of Ryzhkov, whose appointment was announced on November 22, 1982, cannot presently be ascertained.) [16]

The rapid growth of the Muslim population of Central Asia will certainly cause the Soviet leadership to pay more attention to this region, but it will not result in a fundamental change in Russian predominance over the key political institutions. By the same token, unless Islamic fundamentalism acquires much more force in the Middle East than it presently has, Soviet fears that it may spread are unlikely to be a major force shaping that country's foreign policy.

The Economic Slowdown

Of late, western observers have devoted a great deal of attention to the economic difficulties of the Soviet Union. As the economist Philip Hanson has pointed out, there have been two main schools of thought among western experts: the pessimists, who believe that the Soviet economy is in poor shape, and the optimists, who believe it is in truly disastrous condition![17]

The most serious problem confronting the Soviet leadership is that their economy has been experiencing a long-term, continuous, and steady decline in growth rates. During the 1950s, the Soviet GNP grew at the impressive rate of approximately 6% per year. In the 1960s, the rate of growth was about 5½%. In the 1970s, it dropped to 3½%, and in the first half of the 1980s, it is projected by many western economists to decline to 2½% per year or less.[18]

The political implications of this trend toward ever slower growth are profound. In the first instance, it makes the Soviet Union's on-going military build-up an ever more costly process. Over the past fifteen years, from the late 1960s to the early 1980s, it is estimated that the Soviet military budget increased on the order of 4-5% per year. This was at a rate roughly comparable to or only slightly above the rate at which the Soviet economy expanded during this period. As a result, even though military expenditures absorbed a staggering 12-14% of the GNP during this period, the percentage did not change appreciably over the years.[19] The situation in the 1980s, however, will be quite different. If the military budget continues to expand at the past rate of approximately 4-5% per year, while the GNP grows at only 2½% per year, the military will be absorbing an ever greater share of Soviet economic resources, and, consequently, less would remain for reinvestment or consumption.

But if increments of new investment capital are further reduced, then one of the main factors contributing to economic growth would be curtailed, and future slowdown would be that much greater. Alternatively, if consumption is restricted, this would mean that the impressive increases in the Soviet standard of living that occurred in the Brezhnev years of 1965-1980 would largely cease. This in turn would not only adversely affect productivity (by depressing worker morale and leading to increased absenteeism, alcoholism, and carelessness on the job), but would also have potentially far-reaching consequences for the stability of the Soviet political system in the years ahead.

As the eminent American Sovietologist Seweryn Bialer has argued, the preservation of political stability is a matter of grave concern to the Soviet Union's rulers.[20] They are fearful of challenges to their power and have worked hard to enhance Soviet stability. Under Stalin, political terror and brutal repression were the major instruments for eliminating potential challenges to the regime. However, in the post-Stalin era, even though coercion has remained ever present and the Soviet Union continues to be a highly authoritarian society, the ubiquitous terror of the past has receded, and the regime must now provide positive incentives for loyalty. This has taken the form of increased efforts to ensure a steady improvement in the standard of living. Loyalty can no longer be compelled; increasingly it has to be purchased.

The Brezhnev regime has been highly successful in this regard. Major strides were made in providing the Soviet population with improved housing, better clothing, more televisions, refrigerators, and other consumer goods.[21] In the period 1965-1980, per capita consumption increased at the rate of about $3\frac{1}{2}\%$ per year. [22] For the long suffering Soviet consumer, who tends to compare his present situation with his own condition of years past — and not with the much higher standard of living of the west of which he knows relatively little — this represented an appreciable gain. The problem, however, is that future prospects are not very rosy, and it is projected that in the future per capita consumption may increase at only one third the rate of past years (i.e., 1.2%).[23] For the Soviet leadership, which is vividly aware of how past economic problems have provoked instability in Poland, Czechoslovakia, and East Germany, this is indeed a troubling prospect.

Equally disturbing to the Soviet leadership is the challenge that declining growth rates pose to the ideological rationale used to legitimize the Soviet system. The basic premise of Marxism-Leninism is that Soviet-style socialism constitutes a superior economic system, one which will eventually close the economic gap with the west and demonstrate its ability to outproduce the most advanced capitalist countries. With pride the Soviets point to the fact that the backward regime which they inherited in 1917 is now the world's largest producer of oil, coal, steel, pig iron, cement, tractors, chemical fertilizers, etc.[24] Up until quite recently, it has been possible for the Soviet Union's rulers to convince themselves and their subjects that due to superior Soviet growth rates (which were generally in excess of those achieved in the west), it would only be a matter of time before that country's economy was the most advanced in the world. Now they can no longer be so sanguine, yet the acceptance of a position of permanent inferiority runs counter to the whole thrust of the dominant ideology and would be profoundly unsettling to the self-confidence of the leadership and the loyalty of the population.

Thus the on-going decline in Soviet growth rates is bound to create disquiet in the minds of the Soviet leadership since it severely constrains their military options, may induce political instability, and could lead to a serious loss of confidence in the Soviet system. And, the Soviet Union has been hit by the more immediate problem of three disastrous harvests in a row, in 1979, 1980, and 1981. The grain harvest for 1981 has been such an embarrassment that the Soviet Government has broken with past practice and refused to release the final figures. Western estimates are that grain production in 1981 was approximately 70 million tons (i.e., more than 25%) short of the target for that year and some 20 million tons less than the disappointing 1980 harvest.[25] These shortfalls have forced the Soviet Union to purchase massive quantities of grain abroad, a highly undesirable situation since it consumes a large part of the Soviet Union's scarce foreign exchange and opens the Soviet Union to western attempts to use Soviet dependence upon foreign grain as a lever for influencing its policies.

Slowing industrial growth and erratic harvests have put the Soviet Union in a difficult situation. There have been reliable reports that even though the Soviet Union has been selling unusually large quantities of gold, it has been unable to generate enough foreign exchange to cover its commitments. Short term Soviet foreign debt has increased, the Soviet Union has asked a number of suppliers for an extension in meeting outstanding bills, and the Soviet trade deficit for 1981 was approximately $5½ billion (twice that of 1980).[26]

All of this sounds quite ominous, and it has caused some western observers to suggest that the Soviet economy is in a state of near collapse. However, I would argue that a closer examination of the situation discloses a more complicated picture. There is still a great deal of resilience and latent strength in the Soviet economy. Recent economic performance has clearly been disappointing to the Soviet leadership, but compared to Poland — or even the recession-battered countries of the western world — the Soviet Union is not doing nearly as poorly as is often assumed. This can be seen if we look more closely at the matter of declining growth rates. On the one hand, the fact that the Soviet economy is now growing at less than one half the rate it attained in the 1950s and 1960s is highly significant. If the downward trend of the last quarter of a century were to continue, the Soviet regime would eventually face the prospect of zero growth.

On the other hand, it must be realized that while growth is slowing down, *the Soviet economy is still growing.* The post-World War II Soviet economy has yet to experience even a single year of true recession, i.e., throughout this period each year's output has always exceeded that of the previous year.[27] This contrasts rather favorably with the frequent recessions of the western world (or even with those of Poland in 1979-1981 and Czechoslovakia in the early 1960s) during which time an actual shrinkage in output occurred.

Moreover, while the Soviet growth rate of the 1970s of 3½% was low by past Soviet standards, it still compares quite favorably to rates attained in the west. It has been calculated that for the period 1973-1978, the Soviet economy grew faster than those of the United States, the United Kingdom, and West Germany, and only marginally slower than that of Japan, the economic miracle worker of the western world.[28] As far as future trends are concerned, it should be noted that the figure of 2½% growth per year that has been projected for the 1980s is roughly comparable to that which many economists anticipate for the west in the years ahead.[29] The long-cherished

Soviet dream of catching up with and then surpassing the economic performance of the west may have to be jettisoned. But for the foreseeable future, the Soviet economy appears likely to grow, and it shows no sign of falling into the kind of disarray that has afflicted Poland in recent years.

If growth rates continue to decline, there will indeed be a squeeze on Soviet resources. If military expenditures increase more rapidly than the rate of economic growth, less money would be available for improving living standards. Yet we should not magnify the severity of this problem. It has been calculated that even if the growth of the Soviet economy slows to 2½% per year in 1980-1990, the leadership could match the rapid military buildup of the 1970s (i.e., increases of 4½% per year in military expenditures) and still be able to raise living standards by about 1% per year.[30] While a 1% annual increase in per capita consumption is low compared to the rate prevailing in 1965-1980, most western observers would agree that it should be adequate to preserve domestic tranquility. Historically, the Soviet people have proved patient and long suffering. They do not have the Polish tradition of working class militancy, and unless faced with acute food shortages or a sharp decline (as opposed to a leveling off) in living standards, they are unlikely to threaten the stability or orderly functioning of the Soviet regime.[31]

This, then, brings us to the agricultural situation. Here, too, a degree of balance is necessary. Clearly, Soviet agriculture is performing poorly. Output targets are not being met despite the truly massive amounts of scarce capital that the Brezhnev regime has poured into the countryside. The poor performance of the Soviet Union's agricultural sector remains an international embarrassment and a major factor dragging down the rest of the economy. Yet the situation is not quite as bad as is frequently assumed.

The western press tends to compare the actual Soviet harvest to the output targets set in the five-year plans. However, because these targets are often quite ambitious and constantly increase from one plan to the next, such a comparison can produce a one-sided interpretation. This can be seen if one looks more closely at the grain harvests for 1979-1981 which have justly been described in both the Soviet Union and the west as poor.

The harvests for 1979-1981 averaged only 80% of the planned output, resulting in a shortfall of about 50 million tons per year.[32] But if one looks not at planned targets, but at the actual amount of grain produced, a rather different picture emerges. For example, the "disappointing" harvest of 1980 actually exceeded that of the record harvest of 1970. Planning authorities in 1980 regarded the record harvest of ten years earlier as an achievement of the past which was to be surpassed. Similarly, we find that even during the bad years of 1979-1981, grain output was twice that of the early 1950s.[33] It also might be noted that in the 25-year period from 1951-1975, total Soviet agricultural output increased at a rate averaging 3.4% per year compared to an American increase during this period of only 1.6%.[34] Due to climatic and other factors, Soviet grain production has always fluctuated much more widely than it does in North America. Hence we must look not just at the weak years of 1979-1981 (when Soviet grain production averaged 180 million tons), but also at the record harvests of 1976 and 1978 (which were 224 and 237 million tons). In short, there is much room for improvement in Soviet agriculture, but it is not obvious that difficulties have reached crisis proportions.

In regard to foreign exchange and balance of payments, the Soviet position is, if anything, even healthier. Even though the Soviet Union may be experiencing some minor cash flow problems at the present time, its basic foreign currency position is quite sound, and its long term earning potential is more than adequate to cover its debts and pay for its imports. The Soviet Union, with the world's second largest economy, owes less than Poland ($20 billion vs. $27 billion) — or less than Argentina for that matter. The Soviet Union can count on earning large quantities of foreign exchange through the sale of oil, gas, gold, and military hardware. Soviet annual gold production alone is estimated to be worth more than $3 billion on the world market.[35] Whereas Poland is virtually bankrupt (and Rumania and Yugoslavia are in serious trouble), the Soviet Union has gold and hard currency reserves that far exceed its outstanding debt.[36]

What, then, can be said about the foreign policy implications of the Soviet Union's economic difficulties? How apt is the warning of the distinguished British Sovietologist Robert Conquest: "Governments incompetent at home but capable of demagogic expansionism abroad have traditionally — one might almost say automatically — turned to foreign adventure"?[37] Will the Soviet leadership be driven to undertake foreign adventures as a means of arousing patriotism and distracting the population from internal failures? Argentina's seizure of the Falkland Islands is a vivid reminder that throughout history, regimes in domestic trouble have often provoked foreign crises.

Nonetheless, I would argue that on balance there are good reasons for not expecting the present or future Soviet leadership to choose this path. First, as we have noted above, the Soviet regime cannot accurately be said to be experiencing an acute economic crisis. Economic growth may be slowing, but it is still taking place, and it would appear that for the next decade at least, economic conditions will be fully adequate to ensure domestic stability.

Secondly, an examination of the historical record suggests that the Soviet regime has responded to past internal crises not by provoking foreign conflict, but by either retreating inward and isolating itself from the outside world or by making overtures aimed at lessening tension and improving the international climate. This was the case during the massive economic dislocations of the late 1920s (caused by the rapid industrialization and forced collectivization of the first five-year plan), during the upheaval of the mid-1930s (due to the purges), and in 1953-1955, when Stalin's death left a power vacuum. While there is, of course, no guarantee that previous patterns will repeat themselves, past behaviour does at least suggest that the Soviet leadership is perfectly capable of finding other ways of defusing or repressing popular discontent. Thus internal weakness need not automatically result in foreign adventure.

At the same time, we should not fall into the trap of assuming that internal weakness precludes foreign expansion, that because the Soviet economy is already severely strained by the cost of supporting 100,000 troops in Afghanistan, keeping Poland afloat, and subsidizing Cuba at the rate of $3 billion a year, it will be unable to sustain the expense of new client states or afford the cost of a rekindled arms race with the United States. The immense destruction of World War II did not prevent the Soviet Union from embarking upon its most successful period of foreign expansion, in the years 1945-1948.[38] The Soviet economy, with all its difficulties, can still support more Cubas and Afghanistans. Given the clear priority that the Soviet leadership has always assigned to key political objectives — with relatively little concern for economic costs — we should not assume that economic factors alone will compel the Soviet Union to retrench in the third world or to embrace eagerly the cause of arms reduction.

In short, economics will be only one factor shaping Soviet policy in the years ahead. Conditions in the Soviet economy are not likely to compel Soviet leaders either to expand outward or to withdraw inward. The choice will ultimately be a political one, shaped first and foremost by the priorities and policies adopted by Brezhnev's successors. Depending upon how the succession struggle unfolds, upon precisely who consolidates power, upon the strength of various internal political forces, and upon the international dangers and opportunities, very different choices are possible.

The Succession Problem

For years, Brezhnev has been in obvious ill health, and western observers have speculated on the possible consequences of his departure from power. Such speculation was bound to be laced with great uncertainty, since there was no way of knowing when he might leave office, whether he would designate a successor before his departure, or who might take his place. Now suddenly Brezhnev is gone, and Yuri Andropov has swiftly emerged as the most powerful Soviet leader.

Yet the imponderables are still enormous. What are Andropov's political leanings? Does his background as head of the K.G.B. (the secret police) for fifteen years and as Soviet Ambassador to Budapest at the time of the crushing of the Hungarian uprising of 1956 point to a hardening of Soviet policy? Or does his reputed interest in the English language and western world, his association with various liberal Soviet political figures, and his apparent support for Hungarian liberalization over the last two decades suggest that he may lean toward improved relations with the west and economic reform at home?[39] How secure is his position as Secretary-General? What coalitions are forming within the Politburo and will Andropov be able to satisfy their demands? The inner workings of Soviet political institutions are so deeply shrouded in the mists of official secrecy that few of its important features can be discerned by the outside observer. This is true even at the best of times, but the analysis and prediction of the future is even more difficult, since the future is highly contingent and dependent upon the complex interaction of all sorts of unforeseen events that intervene.

One has only to look at the three previous occasions of leadership change to see how limited is our ability to anticipate and predict future events. In the 1920s, most observers thought that Trotsky was far more likely than Stalin to inherit Lenin's mantle. Similarly, no one expected that Khrushchev, who was widely regarded as an uneducated buffoon, would be able to fight his way to the top following Stalin's death. And even though Brezhnev was regarded as the leading contender to replace Khrushchev, it came as a total surprise when the Politburo was able to remove him from power. Writing in 1963, just one year before Khrushchev's dramatic ouster, two distinguished scholars, Zbigniew Brzezinski and Samuel P. Huntington, confidently stated: "In the Soviet system the top leader, like the Czar, always dies in office."[40]

By the same token, western observers have not been any more prescient in anticipating the policies that new leaders would follow once they came to power. Stalin was widely viewed as a pragmatist who would downplay ideology and avoid sharp confrontations with the west. Khrushchev, who turned out to be remarkably innovative and flamboyant in his campaign to discredit hardline Stalinist perspectives on international politics, had been viewed as a colorless bureaucrat of orthodox persuasion.

Nor has there been any consistent pattern as to the consequences of leadership change for Soviet foreign policy. Lenin's death in 1924 had little immediate effect upon the Soviet Union's relations with the west. Stalin's death brought about an instant thaw in east-west relations as the new leadership moved quickly and decisively to end the Korean War and improve relations with the United States, Israel, Yugoslavia, Turkey, and other countries. In contrast, Brezhnev's assumption of power in 1964 brought about a distinct cooling of relations with the west. In short, the only pattern that emerges is that there is no pattern.

Hence it behooves us to be very cautious in speculating about what Brezhnev's demise will mean to domestic and foreign policy. While the transition to Andropov has been more rapid and smoother than most western experts expected, we must remember that only the first round of the succession struggle is over. Malenkov was also quick off the mark as the clear front-runner when Stalin died in 1953, but within two years a coalition headed by Khrushchev forced his resignation. Judging by past experience, it may well be several years before a new leader — be he

Andropov or someone else — is able to consolidate his power. It took Stalin approximately four years to ensure his unchallenged domination over the Soviet system. It was not until June 1957, four years after Stalin's death, that Khrushchev was finally able to push his rivals aside, and while Brezhnev did not face the same bitter opposition, it was not until 1970-1971 that his undisputed primacy was established.[41] Age may also handicap Andropov. He is already 68, whereas Khrushchev was 58 when Stalin died, and Brezhnev was 57 when Khrushchev was removed from power.

In the face of such formidable obstacles to the anticipation of the policies of Brezhnev's successors, most scholars would be tempted to turn to more fruitful lines of inquiry. But Sovietologists are a hardy and resourceful lot, and they have devised another way of attempting to read the tea leaves. It is argued that even though we cannot know how long Andropov will remain at the helm or the precise views of each of the contenders for power, we can say something about the general characteristics of the next political generation which is waiting in the wings of the Kremlin.

Actuarial realities will eventually make themselves felt. Six of the twelve full members of the Politburo are seventy years of age or older. Two others, Andropov and Grishin, are sixty-eight. Sooner or later, they will give way to younger men. These younger men, the argument runs, can be viewed as a distinct political generation with definite tendencies and characteristics distinguishing them from the people now in power. Those prominent Soviet leaders who were born after 1925, and are now in their mid-fifties, constitute a distinct generation, not by virtue of age alone, but because they have had very different formative political experiences. They have come of political age since World War II. The destructive experiences of Stalin's bloody purges of the 1930s or the devastation of the Second World War count less for them than their experience with Khrushchev's efforts at de-Stalinization. They are better educated than their elders, more dynamic, and less willing to accept a continuation of the present uninspired muddling through in domestic and foreign policy.[42]

This line of argument has been skillfully and imaginatively explored by a number of scholars. My own view, however, is that it provides a rather unreliable guide to the future. There are two main reasons for asserting this. The first is that I doubt whether it is really possible to anticipate the politics of a particular individual (or even of a small group such as the Politburo) by reference to the concept of political generations. The attempt to gauge the future direction of Canadian or American politics by reference to the coming of age of a new political generation (e.g., the post-Vietnam generation) would rightly be regarded as highly suspect. Within every age cohort there is a wide range of opinion, and particular individuals who gain the top political positions may diverge greatly from the majority of their contemporaries.

In a highly authoritarian country like the Soviet Union, which lacks many of the balancing mechanisms and restraining influences of a more pluralistic society, the policies and personality of the top leader are all the more important. Brezhnev may perhaps be representative of the mass of Party functionaries, but this cannot be said of Stalin or Khrushchev. Khrushchev was unorthodox, highly individualistic, and surprisingly innovative. He was no more representative of his generation than were his main rivals for power, the arch-conservative Molotov, the sinister Beria, or the reformist Malenkov.

Moreover, even if we accept the concept of political generations in regard to Soviet politics, we run into a second problem. How are we to ascertain the outlook and policy preferences of the younger generation of Soviet officialdom? Given their blandly orthodox and deliberately unrevealing public utterances, we can do little more than engage in wild speculation as to how certain formative political experiences might shape individuals of a particular age.

Thus it is hardly surprising that among those who have attempted this methodological approach, there is a complete lack of consensus. Those inclined toward a bleak view of the Soviet scene argue that younger leaders are likely to be bolder and more assertive than the present gerontocracy. Not only will they possess greater vigor and energy, but they will be under pressure to prove themselves and to demonstrate that they can be effective leaders. In the view of William Hyland:

> some of these people probably have not acquired the temperance and prudence that Brezhnev and Kosygin learned through experience. They might feel, for example, that the risks of the Ethiopian adventure undertaken by this very "old, tired" regime were really not all that great.... When the Brezhnev group retires from the scene, it may be succeeded by people who see interventionism as the norm, who believe that the Soviet Union can intervene in ways that earlier appeared quite risky indeed.[43]

According to this interpretation, if the Soviet economy continues to deteriorate, these new leaders may be driven to seek foreign success so as to compensate for domestic weakness and to distract the people from their hardships.[44]

This certainly is not an implausible scenario, and yet at least as good a case can be made for the opposing view. Thus another group of equally distinguished experts optimistically suggests that the next generation of Party leaders, being better educated, more knowledgeable about the West, more secure in their positions and more conscious of the inefficiencies of the rigid Soviet economy is likely to incline toward "moderate reformism" in domestic policy and to search for a form of "economic, military and political detente" with the west.[45] According to Jerry Hough: "Once the generation of leaders who benefited from the purge has retired, there will be a strong natural tendency for Soviet internal policy to evolve in a more liberal direction — toward the more relaxed type of authoritarian state found in Poland."[46] In foreign policy, this may well bring a desire to reduce east-west tension so as to improve Soviet access to western technology and allow the avoidance of an economically ruinous arms race.

Who is right, the optimists or the pessimists? My own view is that either outcome is possible. The future is not predetermined and the role of generational factors in shaping Soviet foreign policy will be relatively limited. The concrete events, problems, and opportunities of the years ahead will have a major impact in determining not only which individuals from the younger generation have the best chance of gaining power — moderates or those inclined toward confrontation — but also what policies they will follow once they are saddled with the responsibilities of power.[47]

Given such factors as the need for the leadership to grapple with the deterioration of the economy and the likelihood that the advanced age of the members of the Politburo will lead to vacancies and hence sharp conflict over new appointees, it is quite possible that the struggles within the Politburo will be even sharper than those of the past.[48] Soviet foreign policy is bound to be affected. But just how the succession process will unfold, no one can say. Lacking a reliable road map to the future, all we can do is watch developments carefully and expect the unexpected.

Conclusion

A striking example of the unexpected is Soviet policy — or more accurately "non-policy" — during the most recent Lebanese crisis. In the last few years, the Soviet Union has sharply increased its support for Syria and the PLO, its two closest allies in the Middle East. The Soviet Union signed a Treaty of Friendship and Cooperation with Syria in October 1980 and accorded the PLO full diplomatic recognition in October 1981. Yet the Soviet Union did virtually nothing when Israel's forces inflicted a humiliating defeat on the PLO and Syria in the summer of 1982. The Soviet Union sat on the sidelines and was largely irrelevant to the unfolding of the Lebanese conflict.

Soviet inaction is all the more striking when it is compared to the forceful Soviet response during the Arab-Israeli War of 1973. At that time the Soviet Union engaged in a massive airlift of military equipment, sending in approximately one thousand planeloads of supplies.[49] At one point, when Egyptian forces were encircled by Israel's troops, the Soviet Union placed large numbers of airborne troops on standby alert and threatened to send its forces into the region. This threat was regarded with such seriousness by the United States that American personnel were placed on a worldwide alert, and a full blown east-west crisis ensued. Only urgent consultations between the superpowers defused the crisis. In contrast, in 1982 the Soviet Union did relatively little to resupply its allies and its diplomatic response was low key and ineffectual.

How is this unexpected shift in Soviet policy to be explained? It is tempting to attribute this new-found caution to some of the factors discussed in this paper, and a number of commentators have made this argument. It has been suggested that Soviet policy is severely constrained by that country's growing economic difficulties and increasingly infirm leadership. According to this view, the Soviet economy, with its declining growth rates, is already stretched to the limit by Afghanistan, the on-going Polish crisis, and the need to match greatly increased American military expenditures. The aging Soviet leadership, with its lack of dynamism and imagination, is said to fear the economic costs and political risks of a major confrontation with the United States.

There are, however, two problems with this analysis. The first is that its predictive value is very limited. Even if it provides a correct diagnosis of the present, it does not help very much in anticipating the future, since prognosis depends upon which particular factor is given greater prominence. If one believes that economic weakness provides the key to understanding Soviet policy, then one can be relatively optimistic about the future, since the deep-seated and fundamental causes of the Soviet economic decline are not susceptible to short term solution. On the other hand, if one believes that the Soviet loss of dynamism is attributable to the advanced age and ill health of Brezhnev's Politburo, then there is reason to be deeply concerned about what will happen now that Brezhnev has died and a healthier, more vigorous leadership is taking over.

The second and more fundamental problem with this line of analysis is that it may simply not be correct, even as applied to recent events. The secrecy surrounding Soviet decision-making is so all-pervasive that it is often very difficult to fathom the Politburo's motives and to know what considerations are responsible for a particular policy. Thus it might be argued that Soviet policy in regard to Lebanon was not the product of indecision and drift, but resulted from a clear-headed appraisal of basic Soviet interests.

The Soviet leadership may have decided that the Middle East is a hopeless quagmire. Over the years, the Soviet Union has spent billions of rubles trying to win the support of such countries as Egypt, Iraq, Somalia, and the Sudan. Despite these enormous expenditures, it has little to show for its efforts. Rather than squander additional resources on ungrateful clients, the Kremlin may have decided to deescalate its involvement in the Middle East and concentrate on more pressing goals such as encouraging Western Europe's estrangement from the United States and attempting to reduce China's animosity toward the Soviet Union. An acute crisis in the Middle East would tend to work against progress toward these far more important objectives.

Having considered all its options in regard to the Middle East, the Soviet leadership may have concluded that the best policy was one in which the Soviet Union assumed a low profile and let the United States pay the costs of the inevitable failure of its attempt to promote peace in that volatile and uncontrollable region. The United States had staked its reputation on the shuttle diplomacy of Philip Habib and President Reagan's peace plan, and one of the many parties to the Arab-Israeli conflict would certainly challenge the American initative. In the interim, the Soviet Union would seek to widen the breach between the United States and the Arab world by blaming the Americans for all that happened. To this end, Soviet spokesmen have asserted that the United States was an "accomplice" to the massacre of civilians in Beirut and "the world has witnessed not simply an Israeli aggression but an American-Israeli one."[50] In short, given the ambiguous record of Soviet behaviour, it is difficult for the western observer to say whether the Soviet Union's Middle East policy reflects weakness or sober calculation.

Finally, even if one were to conclude that Soviet behaviour in Lebanon is indeed the product of internal weakness, it would be a mistake to generalize from Soviet policy in this crisis to future Soviet conduct in subsequent conflicts. If the members of the Politburo come to believe that western policy-makers view the Soviet Union as an enfeebled giant with feet of clay, then they may well feel the need to over-compensate during some future crisis to demonstrate that the Soviet Union is not an international weakling to be pushed around with impunity. Present passivity may give way to future truculence.

Lacking a crystal ball, our examination of some of the internal factors shaping Soviet foreign policy can provide only a very general picture of the highly uncertain and contingent Soviet future. Nonetheless, several conclusions emerge. The first is that two of the problems we have discussed, the burgeoning Muslim population and the leveling off of Soviet oil production, are not likely to be major factors influencing Soviet foreign policy. There does not seem to be much basis to the alarmist scenarios that depict a Soviet compulsion to drive southward in order to insulate the Muslims of Central Asia from contaminating influences or to acquire Persian Gulf oil.

On the other hand, it would appear that the slowdown of the Soviet economy and the post-Brezhnev succession struggle are much more important factors. They are likely to have a major impact upon the thrust of Soviet policy in the years ahead. Battles over contending economic remedies will complicate the selection of new leaders, and conversely the struggle for political primacy will make the adoption of effective economic policies more difficult. The relative continuity of the Soviet leadership and of Soviet policies during the past decade is likely to give way to a highly unstable and unpredictable period. This is hardly a cheery prospect given the Soviet Union's vastly expanded global power and the tempting opportunities for intervention that are sure to arise in the volatile countries of the Middle East and elsewhere.

The outward thrust of Soviet foreign policy, which has been so prominent in recent years, is the product of factors deeply imbedded in Soviet perceptions of the international scene: the desire to be recognized as a global superpower fully equal to the United States with the same broad prerogatives to shape international events; the pursuit of clients and bases throughout the world; the continued influence of an ideological outlook which sees the world in terms of irreconcilable class forces and unceasing struggle; the tendency to accord great value to military strength as the one reliable instrument of Soviet power, now that Soviet inability to compete in the economic, political, and ideological realms has become so manifest; and a sense of weakness and vulnerability which leads to policies (such as the invasion of Afghanistan), which whatever their defensive component, cannot but threaten the security of other nations.[51]

I for one doubt that even a new leadership under pressure to concentrate on reviving the economy is likely to be free of this troublesome mind-set. The precise shape of future events is impossible to discern, but it would appear that storm clouds are more probable than calm seas. The Soviet Union is far more likely to fish in the troubled waters of the Middle East than engage in a constructive search for even-handed solutions. Even though the Soviet Union decided to sit on the sidelines during the Lebanese crisis of 1982, there is no guarantee that it will do so in the future or that it will lend its weight to promoting a genuine dialogue between Israel and her neighbors.

FOOTNOTES

NOTE: The research for this paper was assisted by the funding provided by the Donner Canadian Foundation, through a grant in support of the Institute of International Relations' research project on "Canada and International Trade" at the University of British Columbia. An earlier version of this paper has been published in *Etudes Internationales*, December, 1982.

[1] The C.I.A. report is discussed in: Abram Bergson, "Soviet Economic Slowdown and the 1981-85 Plan," *Problems of Communism*, vol. 30, no. 3 (May-June 1981), p. 27; Philip Hanson, "Economic Constraints on Soviet Policies in the 1980s," *International Affairs*, vol. 57, no. 1 (Winter 1980-81), pp. 27-28, 36-37; *The New York Times*, April 28, 1977, p. 35, May 22, 1978, p. D3, July 30, 1979, p. D1, November 20, 1979, p. D1.

[2] *The New York Times*, April 15, 1980, p. 1.

[3] *Ibid.*

4 Helmut Sonnenfeldt, "Implications of the Soviet Invasion of Afghanistan for East-West Relations," and Raymond L. Garthoff, "Detente and Afghanistan," in Erik P. Hoffmann and Frederick J. Fleron, Jr., eds., *The Conduct of Soviet Foreign Policy* (2nd ed.; New York: Aldine, 1980), pp. 748-755, 756-761.

5 *The New York Times*, April 28, 1977, p. 35 and April 17, 1980, p. A27; Marshall I. Goldman, "The Soviet Union and a Multilateral Oil Agreement," in *The Soviet Union and the World Economy* (New York: Council on Foreign Relations, 1979), pp. 81-100.

6 *The New York Times*, May 19, 1981, p. A1 and Sept. 3, 1981, p. A1.

7 Bergson, "Soviet Economic Slowdown and the 1981-85 Plan," p. 27; Goldman, "The Soviet Union and a Multilateral Oil Agreement," p. 85.

8 *The New York Times*, January 24, 1981, p. 1.

9 Thane Gustafson, "Energy and the Soviet Bloc," *International Security*, vol. 6, no. 3 (Winter 1981-1982), pp. 74-78.

10 In 1981, 465 billion cubic meters of natural gas were produced compared to 435 the year earlier. *The New York Times*, January 24, 1982, p. 1.

11 Miriam Karr and Roger W. Robinson, Jr., "Soviet Gas: Risk or Reward?," *The Washington Quarterly*, vol. 4, no. 4 (Autumn 1981), pp. 3-11; *The New York Times*, March 14, 1982, p. A20.

12 The statistics cited in this discussion are drawn from: Murray Feshbach, "Between the Lines of the 1979 Census," *Problems of Communism*, Vol. 31, no. 1 (January-February 1982), pp. 29, 35; Jeremy Azrael, "The 'Nationality Problem' in the USSR: Domestic Pressures and Foreign Policy Constraints," in Seweryn Bialer, ed., *The Domestic Context of Soviet Foreign Policy* (Boulder: Westview Press, 1981), p. 145; *The New York Times*, February 28, 1980, p. A9.

13 Steven L. Burg, "Soviet Policy and the Central Asian Problem," *Survey*, vol. 24, no. 3 (Summer 1979), pp. 65-82; Hélène Carrère d'Encausse, *Decline of an Empire* (New York: Harper & Row, 1981), pp. 277-284.

14 Edward A. Corcoran, "Soviet Muslim Policy: Domestic and Foreign Policy Linkages," in Robert H. Donaldson, ed., *The Soviet Union in the Third Word: Successes and Failures* (Boulder: Westview Press, 1981), pp. 306, 311; Azrael, "The 'Nationality Problem' in the USSR," pp. 139-153.

15 Stanley Rothman and George Breslauer, *Soviet Politics and Society* (St. Paul: West Publishing Co. 1978), pp. 139-145, 150; *The New York Times*, April 12, 1980, p. A1.

16 The nationality of Soviet leaders may be ascertained from Alexander G. Rahr, *A Biographic Directory of 100 Leading Soviet Officials* (Munich: Radio Free Europe/ Radio Liberty, 1981). It might be noted that 68.3% of the full members of the Central Committee elected at the Twenty-Sixth Party Congress in 1981 were Russian. Boris Meissner, "The 26th Party Congress and Soviet Domestic Politics," *Problems of Com-*

munism, vol. 30, no. 3 (May-June 1981), p. 21.

[17] Hanson, "Economic Constraints on Soviet Policies in the 1980s," p. 21.

[18] *Ibid.*, p. 22. Official Soviet statistics for any particular time period are invariably higher than those calculated by Western economists. However, they show precisely the same pattern of decline. *Ibid.*, p. 22. For slightly different Western calculations, which also show the same trend, see: Bergson, "Soviet Economic Slowdown and the 1981-1985 Plan," p. 26 and Herbert S. Levine, "Soviet Economic Development, Technological Transfer, and Foreign Policy," in S. Bialer, ed., *The Domestic Context of Soviet Foreign Policy*, p. 178.

[19] Since the Soviet Union does not provide any reliable statistics on its actual military expenditures, we are forced to rely upon western estimates. The percentages cited are those estimated by the C.I.A. They are accepted as being relatively accurate by most western observers and accord with what we know about the massive increases in Soviet hardware. The American economist, Franklyn D. Holzman has raised a number of sophisticated methodological questions about the C.I.A.'s calculations, but even if he is correct, only minor reductions (in the order of 1-2%) would have to be made in the C.I.A.'s figures. Holtzman's major challenge is to the C.I.A.'s comparison of Soviet vs. American military expenditures. "Soviet Military Spending: the Numbers Game," *International Security*, vol. 6, no. 4 (Spring 1982), pp. 78, 97, 99-101.

[20] Seweryn Bialer, *Stalin's Successors* (Cambridge: Cambridge University Press, 1980), pp. 141-182; Seweryn Bialer, "The Harsh Decade: Soviet Policies in the 1980s," *Foreign Affairs*, vol. 59, no. 5 (Summer 1981), pp. 999-1020.

[21] Jerry F. Hough, "The Man and the System," *Problems of Communism*, vol. 25, no. 2 (March-April 1976), pp. 11-13; Walter D. Connor, "Mass Expectations and Regime Performance," in S. Bialer, ed., *The Domestic Context of Soviet Foreign Policy*, pp. 155-173.

[22] Bialer, *Stalin's Successors*, p. 293.

[23] *Ibid.*

[24] *Ibid.*, p. 150.

[25] *The New York Times*, January 24, 1982, p. 1; Karl-Eugen Wädekin, "Soviet Agriculture's Dependence on the West," *Foreign Affairs*, vol. 60, no. 4 (Spring 1982), p. 888.

[26] *The New York Times*, March 14, 1982, p. A1.

[27] Hanson, "Economic Constraints on Soviet Policies in the 1980s," p. 24.

[28] *Ibid.*, pp. 24-25.

[29] For example, Wharton Econometric Forecasting Associates predicts that the economies of the Common Market nations (which *contracted* by an average 0.5% in 1981) will grow by about 1% in 1982 and by about 2.8% in 1983-1986. *The New York Times*, March 21, 1982, p. F1.

[30] Hanson, "Economic Constraints on Soviet Policies in the 1980s," pp. 29-32.

31 Connor, "Mass Expectations and Regime Performance," pp. 155-176.
32 *The New York Times*, January 24, 1982, p. 1; Wädekin, "Soviet Agriculture's Dependence on the West, " p. 888.
33 James R. Millar, "The Prospects for Soviet Agriculture," *Problems of Communism*, vol. 26, no. 3 (May-June 1977), p. 7.
34 *Ibid.*, p. 8. Also see Wädekin, "Soviet Agriculture's Dependence on the West," pp. 882, 889. Needless to say, these statistics — like any one set of statistics — do not tell the full story. The Soviet Union started from a very low base, while the American Government was trying to restrict output during much of this period. However, they do serve as a useful corrective to the prevalent image of Soviet agriculture as being in a state of total collapse.
35 *The New York Times*, March 14, 1982, p. A20.
36 *Ibid.* Hanson, "Economic Constraints on Soviet Policies in the 1980s," p. 37.
37 Robert Conquest, "A New Russia? A New World?" *Foreign Affairs*, vol. 53, no. 3 (April 1975), p. 492.
38 Adam Ulam, "How to Restrain the Soviets," *Commentary*, vol. 70, no. 6 (December 1980), pp. 38-41.
39 Andropov's background and views are examined in Jerry F. Hough, "Soviet Succession: Issues and Personalities," *Problems of Communism*, vol. 31, no. 5 (Sept.-Oct. 1982), pp. 32-34 and Harrison E. Salisbury, "Andropov Reads America, Fluently," *The New York Times*, November 16, 1982, p. A27.
40 Zbigniew Brzezinski and Samuel P. Huntington, *Political Power: USA/USSR* (New York: Viking Press, 1965), p. 182.
41 Myron Rush, "Brezhnev and the Succession Issue," *Problems of Communism*, vol. 20, no. 4 (July-August 1971), pp. 9-15.
42 The logic behind this approach is cogently set out in Bialer, *Stalin's Successors*, pp. 97-126.
43 William F. Hyland, "Implications for U.S.-Soviet Relations," in Dimitri K. Simes, et al., *Soviet Succession: Leadership in Transition, The Washington Papers*, no. 59 (1978), p. 78.
44 Ulam, "How to Restrain the Soviets," pp. 38-41; Walter Laqueur, "Russia Beyond Brezhnev," *Commentary*, August 1977, pp. 39-44.
45 George W. Breslauer, "Political Succession and the Soviet Policy Agenda," *Problems of Communism*, vol. 29, no. 3 (May-June 1980), p. 46.
46 Jerry F. Hough, "The Soviet Succession," *Washington Post*, April 17, 1977, pp. C1-C2, cited in Connor, "Mass Expectations and Regime Performance," p. 170. Also see: Hough, *Soviet Leadership in Transition*, pp. 156-157; Bialer, "The Harsh Decade," pp. 1011-1015; Bialer, *Stalin's Successors*, pp. 283-305; Dimitri K. Simes, "The Soviet Succession: Domestic and International Dimensions," *Journal of International Affairs*, vol. 32, no. 2 (Fall/Winter 1978), pp. 211-221.

47 Different scenarios are effectively set out in Breslauer, "Political Succession and the Soviet Policy Agenda," pp. 49-52 and Connor, "Mass Expectations and Regime Performance," pp. 168-171.

48 Bialer, "The Harsh Decade," p. 1015.

49 Joseph L. Nogee and Robert H. Donaldson, *Soviet Foreign Policy Since World War II* (New York: Pergamon, 1981), p. 270.

50 The treatment of the Lebanese crisis in the Soviet press is discussed in *Soviet World Outlook*, vol. 7, no. 9 (September 15, 1982), p. 2 and Robert Rand, "Brezhnev's Remarks on Foreign Policy in His Speech in Baku," *Radio Liberty Research Bulletin*, RL 390/82 (September 27, 1982), pp. 1-3.

51 Bialer, *Stalin's Successors*, pp. 229-279.

AMERICAN FOREIGN POLICY IN THE MIDDLE EAST: A STUDY IN CHANGING PRIORITIES

Blema S. Steinberg
Department of Political Science
McGill University

Introduction

What are the basic underlying factors that explain American foreign policy in the Middle East? If there are no easy answers to this question it is not because scholars, practitioners, and journalists have failed to address the problem. Quite the contrary. There is a plethora of detailed and fascinating accounts of American foreign policy in the Middle East written from a wide variety of perspectives. Many of these, however, are crisis-oriented, instant histories. What we lack is a systematic attempt to explore the pattern of American foreign policy over time within a broad historical context. There have been numerous efforts to explain, for example, the decision to sell AWACS to Saudi Arabia, but little attention to the pattern of American arms sales to the Middle East and the factors that explain the differences in policy over the years.[1]

In an effort to fill this gap, this paper explores two specific dimensions of American foreign policy behaviour in the Middle East: patterns of conflict management — intense involvement vs. benign neglect — and patterns of military commitment — the extent of U.S. arms sales and formal treaty arrangements. Between 1948 and 1982, U.S. management of the conflict in the Middle East oscillated between periods of intense involvement and periods of benign neglect. Sometimes the United States involved itself heavily in trying to find solutions to the Arab-Israeli conflict, while at other times it left the conflict quietly simmering on the backburner. What explains these different patterns of behaviour? The nature of U.S. military involvement in the Middle East since 1948 also varied widely. At times the United States worked to create formal treaty arrangements, at other times to develop a strategic consensus; at times it has embargoed arms to the region, or supplied limited amounts of weaponry to selected states, and most recently, it has sold huge amounts of sophisticated weapons systems to an increasing number of actors in the region. Again the question arises: what factors might explain those differences?[2]

Among foreign policy analysts there appears to be general agreement that U.S. interests in the Middle East were both global and regional in scope. At the global level, the United States was engaged in an ongoing world-wide struggle for power and influence with the Soviet Union. In this context, the Middle East provided an important arena of superpower competition. At the regional level, the United States pursued two major sets of interests — one that focused on Israel and its security, the other on the Arab world and secure access to oil and petro-dollars.

At the global level, American interest in competing with the Soviet Union for power and influence was reflected in two quite different approaches. At certain times the United States adopted a strategy of overt containment in which its primary goal was to prevent any further expansion of Soviet influence through a forceful American posture of deterrence. Underlying this approach was a perception of U.S.-Soviet relations as a zero-sum game — a win for one side was automatically a loss for the other side. Quite different was the strategy of 'tacit' containment or détente. The United States still competed with the Soviet Union, but it conceived of superpower relations in less than zero-sum terms. American leaders argued that their Soviet counterparts were interested in co-operating with the United States, or at least in modifying their policies either for economic benefits — technology transfers, investments, and more advantageous terms of trade — because they recognized the risks inherent in a superpower confrontation arising from escalating local wars.[3]

At the regional level, U.S. interests focused on Israel and the Arab world. Ever since the birth of the state of Israel in 1948, the United States demonstrated a basic commitment to Israel's security. Although no formal treaty bound the two countries, successive American presidents and the Congress repeatedly spoke of a commitment to Israel's survival. Whatever the sources of that commitment — and differences of opinion do exist as to the relative importance of such factors as Israel's role as a free and democratic society deserving of American support, its value as a strategic asset, the legacy of the Holocaust, the role of domestic politics and the existence of a well-organized and effective Zionist lobby — American support for Israel's security and well being was both constant and of long-standing duration.

Quite different in scope were American interests in the Arab world. These are primarily economic in nature. The Arab world contains approximately two-thirds of the known reserves of oil in the world — a commodity that remains vital to the economic health of advanced industrial societies. At times, American interest in Arab oil translated into an effort to protect American oil companies worried about their profits, the rate of return on their investments, and nationalization of their assets. As well, U.S. government officials were not unmindful of the financial contribution that U.S. oil companies earning over $2 billion annually in repatriated revenues, particularly since the late 1960s, could make to easing U.S. balance of payment problems.[4] Since 1973 and the Arab oil boycott, American interests in Arab oil shifted from an emphasis on protecting American oil companies to a concern with assuring western access to Middle East oil and sufficient production at reasonable prices.

It would be an over-simplification, however, to subsume American interests in the Arab world under the single heading of oil. The economic spin-off of a fourteen-fold increase in the price of crude oil per barrel since 1971 was an enormous increase in American interest in re-cycling Arab petro-dollars. The Arab world, and more particularly Saudi Arabia, became important investors in American financial and commercial institutions and significant purchasers of American military and non-military goods and services both from government and the private sector. The American interest in petro-dollar reserves undoubtedly explains some of the changes in American patterns of conflict management and military involvement in the Middle East.

American Interests And American Behaviour

In this paper, we focus particularly on two dimensions of American foreign policy behaviour in the Middle East — patterns of conflict management and patterns of military commitment. We begin by exploring the impact that alternating American global interests — containment vs. détente — have had on American policy. At times, American policy makers argued that the Soviet Union was ambitious and hostile, that it could be deterred only by countervailing U.S. military, political, and economic power. When U.S. decision-makers emphasize deterrence and containment of the Soviet Union, they should logically strengthen regional powers militarily to resist Soviet expansionism and second, de-emphasize the importance of resolving the conflict between Israel and the Arab states because of the pre-eminent Soviet threat to American security interests.

At other times, when American leaders had a much less antagonistic view of their superpower opponent, and, consequently, moved to a strategy of détente, then they assumed that both superpowers shared an equal interest in global stability and the major threat to that stability lay less in the threat of Soviet expansionism than in escalating regional conflicts. Consequently, decreasing the level of U.S. military commitments in the region and finding a solution to the Arab-Israel conflict become crucial elements in the maintenance of détente and global stability.

Four key questions structure our examination of the relationship between American global interests and American policy:

(1) Will increased American interest in containing the Soviet Union be associated with decreased efforts to resolve the Arab-Israeli dispute (i.e., a policy of benign neglect)?
(2) Will increased American interest in détente with the Soviet Union be associated with increased efforts to resolve the Arab-Israeli dispute (i.e., a policy of intense and active involvement)?
(3) Will increased American interest in containing the Soviet Union be associated with increased American weapons supplies to regional actors?
(4) Will increased American interest in détente be associated with decreased American arms supplies to regional actors?

Equally important, changes in American views of their regional interests may influence American foreign policy behaviour. Did changes in the importance to American leaders of Arab oil and/or petro-dollar

113

investments have an impact on their efforts to find a solution to the Arab-Israeli conflict and on the level of American military assistance to regional actors? When American interest in Arab oil and/or petro-dollar investments was relatively low, U.S. decision-makers very likely attached lower priority to finding a solution to the Arab-Israeli conflict; conversely, when American interest in Arab oil and/or petro-dollar investments was relatively intense, the United States probably gave higher priority to solving the conflict. Why should this be so? Since 1948, Israel continually stressed the importance of direct bilateral negotiations with its Arab neighbours as the correct approach to resolving the conflict. It feared that U.S. involvement in managing the conflict would translate into American pressure to relinquish Arab lands captured on the battlefield without securing an equivalent trade-off, a secure and lasting peace. The position of the Arab states provided a sharp contrast. In the aftermath of successive military defeats, some Arab leaders expressed interest in U.S. efforts to help them regain their lost territories. They recognized that while the Soviet Union could provide the instruments of war, only the United States could supply the requisite political leverage to extract concessions from Israel.

Faced with two competing perspectives — Israel's disinterest and Arab interest in American mediation efforts — on what basis did American foreign policy makers choose among alternative strategies to manage the Middle East conflict? American interest in Israel's security was largely constant, but what did change was America's interest in placating the Arabs. When the United States was not overly concerned about Arab economic power, it could afford to ignore Arab pressure for territorial changes in the Middle East; when it felt itself vulnerable to Arab economic reprisal, it was more inclined to work for changes in the existing status quo in the region. To examine the relationship between American interests in the region and their strategies of conflict management, we ask the following questions:

(5) Will low to moderate U.S. interest in Arab oil and/or petro-dollar investments be associated with limited U.S. efforts to find a solution to the Arab-Israeli conflict (i.e., a policy of benign neglect)?

(6) Will strong U.S. interest in Arab oil and/or petro-dollar investments be associated with active American involvement in conflict resolution?

A focus on changes in U.S. interests in the Arab world also contributes to an understanding of the pattern of U.S. military assistance to states within the region. Once again the key factor is the fluctuation in American desires to placate the oil-rich Arab states. If we assume first that an increase in American estimates of its dependency on Arab oil and/or petro-dollars would be reflected in greater willingness to meet Arab requests for military goods and services, and second, that increased

American interest in the Arab world would not decrease concern for Israel's security, then increases in arms sales to the Arab world would be matched by corresponding increases in arms supplies to Israel to prevent any significant alteration in the regional balance of power between Israel and its Arab neighbours.

To explore the relationship between American regional interests and arms sales we ask two final questions:

(7) Will low to moderate U.S. interest in Arab oil and/or petro-dollar investments be associated with moderate arms sales to the Arab world?
(8) Will strong U.S. interest in Arab oil and/or petro-dollar investments be associated with major arms sales to Israel and to the Arab states?

These assumptions and questions link global and regional interests independently to foreign policy. But what is the combined effect of particular combinations of global and regional interests on the patterns of conflict management and arms sales? For example, is active U.S. involvement in managing the Middle East conflict most likely when the U.S. has a strong interest in détente and a strong interest in Arab oil and petro-dollars? Conversely, can we expect a policy of benign neglect when the U.S. is interested in containment and relatively disinterested in Arab oil and petro-dollars? By the same token, will the heaviest volume of U.S. arms sales to the Arabs occur when the U.S. is interested in containing the Soviet Union and assuring access to Arab oil and petro-dollars; conversely, are arms sales likely to be limited when the U.S. is interested in détente and relatively disinterested in Arab oil and petro-dollars?

American Behaviour In The Middle East

Before examining the relationship between interests and policy, we set the scene with a brief look at changes in American management of the Arab-Israeli dispute. When we examine the extent of U.S. involvement, we distinguish between periods of 'intense involvement' and periods of 'benign neglect'.[5] We look also at changes in the nature of American military involvement in the region, paying particular attention to American efforts to create pacts or alliances in the region and to the scope of U.S. arms sales.[6]

a. U.S. Management of the Arab-Israeli Conflict
(i) 1948 to 1968: 'Benign Neglect'

Generally from 1948 to 1968, American interest in finding a solution to the Arab-Israeli conflict appears limited. The United States did recognize that termination of the Arab-Israel dispute by peaceful means was essential to achieve peace and stability in the region. In a statement to Eliahu Elath, Israel's first ambassador to the United States, President Truman expressed this recognition:

> I am firmly convinced of the necessity of the speedy establishment of a true and equitable peace between Israel and its neighbours and for the resolution of all problems outstanding between them, in accordance with the solemn recommendations of the United Nations with respect to Palestine. The Government of the United States is deeply desirous of assisting by all appropriate means in the fulfillment of these objectives.[7]

The United States did not attempt, however, to mediate between Israel and its Arab neighbours, nor did it attempt to press either Israel or the Arab states to make concessions that might encourage the development of a genuine rapprochement. Before Arab-Israel relations could improve, American leaders argued, the Arab view of Israel would have to change. U.S. decision-makers, particularly during the Eisenhower Administration, believed that a more reasonable Arab view of Israel could be achieved through accelerated Arab economic development and this analysis led to an increase in U.S. economic aid.[8]

In October 1953, as part of Dulles' increased interest in improving conditions between Israel and its Arab neighbours, President Eisenhower sent Eric Johnston to the Middle East as his personal representative with the rank of Ambassador "to explore with the governments of the countries of that region certain steps which might be expected to contribute to an improvement of the general situation in the region".[9] One of Johnston's major purposes was to undertake discussions concerning the mutual development of the water resources of the Jordan River in an effort to benefit all the inhabitants of the area. A comprehensive Jordan Valley development plan would, it was hoped, contribute to regional stability and economic progress and thus help to reduce tension and to promote accommodation between Israel and the Arabs. Despite some initial support for the Johnston Plan on the part of the technical and professional advisers representing Israel, Jordan, and Syria, the mission came to naught.

In the two years that followed, U.S. efforts to promote an Arab-Israeli settlement benefitted from the 'advice' and proposals of senior American officials. By mid-1955, however, the U.S. recognized that its efforts had achieved no tangible results and on 26 August 1955 Secretary Dulles, in an address to the Council on Foreign Relations in New York City, reviewed the problems of the region and suggested a multi-faceted approach. To solve the refugee problem, he proposed resettlement and repatriation along with an increase in arable land through practical projects for water development. The necessary funds would be made available partly by the United States, which would also participate substantially in an international loan to enable Israel to pay the compensation due to the refugees. In an effort to alter the climate of fear and insecurity in the region, the United States "would join in formal treaty engagements to prevent or thwart any effort by either side to alter by force the boundaries between Israel and its Arab neighbours".[10] In summary, from 1953 until September 1955 the United States demonstrated somewhat greater interest in promoting a solution to the Arab-Israeli conflict. The extent of American involvement, however, remained limited — the U.S. would provide the infrastructure of economic and technical assistance to finance change as well as a political guarantee that boundaries could not be altered by force.

With the onset of the Suez Crisis, the United States concentrated first on preventing escalation of the conflict and then on ensuring that the "aggressor" states not reap the fruits of their military action. With the withdrawal first of British and French, and then of Israel's forces, the U.S. renewed its efforts to resolve the Arab-Israeli conflict. Again, the United States stressed the importance of creating the conditions appropriate to a long-term resolution of the underlying issues of the conflict, rather than any direct American role as a conciliator or mediator.

By the end of the Eisenhower years, even limited U.S. efforts to encourage a permanent settlement of the Arab-Israeli conflict had failed. Consequently the United States seemed to prefer the status quo to new initiatives. In its approach to the region, the Kennedy Administration made stylistic rather than substantive changes. Symptomatic of increasing American interest in improving relations with the Arab world was the appointment of John S. Badeau, former president of the American University in Cairo, as U.S. Ambassador to Egypt. The United States also gave the Arab refugee question increased attention. Joseph Johnson, the President of the Carnegie Endowment for International Peace in New York, was appointed as Special Representative of the Palestine Conciliation Commission to explore means of resolving the Arab refugee problem. Once again, the United States stressed the importance of improving the atmospherics — in this case, relations with the Arab world — to improve the prospects of a peaceful solution.

In the years that preceded the 1967 war, the Johnson Administration made no significant effort to resolve the Arab-Israeli conflict. Like its predecessors, it continued to emphasize regional security and stability and the maintenance of a military balance to prevent conflict. It was the June War that precipitated a major change in American thinking. Rather than focusing primarily on the need for regional stability, the United States tried to promote a peaceful resolution of the conflict. Unlike President Eisenhower's emphasis, after the Suez War, on Israel's withdrawal from all occupied Egyptian territory, President Johnson believed that Israel should be prepared to give up the conquered territories only in exchange for a genuine peace agreement. A diplomatic framework for a peace settlement was the priority. Once this was in place, with time the Arabs would be prepared to negotiate to recover their territories, or so American leaders expected. The American administration did not, however, consider a high level, intensive peace-making effort useful in the immediate future. Very likely, Johnson considered that such a move would fail, given the limited influence of the United States in Arab capitals and he did not feel that he could sustain such an effort at a time when Vietnam was demanding so much of his attention. The Johnson Administration never seriously considered such an option.[11]

In a major policy statement issued on 19 June 1967, on the eve of President Johnson's meeting with Soviet Premier Kosygin at Glassboro, the American president spelled out the general lines of a settlement. Johnson placed the major responsibility for the war on Egypt, terming the closure of the Straits of Tiran an "act of folly". He stated that the United States would not press Israel to withdraw in the absence of peace and he proceeded to spell out five principles essential to such a peace: the recognized right to national life; justice for the refugees; innocent maritime passage; limits on the arms race; and political independence and territorial integrity for all the states in the region. Although Johnson did envision a comprehensive settlement of all the issues stemming from 1947-49 and 1967, American diplomatic efforts focused on the passage of a UN Security Council resolution that would incorporate Johnson's five points. On 22 November 1967, Resolution 242 was adopted. It incorporated Johnson's five points as well as a delicately balanced call for "withdrawal of Israeli armed forces from territories occupied in the recent conflict" and "termination of all claims of belligerency and respect of and acknowledgement of the sovereignty, territorial integrity and political independence of every state in the area and their right to live in peace within secure and recognized boundaries free from threats or acts of force". The United Nations also appointed Gunnar Jarring as its representative and charged him with the responsibility for finding a solution to the Arab-Israeli conflict within the parameters of Resolution 242. Throughout most of 1968, the Johnson Administration assumed a comparatively low profile in Arab-Israeli diplomacy, leaving the main task to Jarring.[12]

This review of the years from 1948 to mid-1967 suggests that American involvement in managing the Arab-Israeli conflict was minimal. It did not address itself directly to the achievement of a permanent and secure peace in the region. Rather, U.S. policy was active only at the margins — it sought to improve the environment among the protagonists by attempting to resolve such elements of the conflict as the Arab refugee problem and to promote economic growth in the Arab states. In the aftermath of the June War, the Johnson Administration did acknowledge the need for a just and lasting peace in the region, but it chose not to insinuate itself directly into the diplomatic process, preferring to rely instead on the United Nations

Security Council and UN Special Envoy, Gunnar Jarring. This entire phase, from 1948-1968, can best be characterized as one of 'benign neglect'.

(ii) 1969 to 1970: 'Intense Involvement'

If the American approach to the Arab-Israeli conflict from 1948-68 was one of 'benign neglect' or limited involvement at the margins, the period from 1969-82 reveals much greater oscillation between 'intense involvement' and 'benign neglect'. From early 1969 to August 1970, the approach of the Nixon Administration reflected a much greater sense of urgency and involvement. A broad consensus developed that the United States should play a more active role in promoting a political settlement based on the principles embodied in UN Resolution 242. Nixon's advisors considered the efforts of the Johnson Administration too passive, those of UN Ambassador Gunnar Jarring as too cautious. Between February and October 1969, the Nixon Administration was actively involved in bilateral negotiations with the Soviet Union and four power negotiations with the U.S.S.R., Britain, and France to promote a solution to the conflict.[13]

In late October 1969, Secretary Rogers outlined the terms of an American proposal calling for the conclusion of a final and reciprocally binding accord between Egypt and Israel, to be negotiated under the auspices of UN Ambassador Jarring, following procedures used at Rhodes in 1949. Rogers referred to the basic elements of an accord: binding commitments by the parties to peace, including the obligation to prevent hostile acts originating from their respective territories; Rhodes-style negotiations to work out details of an agreement; issues to be negotiated between Egypt and Israel to include safeguards in the area of Sharm el-Sheikh, the establishment of demilitarized zones, and final arrangements in Gaza; and, in the context of peace and agreements on security, Israel's forces would be required to withdraw to the international border between Egypt and Israel. On 18 December the United States presented a parallel plan for peace between Israel and Jordan, but the rejection by both Israel and the Soviet Union in late December of the Rogers Plan ended the first major Middle East initiative of the Nixon Administration.

Faced with an escalation of Soviet involvement in Egypt early in 1970, intensified fighting along the canal, and the increasingly important role of the Palestinian fedayeen in Jordan, State Department specialists decided that the best way to reverse the trend was a new diplomatic initiative, this time less ambitious in scope than the Rogers Plan and less dependent on Soviet cooperation. A simple "stop shooting-start talking" formula was proposed directly to each party on 19 June 1970. After discussions in Moscow in early July, Nasser announced his willingness to accept the proposals for a cease-fire and on 26 July, Jordan also accepted. Israel was finally persuaded to accept the proposals on 31 July in exchange for permission to purchase Shrike missiles and Phantom jets. On 7 August

1970, a three-month cease-fire with a provision for a complete military stand-still in a zone 50 kilometers wide on each side of the Suez Canal went into effect.

(iii) 1971 to 1973: 'Benign Neglect'

The stand-still cease-fire agreement marked the last major effort of the U.S. Government to intervene actively in managing the Arab-Israeli conflict until the October War. Faced with unmistakeable evidence of Egyptian violations of the cease-fire agreement and a recognition that Egypt was not acting alone — Soviet missiles were moved with the help of Soviet technicians — the U.S. accorded much lower priority to achieving peace in the Middle East than it did to assuring the stability of the region. American leaders emphasized the Soviet-American relationship in the area and tried to maintain the balance of power in Israel's favour. Periodically, the State Department tried to launch new initiatives: the Jarring talks, the interim settlement along the Suez Canal, and proximity talks, but the White House was only mildly supportive at best and on occasion distinctly negative. In retrospect, this period was quite aptly referred to as one of "stand-still diplomacy".[14]

(iv) 1974 to 1979: 'Intense Involvement'

From October 1973 until the middle of 1979, through three administrations — Nixon, Ford, and Carter — the United States shifted from a policy of 'benign neglect' to one of active involvement in fashioning a solution to the Arab-Israeli conflict. During the hostilities in October 1973, Kissinger and Nixon both promised an active American diplomatic initiative to implement Resolution 242 after the war ended. With the achievement of the shaky cease-fire of 25 October 1973, Nixon and Kissinger began to define the contours of their policy. Two key elements quickly emerged. First, the U.S. would play an active role in trying to resolve the Arab-Israel conflict. Unlike Johnson after 1967 and their own policy after 1970, Nixon and Kissinger felt that the situation in the Middle East was too dangerous — American interests were too important — to permit anything but an active effort. Perhaps even more importantly, the opportunity for a successful American initiative existed. Kissinger believed that the United States held the important cards: Israel was isolated internationally, heavily dependent on Washington for arms, for economic aid, and for diplomatic support, while the Arabs knew that only the United States could produce territorial concessions from Israel.[15]

The second element of American strategy was to decouple initial diplomatic steps from a final peace settlement. Step-by-step soon became the hallmark of Kissinger's diplomacy. Under Kissinger's indefatigable prodding, first Egypt and Israel and then Syria and Israel concluded a disengagement agreement by mid-1974, capped by a second agreement between Israel and Egypt, the Sinai II Accord (15 September 1975) that provided for additional withdrawals by Israel. Throughout this entire period, the United States struggled to 'fractionate' the conflict in order to resolve those issues capable of a solution.

After Sinai II, American officials debated the next appropriate step. After an initial flurry of activity, the Administration was increasingly preoccupied by the bloody civil war in Lebanon (1975-76) and the establishment of a 20,000 man Syrian 'peace-keeping' force. Shortly after his inauguration in January 1977, President Carter developed a plan that was substantially different in conception from the approach articulated by former Secretary of State Kissinger. Rather than approaching a solution of the conflict through gradual steps, the president argued that the time had come to spell out the central and indispensable elements to a comprehensive Middle East settlement. He identified three core components: the creation of permanent peace — the termination of belligerence toward Israel by her neighbours — and recognition of Israel's right to exist in peace; second, permanent, secure, and recognized borders between Israel and her Arab neighbours that would involve substantial withdrawals by Israel from the occupied territories and minor adjustments to the pre-1967 lines; third, the establishment of a Palestinian 'homeland' or 'entity', which would meet the legitimate interests of the Palestinian people. The precise political status of a Palestinian entity would be subject to negotiation. The Carter Administration also believed that the Soviet Union would have to participate in the negotiating process. Between January and October 1977, officials concentrated on reconvening the Geneva Conference.

President Sadat's visit to Jerusalem in November 1977 effectively undercut the American effort to reach a comprehensive settlement at Geneva. It did not, however, diminish American enthusiasm for its strategy. President Carter reiterated the need to "build on the momentum" created by Sadat's visit to fashion a comprehensive settlement. Oblivious to the fact that Sadat's peace initiative was an attempt to accomplish the achievable good rather than the unachievable best, U.S. policy makers from November 1977 to August 1978, opposed a separate Egyptian-Israeli peace. Faced, however, with the grim prospect of a collapse of the negotiating process and confronted with continued turmoil in Iran and a coup d'état in Afghanistan, President Carter spent 13 days at Camp David in September 1978 negotiating with President Sadat and Prime Minister Begin to hammer out the Camp David Accords which were signed on 17 September.

Alarmed by indications of Sadat's growing isolation in the Arab world, the administration redoubled its efforts to seek an overall settlement. Assistant Secretary of State Harold Saunders argued that the framework for peace between Egypt and Israel was not an isolated bilateral agreement but part of a broader regional process of political accommodation. Israel's acceptance of the principle of withdrawal from the Sinai Peninsula was, in his view, a "model" for the West Bank. Faced with opposition by Israel to Saunders' interpretation of the Camp David Accords, Arab opposition to the agreements, and the loss of a major regional ally in Iran, American diplomacy reversed itself once again to concentrate on solidifying the Egypt-Israel peace. President Carter made an intense effort at mediation in a personal visit to the Middle East, and shortly thereafter, Egypt and Israel signed a peace treaty in Washington on 26 March 1979. The United States wished to move ahead as quickly as possible on the negotiation of Palestinian autonomy and consequently, President Carter appointed Robert Strauss as Special Middle East Envoy to oversee the negotiations. He, in turn, was replaced in December 1979 by Sol Linowitz as special U.S. negotiator for the autonomy talks.

(v) 1980 to mid-1982: 'Benign Neglect'

Despite numerous trips to the Middle East by special White House negotiator Sol Linowitz during 1980, there was a perceptible decline in American interest in resolving the Arab-Israeli conflict. The seizure of the American embassy in Iran and the Soviet invasion of Afghanistan led to an emphasis on 'balance of power' politics rather than conflict resolution. Faced with a significant Soviet challenge to American global and regional interests in the region, the United States under both the Carter and Reagan Administrations tried to avoid escalation of regional conflicts. The Reagan Administration quickly confronted its first dangerous crisis in the Middle East. As the fighting in Lebanon intensified, Syria emplaced six Soviet SAM-6 missile batteries in the Bekaa Valley in April of 1981 and Prime Minister Begin threatened to remove them with force. The U.S. sent special envoy Philip Habib to the Middle East to try to defuse the crisis, but despite prolonged shuttling back and forth between Damascus and Jerusalem, Habib was unable to secure the withdrawal of the Syrian missiles. He did succeed, however, in obtaining Israeli and Palestinian agreement to a cease-fire across the Israel-Lebanese border on 24 July 1981. Throughout this period, American involvement was largely reactive: Habib concentrated on restoring the *status quo ante*, not on resolving the underlying issues in conflict.

(vi) June 1982 — : From 'Benign Neglect' to Active Involvement?

When Israel invaded Lebanon in June 1982 and encircled the PLO in West Beirut, the United States assumed a much more active role in managing the escalating crisis. Again, Philip Habib returned to the Middle East and engaged in tortuous negotiations to secure the withdrawal of PLO forces from Lebanon. Although American involvement in the crisis was intense, it still did not attempt to solve the broader issues in dispute. And, unlike the periods from 1969-70 and 1974-79, when the Secretary of State (William Rogers, Henry Kissinger or Cyrus Vance) or the President (Jimmy Carter) were personally involved, during the crisis in Lebanon negotiations were conducted by lower-level officials. Even more significantly, the mediation of Philip Habib focused almost exclusively on the narrow question of the terms and conditions of the PLO's withdrawal from Lebanon. While the U.S. paid lip-service to the need to take advantage of the opportunities provided by the elimination of the PLO's military potential — in particular, the re-establishment of a strong central Lebanese government whose authority would extend throughout the country — the United States did not address itself to the future of the Palestinian Arabs living in the West Bank and Gaza nor to the establishment of a lasting peace between Israel and its Arab neighbours. Once again, American behaviour was largely reactive. American diplomacy concentrated on defusing the crisis and ending the PLO presence in the country; it did not, however, articulate a more comprehensive vision of a Middle East peace. Nevertheless there were a number of indications from senior government officials that, in the aftermath of the crisis, the U.S. would renew its efforts to move Israel and the Arabs to the negotiating table.[16] That move came on 1 September 1982 with the announcement of the Reagan Peace Plan.

b. U.S. Military Involvement
(i) 1948 to 1961: Arms Embargo and Military Alliances

American military involvement is also an important, if somewhat neglected, component of American policy in the Middle East. From 1948 to 1961, we can see two major themes: first, an emphasis on preventing a local arms race and, second, the attempt to create a structure of military alliances. Both the 1947 arms-embargo and the Tripartite Declaration of 25 May 1950 were important elements in this approach. After the Arab-Israeli armistice agreements in 1949, England resumed arms shipments to Egypt, Iraq, and Jordan in accordance with its treaty obligations to those states. As Arab leaders threatened a second round against Israel and Israel concentrated on increasing its military strength, the three western powers became increasingly concerned about the prospect of an arms race. The United States, England, and France sought to clarify their policy on arms supply and related defense matters in the Tripartite Declaration of 25 May 1950. In that statement, they recognized the need of both Israel and the Arab states to maintain a certain level of armed forces to assure their internal security and legitimate defense as well as to participate in the defense of the area as a whole. Consequently, requests for arms or war material by the regional states would be considered by the three powers "in the light of these principles" and their "declared opposition to the development of an arms race between the Arab states and Israel".[17] Even after the Czech-Egyptian arms deal in 1955, and despite an intense campaign of persuasion and lobbying, Secretary of State Dulles refused to allow the sale of American arms to Israel to match Egyptian acquisitions.

At the same time as the U.S. embargoed arms, from 1948-1961, American leaders tried to strengthen the security of the region through military alliances. In October 1951, the United States, England, France and Turkey invited Egypt to become a member of a proposed allied Middle East Command for the defense of the area. This proposal was designed to protect the Suez Canal Zone while meeting Egyptian objections to the continued presence of British troops on its soil. The proposal proved unacceptable to Egypt. It was the first of a series of American attempts to formulate a regional defense system against external threats, particularly the Soviet Union. American pre-occupation with containing the Soviet Union led to the establishment of the Baghdad Pact in 1955 embracing Turkey, Iraq, Iran, Pakistan, and Britain. From the outset, the Baghdad Pact was regarded with suspicion and animosity by Syria, Jordan, and Egypt who feared the build-up of their rivals in the northern tier as well as the intrusion of cold-war politics into the region.

The conclusion of the 1955 Czech-Egyptian arms deal demonstrated that American efforts to contain Soviet influence in the Middle East through military defense pacts had failed. After Iraq defected in 1958, the alliance was forced to move its headquarters from Baghdad to Ankara and the organization was renamed the Central Treaty Organization. The U.S. made no further efforts to organize regional military alliances or pacts until more than 25 years later when the Reagan Administration tried to create a 'strategic consensus'.

(ii) 1962 to 1968: Limited Arms Sales to Israel, Jordan, and Saudi Arabia

In response to Soviet supplies to Egypt of the latest model MIG-21s and TU-16s in the spring of 1962, the Kennedy Administration agreed, for the first time, to sell Israel short-range defensive Hawk anti-aircraft missiles as a partial defense against UAR jet fighters and bombers. During 1964, prompted by increased Soviet arms supplies to Egypt, Syria, and Iraq, the Johnson Administration agreed to provide Saudi Arabia with Hawk missiles and Israel and Jordan with 'offensive' weapons such as Patton tanks. In February 1966, a new arms agreement was signed in which the U.S. promised to supply Jordan with F-104 Starfighters and Israel with A-4 Skyhawk jets. In the aftermath of the June War, the State Department announced that the 48 A-4 Skyhawk jets previously promised to Israel would be delivered and subsequently it raised the number to 100. On 9 October 1968, President Johnson publicly endorsed Israeli Prime Minister Eshkol's previous request to purchase the high performance F-4 Phantom jets. A deal for 50 F-4s was signed at the end of December 1968 providing for the delivery of 16 aircraft late in 1969 and the rest in 1970.[18]

(iii) 1969 to 1970: Limited Arms Sales to Israel

Faced with an intensification of fighting along the Canal between the forces of Egypt and Israel, on 15 September 1969, Prime Minister Meir informally requested an additional 100 A-4 Skyhawks and 25 F-4 Phantoms to compensate for the Mirage jets embargoed by France. But throughout 1969, the period of active American effort to manage the Arab-Israeli conflict, the U.S. appeared reluctant to supply Israel even with those weapons systems previously agreed to in December 1968, lest this antagonize the Arab states. With the rejection of the Rogers Plan by both Israel and the Arab states, the United States became somewhat more sympathetic to new requests by Israel for arms assistance, particularly in view of the large quantities of arms and advisers arriving in Egypt. By mid-April 1970, Soviet pilots had begun to fly combat sorties in the Canal Zone. Despite the enhanced Soviet presence, however, American leaders were still divided about selling new arms to Israel. Nixon favoured a positive response to Prime Minister Meir's request, while the State Department opposed the supply of more Phantoms, arguing that Israel's military superiority was unquestioned and that Soviet arms shipments were a response to Israel's reckless campaign of deep penetration bombing raids.[19]

On 23 May 1970, Secretary of State Rogers announced that the President had decided to hold Israel's request for the 100 A-4s in abeyance pending new developments in the region. One month later, President Nixon assured Israel's Foreign Minister Eban that the remainder of the arms committed in December 1968 would be forthcoming, but he urged Israel not to publicize the deliveries. At the same time, Nixon requested a public statement by Israel indicating some flexibility on the terms of a Middle East peace settlement and five days later, Prime Minister Meir announced Israel's continued acceptance of UN Resolution 242 as the basis for a settlement and its willingness to accept something akin to the Rhodes formula for further talks.[20]

Responding to the accelerating pace of the Soviet military build-up of Syria and Egypt, on 2 July 1970, Prime Minister Meir appealed to the U.S. for help in dealing with the threat posed by the SAMs that were then being moved closer to the Canal. Two days later, President Nixon authorized the shipment of electronic counter measure (ECM) equipment to be used against Soviet SAMs in the Canal Zone. Although he still held back on new commitments of aircraft, on 10 July 1970, President Nixon ordered that the remaining A-4s and F-4s committed in December 1968 be shipped to Israel at an accelerated pace.[21]

An examination of U.S arms policy from January 1969 to August 1970 suggests that the U.S. administration was initially reluctant to supply

Israel even with those weapons that been previously agreed to in December 1968. Even when the administration decided to honour its previous commitments, the United States attempted to make American arms supplies contingent on Israel's receptivity to American peace initiatives.

(iv) 1971 to 1973: Major Arms Supplies to Israel, Jordan, and Saudi Arabia

From August 1970 until October 1973, the U.S. concentrated on enhancing Israel's military capability. On 14 August 1970, in the wake of unmistakable evidence of forward deployment of Soviet missiles in the Canal Zone, in violation of the 7 August 1970 stand-still cease-fire agreement, President Nixon authorized a $7 million arms package for Israel. In the package were sophisticated electronic equipment, Shrike missiles, and cluster bomb units that could be used to attack the missile sites. On 1 September 1970, the U.S. agreed to sell Israel at least 18 F-4 Phantom jets, to inform Egypt of the sales, and to explain the decision as a reaction to Egyptian violations of the cease-fire agreement.

American mililtary assistance to Israel was accelerated by the civil war in Jordan and joint efforts by the U.S. and Israel to keep Hussein on his throne. Nixon authorized $500 million in supplemental military aid to Israel and agreed to accelerate delivery of the 18 F-4s. Indicative of the dramatic shift in American policy on arms sales to Israel was the dollar value of American military credits to Israel from 1968-1973. The United States extended military credits to Israel worth $25 million, $85 million, and $30 million in fiscal years 1968, 1969, and 1970 respectively.[22] After the crisis in Jordan, in fiscal years 1971, 1972, and 1973, the U.S. extended Israel military credits of $300.5 million, $399.8 million, and $162.4 million respectively.[23] The American role as a major arms supplier to Israel was highlighted during the October War. From 14 October until the ceasefire of 25 October, the U.S. delivered approximately 11,000 tons of equipment, 40 F-4 Phantoms, 36 A-4 Skyhawks, and 12 C-130 transports. Another 11,000 tons of equipment were delivered from 26 October until the airlift ended on 15 November. During the same period El Al aircraft carried about 11,000 tons of military supplies to Israel,[24] and President Nixon formally requested Congressional approval of $2.2 billion in military assistance for Israel.

Less well publicized was the on-going American role as a major arms supplier to Jordan and Saudi Arabia. During fiscal years 1971, 1972, and 1973, the United States sold $16.2 million, $18.2 million, and $6.8 million worth of arms to Jordan and $15.2 million, $305.4 million, and $1.5 billion to Saudi Arabia.

(v) 1974 to 1982: Heavy Arms Sales to Israel, Saudi Arabia, Egypt, and Jordan

The pattern of American military involvement in the Middle East in these years was quite different from earlier periods. First, the United States sold increasingly sophisticated weaponry to the Arab world; second, America supplied new customers — Egypt, Kuwait, Oman, and the United Arab Emirates; third, the total volume of military sales to the region increased dramatically; and, fourth, Saudi Arabia became the largest single recipient of arms assistance, a position previously held by Iran.

After the signing of the 1974 Egypt-Israel Disengagement Agreement and the 1975 Sinai II Accord, Egypt requested American military assistance amounting to over $5 billion for the ensuing ten years. The U.S. supported, in principle, the Egyptian shift to reliance on American weaponry rather than Soviet military equipment and agreed to the sale of 1,350 AMC jeeps and 1,000 trucks in June 1975. But it was only in April 1976 that the United States fully lifted its arms embargo against Egypt and agreed to sell it 6 C-130 Hercules transport aircraft. During 1975 and 1976, Jordan and Saudi Arabia also signed important new arms agreements with the United States. In January 1975, the United States agreed to sell Saudi Arabia 30 F-E fighters while Jordan continued to take delivery of 26 F-E fighters committed in February 1974. Jordan also signed an agreement to purchase 2,000 TOW anti-tank missiles, 150 tanks, 740 Dragon anti-tank missiles, and 940 sidewinder air-to-air missiles. In April 1975, the U.S. offered to supply Jordan with an air defense system, including 14 batteries of Hawk SAMs, but the offer was withdrawn in July in the face of Congressional opposition to the sale of equipment that could be used in offensive operations against Israel. Discussions resumed in 1976, however, and in addition to the 14 fixed Hawk batteries, the U.S. agreed to sell Jordan 300 Redeye missiles and 8 Vulcan batteries for an estimated total cost of $540 million.

In the aftermath of President Sadat's visit to Jerusalem, Egypt became a major recipient of American arms. In May 1978, Congress approved a package agreement that provided 42 F-5E fighters to Egypt, 62 F-15 fighters to Saudi Arabia, as well as an increase in the number of F-15s previously promised to Israel in mid-1975. When the U.S. Senate approved the sale of the F-15 jet fighters to Saudi Arabia, the Carter Administration gave assurances that bomb racks, range extending fuel tanks, and other equipment to enhance the offensive capabilities of the F-15s would not be sold.

October 1981 marked the date of the single most sophisticated and extensive arms sale to the Arab world — the $8.5 billion AWACS deal for Saudi Arabia. The following elements were in the package: 5 Boeing E-3A radar planes (AWACS); 1,177 Sidewinder air-to-air missiles for use by the F-15 fighters; 101 pairs of fuel tanks for the F-15s adding to the plane's range; 6 KC 707 tanker planes for inflight refuelling of the AWACS and the F-15s as well as for the F-E fighters already in the Saudi Air Force; and a complex of ground facilities including stations for receiving electronic and voice messages from the patrolling radar planes and ground radar stations.

Early in 1982, the U.S. Defense Department indicated its willingness to sell new improved mobile Hawk anti-aircraft missile batteries to Jordan along with a number of F-16 fighters. Unwilling to face a bruising battle in Congress of the type that attended the passage of the AWACS sale, the Reagan Administration told Congress on 26 February 1982 that it would not press the issue before the Congressional elections in November because Jordan needed time to secure adequate financing. At no time did the administration indicate any reservations in principle about the sale; it dealt only with issues of feasibility and timing.

American policy on arms sales to Arab governments had changed dramatically. One indicator was the growing sophistication in the type of weapons systems that were sold, a second was an increase in the number of recipients, and a third was the sharp increase in the volume of military sales agreements.[25] Until 1975, Bahrain had not received any American military assistance, and between fiscal years 1975 and 1979 the value of military aid was only $157,000. But by 1980, the U.S. had agreed to sell Bahrain over $6 million worth of military equipment. Kuwait had also received no American military assistance prior to 1972 and in 1973 U.S. military sales agreements to Kuwait totalled only $40,000. Beginning in 1974, U.S. arms sales increased to $31.6 million and then to $356.2 million in fiscal year 1975. Between 1976 and 1980, the total value of U.S. arms supplies to Kuwait was $457.5 million.

Very much the same pattern held for Oman, the United Arab Emirates, and Yemen. Oman received no American military assistance until fiscal year 1975 when the U.S. agreed to sell $1.6 million worth of equipment. Between 1976 and 1979, U.S. military sales to Oman were just over $1 million in total, and in fiscal year 1980 the value of American military sales soared to $23.7 million. Like Oman, the United Arab Emirates had not received any military arms assistance from the United States prior to fiscal year 1976. Between 1976 and 1980, however, the total value of U.S. arms sales was $5.4 million. U.S. arms sales to Yemen (Sana) began in 1974 with an initial agreement of $2.6 million. Sales in fiscal year 1976 amounted to $130.4 million. Even Qatar became a recipient of U.S. military equipment in 1980 with an arms package valued at $78,000.

Among those Arab states that had received virtually no American military assistance prior to 1973, Egypt emerged as the largest single benefactor of American military assistance. Between 1950 and 1970 the total value of American military assistance to Egypt was only $373,000. Beginning in fiscal year 1976 with an arms package worth $62 million, U.S. military sales to Egypt increased to $2.4 billion in fiscal year 1980. [26] The increase in the value of U.S. military sales to traditional Middle East recipients of American military assistance — Israel, Jordan, and Saudi Arabia — was also noteworthy. Equally striking is the growing preeminence of Saudi Arabia. From 1950 to 1970, the U.S. agreed to sell Israel $686.9 million worth of military equipment; the comparable figures for Jordan were $147.0 million and for Saudi Arabia, $859.8 million. From 1970-1980, U.S. arms sales to Israel were $8.6 billion, to Jordan $1.1 billion and to Saudi Arabia $34 billion. But even these figures fail to convey the full impact of the shift in the American pattern of arms sales. From 1970-1975, U.S. arms sales to Israel totalled $4.1 billion, those to Saudi Arabia $9.2 billion; from 1976-1980, U.S. military sales to Israel were $4.4 billion, while those to Saudi Arabia were $24.7 billion — a six-fold differential.[27] With the conclusion of the $8.5 billion AWACS deal in 1981, the gap in the value of American arms sales to Saudi Arabia and Israel was evident.

American Interests In The Middle East

a. U.S. Global Interests
(i) 1948 to 1968: Containment

American policy toward the management of the Arab-Israel conflict and its arms sales reflected a complex variety of interests. In the global system, America struggled to 'contain' the Soviet Union from 1948 to 1968. Containment was predicated upon the "innate antagonism between capitalism and socialism." George Kennan, the intellectual father of containment, argued that "there can never on Moscow's side be any sincere assumption of a community of aims between the Soviet Union and powers which are regarded as capitalist."[28] While he acknowledged the fundamental and insurmountable obstacles to accommodation between the two superpowers, Kennan insisted that the Soviet Union felt little urgency in its bid for hegemony. It would seek to exploit available opportunities, but it was prepared to be patient, given its leaders' belief in the ultimate triumph of communism. Kennan concluded that "Soviet pressure against the free institutions of the western world is something that can be contained by the adroit and vigilant application of counter-force at a series of constantly shifting geographical and political points, corresponding to the shifts and manoeuvers of Soviet policy, but which cannot be charmed or talked out of existence."[29]

In the late 1940s and the 1950s the United States tried to contain Soviet expansionism through military pacts. Members would act collectively to deter the Russians from expanding their influence. Containment — and the search for pacts — was extended beyond Western Europe to South East Asia and the Middle East. The United States regarded the Middle East as vital from a geo-strategic perspective, given its location at the right flank of NATO and to the south of the Soviet Union. Because the United States relied on strategic bombers and intermediate range ballistic missiles (IRBMs) as the principle means of delivering nuclear and thermonuclear weapons, it considered bases in the Middle East as essential staging areas to reach crucial centres in the Soviet Union.

By the early 1960s the United States, while remaining committed to containment, began to search for new ways to cope with the Soviet Union. That search was stimulated by the recognition that neither the Baghdad Pact nor CENTO had prevented Soviet penetration of the Middle East and the creation of client states in Egypt, Syria and Iraq. American interest in Middle East bases and pacts also diminished as its capacity to deter the Soviet Union generally improved — given the development of ICBMs stationed on American soil and submarine-based Polaris missiles. Rather than focusing on military pacts, the United States began to emphasize the military build-up of regional actors as a deterrent to the geo-political ambitions of Soviet client states.

(ii) 1969 to 1979: Détente

John Gaddis suggests that historians are likely to regard 1969 as a major turning point in the history of the Cold War, "for it was in that year that the internal situation in each of the major countries involved simultaneously came to favour détente".[30]During 1969, the Soviet Union achieved its long-sought goal of strategic parity with the United States. At the same time, however, it recognized that its objective of economic parity with the United States could not be achieved without the import of 'capitalist' technology — technology needed to solve some of the pressing industrial and agricultural problems that it faced. In the United States, the slow process of disengagement from Vietnam had begun and a new administration with a solid reputation of opposition to international communism had come to power in Washington. Paradoxically, Richard M. Nixon's credentials as an implacable foe of communism both domestically and externally gave him greater latitude in negotiating with his ideological adversaries.

In his inaugural address in 1969, Nixon set the tone for the new era in superpower relations when he declared: "After a period of confrontation we are entering an era of negotiation."[31] Nixon and his chief foreign policy adviser, Henry Kissinger, were intrigued by the possibility of establishing a new relationship with the Soviet Union that would help to ensure global stability and minimize the risks of confrontation. Both were prepared to transcend the ideological rivalry of the Cold War and to establish ties with adversaries based on mutual interests. In the new relationship with the U.S.S.R., issues that divided the superpowers would not be negotiated in isolation but would be linked to each other. Thus, the United States, in its talks with the Soviet Union, would seek a global settlement of issues that would permit simultaneous progress in Vietnam, the strategic arms negotiations, and the Middle East.

To facilitate the process of détente in the Middle East, the U.S. initially tried to involve the Arab states and the Soviet Union in the negotiation process. This effort ended abruptly after the failure of the Rogers Plan and the escalation of Soviet involvement in Egypt early in 1970, culminating in the Egyptian violations of the August 1970 stand-still cease-fire agreement. Although the United States was still preoccupied with the dangers of a superpower confrontation in the Middle East, American leaders now opted to encourage Soviet restraint not by emphasizing negotiations but by strengthening deterrence through increased arms shipments to Israel. Notwithstanding American objections to Soviet behaviour in the region, the U.S. remained committed to détente; negotiations with the Soviet Union on strategic arms limitation were successfully concluded in May 1972 when the SALT I Accords were signed.

Détente appears to have had little impact in restraining Soviet behaviour during the October War. American expectations that the spirit of détente would minimize the degree of Soviet military commitment to its client states proved to be an illusion. Détente remained, nevertheless, the dominant leitmotif in superpower relations for the next five years. Increasingly, however, Soviet behaviour in Angola, Ethiopia, Yemen, and the coup d'état in Afghanistan raised serious doubts in the United States about the value of détente as the cornerstone of its policy toward the Soviet Union.

(iii) 1980 to 1982: Containment

By the end of 1979, détente as an organizing principle animating the conduct of American foreign policy toward the Soviet Union had suffered irreparable damage. Beset by the collapse of the pro-western regime of the Shah of Iran, the continued domestic Soviet military build-up,
controversies over trade and human rights, and the Soviet invasion of Afghanistan in December 1979, the United States abandoned détente and reverted to a policy of containment. American leaders considered that the Soviet decision to send its armed forces outside the Warsaw Pact area and into a non-aligned country violated the norms that governed superpower behaviour. In an interview, President Carter told a reporter that the Soviet Union's aggression "has made a more dramatic change in my own opinion of what the Soviets' ultimate goals are than anything they've done in the previous time I've been in office."[32] Within weeks, Carter outlined a strong and concerted response: a declaration of vital American interests in the Persian Gulf; a partial embargo of grain and technology sales to the U.S.S.R.; acceleration of plans for a new Rapid Deployment Force that could operate in the Persian Gulf region; and a boycott of the Moscow Olympics. Significantly, there were no public apologies and few sympathetic explanations of the Soviet invasion of Afghanistan from American analysts or politicians. The argument that the Soviets were not aggressive and were genuinely interested in a stable relationship of détente, an argument made by many a few years earlier — simply disappeared; it

131

was the principal political victim of the Soviet invasion of Afghanistan.[33]

The new Reagan Administration proceeded to spell out and strengthen the commitment to containment. The renewed emphasis on deterrence was reflected in a sizeable increase in the defense budget, in the decision to develop the MX missile system to deal with America's 'window of vulnerability', and in vigorous criticism of Soviet support for guerrilla movements in Nicaragua, Guatemala, and El Salvador. Within the Middle East, the United States tried to build, albeit unsuccessfully, a 'strategic consensus' that would encompass Pakistan, Saudi Arabia, Egypt, Israel, and Turkey. The creation of such a strategic understanding would, it was hoped, persuade some of the regional states, particularly Egypt and Saudi Arabia, to accept the pre-positioning of U.S. military forces and permanent American naval and military bases. Despite America's best efforts, the Reagan Administration was unable to convince Arab leaders to accept the policy implications that flowed from containment. Both the 'strategic consensus' and permanent U.S. naval and military bases in the region were still-born.

b. **U.S. Regional Interests**
(i) 1948 to 1973: Low to Moderate Salience of Arab Oil

From 1948 until the end of the 1950s, American leaders regarded Middle East oil as strategically important. It was an indispensable resource for the reconstruction of Europe, at a time when Europe was vulnerable strategically and disorganized economically. By the 1960s, however, the United States placed less emphasis on the strategic importance of oil and more on its economic significance. Paradoxically, Europe's dependence on Middle East oil had not decreased; on the contrary, it had increased. Rather, an economically strong and assertive Europe assumed full responsibility for securing its own oil supply.[34] From the American perspective, the strategic significance of Middle East oil was offset by the fact that its own domestic production covered the bulk of U.S. domestic needs. Nevertheless, the U.S. government wished to protect American oil companies against seizure of their profitable operations to ensure the continued repatriation of over $2 billion annually in profits to offset deficits in the American balance of payments.[35]

(ii) 1974 to 1982: High Salience of Arab Oil and Petro-Dollars

In the 1950s, American leaders emphasized secure access to Arab oil and in the 1960s, they focused on assuring the profits of the oil companies, but a qualitative and a quantitative change in American interest occurred after the OAPEC oil boycott in October 1973. Even as late as 1971, imported oil represented only 10% of total U.S. energy needs and of this only 1.5% came from the Middle East. Middle East oil represented 3.4% of total U.S. oil consumption. America's allies, however — Western Europe and Japan — were far more dependent on Middle East oil. Imported oil represented 52% of Western Europe's energy requirements and 63% of Japan's. As a percentage of total oil consumption in Western Europe and Japan, Middle East oil imports accounted for 82.3% and 83.8% respectively.[36]

Beginning in 1970, however, U.S. energy consumption began to grow rapidly in a period of world economic growth. U.S. policy-makers then began to focus increasing attention on the geo-politics of the only easily expandable source of energy: the Middle East. Saudi Arabian oil fields alone contained 62% of the world's proven oil reserves of 550 million barrels within 29% of its territory.

Recognizing that the 1970s would be a seller's market, OAPEC began to raise prices in the last quarter of 1970 and continued to do so throughout 1971 and 1972, with the price per barrel moving up from one dollar to three dollars. In the midst of the October 1973 War, the six Gulf States meeting in Kuwait unilaterally announced a 70% hike in posted prices from $3.01 per barrel to $5.11 per barrel. On 23 December, OAPEC further raised the posted price to $11.65 per barrel, a price level more than twice that of October and nearly four times that of the previous year.[37]

After its initial price increase from $3.01 per barrel to $5.01 per barrel, OAPEC announced that it would cumulatively cut oil exports by a minimum of 5% per month until Israel withdrew from all occupied Arab territory and the legitimate rights of the Palestinian people were restored. Following President Nixon's request to Congress for $2.2 billion of military assistance for Israel, on 19 October 1973, Saudi Arabia immediately cut oil exports by 10% and two days later decreed a total embargo on oil supplies to the United States and the Netherlands.

Although the United States, as the prime target of the embargo, was much less vulnerable to a cut-off in Middle East oil supplies than was Western Europe or Japan, the embargo had a profound psychological impact on American policy-makers. Over the next nine years, successive American administrations responded by encouraging conservation, creating a strategic oil reserve, and developing alternative energy resources. These initiatives must be understood in the context of growing American dependency on OAPEC oil. As in 1970, imported oil continued to represent about 10% of total U.S. energy needs in 1978, but the total volume of U.S. crude oil imports went up from 483 million barrels in 1970 to 2,320 million barrels in 1978 — a reflection of the rapid growth in energy consumption. In 1971, U.S. consumption of Middle East oil was 3.4% of its total oil consumption but by 1978 that figure was up to 25%. As a percentage of U.S. crude oil imports, OAPEC's share rose from 46% in 1970 to 79.6% in 1979.[38]

In retrospect, the period from 1974-1978 appears almost as an Indian summer for world oil prices. From $11 per barrel at the end of 1973, oil prices moved gradually upwards to $13.34 per barrel on January 1, 1979.

The overthrow of the Shah in November 1978 and a strike by Iranian workers in the oil fields in December 1978 removed over 5 million barrels a day from the world market. In response to the ensuing shortages, Saudi Arabia increased its oil production somewhat, but far more significant was a massive rise in oil prices beginning in June 1979 with a posted price of $18 per barrel, moving steadily upwards to $24 per barrel in December 1979, to $26 in January 1980 and from there to $28, $30, $32, and finally to $34 by the end of 1980.[39]

Nevertheless, by the beginning of 1982, there were growing signs that OAPEC's strength was beginning to erode. Demand for OAPEC oil declined significantly from a record high of 31 million barrels per day and OAPEC was forced to reduce its output by about 10 million barrels per day in order to maintain price levels. Although OAPEC, at its meetings in March 1982, held the official price of oil to $34 per barrel, oil was sold unofficially at two to four dollars a barrel below the posted price. In retrospect, it appears that the fourteen-fold increase in world prices from 1971 to 1981 had successfully encouraged wide-spread conservation. In addition, growth in the use of coal, nuclear energy, and natural gas, in conjunction with a world wide economic recession — partially fuelled by the spiralling costs of energy — enabled the U.S. to decrease its imports of crude oil by more than 50% between 1979-1981.[40] U.S. oil independence, however, may be limited by market forces.

The decrease in the demand for oil and the softening of prices depressed oil development projects within the United States. During the first half of 1982, the number of drilling rigs working in the United States declined, there was a slide in the level of seismic exploration, and a number of oil, shale, coal, gasification, and other synthetic fuel projects were abandoned.

Since the mid-70s, American interest in the oil-producing Arab states has not been confined to oil. Important also was the increased pool of petro-dollars developed as a result of the exponential increase in the price of oil, and its availability for investments and purchases in the United States. By the end of 1977, analysts estimated that American goods accounted for approximately 15% to 20% of the $8.2 billion worth of Arab imports.[41] Nor did these figures include contracts for services with U.S. firms, estimated at over $25 billion.[42]

Arab investment in the United States paralleled the growth of American exports to the Middle East. Data from the U.S. Treasury indicate that between 1974 and 1977, some $43.2 billion (about 25% of the U.S. Treasury's estimate of OAPEC's investible surplus) were placed in U.S. Treasury instruments, corporate bonds, and stocks. Of that amount, commercial bank investments accounted for $31.8 billion, while direct investment, prepayment on U.S. exports, and debt amortization made up the remaining $11.4 billion. Adding the funds of OAPEC members placed through third parties and the substantial holdings in foreign branches of U.S. banks (neither of which are represented in these figures), the total

134

comes closer to $60 billion than to $43.2 billion. Of this $60 billion, close to $55 billion (90%) were invested by Saudi Arabia, Kuwait, and the United Arab Emirates.[43] The Saudi share alone was close to $50 billion and increased by about $10-12 billion in 1978; by 1982 it was estimated at $100 billion.[44]

The glut in world oil markets in 1982, the sudden shortfalls in revenue, and the consequent threats to the payments, balances, and budgets of even the highest surplus Arab oil exporters somewhat dimmed the luster of the petro-dollar. Nevertheless according to a report prepared for the American business monthly, *Institutional Investor*, a second-generation Arab petro-dollar, based not on oil in the ground or surpluses accruing passively in Middle East and international banks, but rather on increasingly skillful management of investment funds by Arabs themselves, is now available for investment. According to the report, "the mobilization of these financial reserves already accumulated by private individuals and institutions is largely immune to the current oil glut and will ensure a continuing and strong Arab influence in world financial affairs".[45]

The Relationship Between American Interests And Behaviour: An Examination Of The Evidence[46]

We have now looked at two distinct patterns of American conflict management — intense involvement and benign neglect — and three types of American military involvement in the Middle East — arms embargo, moderate supplies to regional actors, and heavy supplies to regional actors. We have looked as well at two sets of American interests — global (containment vs. détente) and regional (moderate vs. heavy reliance on Arab oil and petro-dollars). Are these patterns of interests linked to patterns of behaviour? More specifically, are particular U.S. global or regional interests associated with particular types of conflict management or patterns of military commitment?

a. U.S. Global Interests and U.S. Conflict Management

Our evidence does indicate, as expected, that when the United States pursued a policy of containment toward the Soviet Union, it demonstrated comparatively little interest in managing the Arab-Israeli conflict. From 1948 to 1968 and from 1980 to mid-1982, U.S. interest in containing the Soviet Union was matched by a corresponding disinclination to intervene actively to resolve the outstanding issues in conflict. Although the U.S. moved from a policy of benign neglect to a more activist posture following Israel's invasion of Lebanon in June 1982, it nevertheless demonstrated less concern with the broader issues and greater interest in defusing the crisis by preventing the destruction of Beirut and ensuring the departure of the PLO from Lebanon. In general, when American leaders considered the Soviet Union aggressively expansionist, they gave priority to ending regional hostilities rather than to resolving the Arab-Israel conflict. In part, policy makers recognized that opportunities and inducements for Soviet expansion in the Middle East would not disappear even if the Arab-Israel conflict were resolved. Inter-Arab rivalries and hostilities as well as internal governmental instability would continue to provide fertile ground for Soviet political and military penetration of the region.

If a policy of containment was associated with a conflict management strategy of 'benign neglect', does the evidence suggest an equally powerful relationship between an American interest in détente and intense U.S. involvement in managing the Arab-Israeli conflict? Here, the evidence is less persuasive. For ten years, (1969-1979), U.S. policy toward the Soviet Union centred on détente and, between 1969-1970 and from 1974-1979, détente was associated with an active U.S. role in managing the Arab-Israel conflict. From 1971 to 1973, however, at the very apogee of U.S.-Soviet détente, the United States decreased its efforts to find a solution to the conflict and pursued a policy of 'benign neglect'. How can we explain these different policies? In 1969-1970 and 1974-1979, active American efforts to resolve the Arab-Israeli conflict followed the wars of June 1967 and October 1973 and reflected American concern that future rounds of regional conflict would pose serious risks of superpower involvement in a global confrontation. The United States considered that both superpowers shared a common interest in managing their relations to avoid a confrontation in the Middle East, and consequently, the United States tried between 1969-1970 and 1974-1979 to find a solution to the Arab-Israeli conflict lest it produce a superpower confrontation that neither the United States nor the Soviet Union wanted.

Between 1971-1973, however, the American interest in détente did not produce a corresponding involvement in managing the conflict. The reasons are not difficult to comprehend. Despite intense American diplomatic efforts during 1969-1970, none of the regional actors was prepared to accept more than a stand-still cease-fire agreement. Subsequent Egyptian violations of that agreement in August 1970, in conjunction with a significant Soviet military build-up in the region, persuaded U.S. policy makers that there was little immediate prospect for successful conflict resolution between Arabs and Israelis.

b. U.S. Global Interests and U.S. Military Involvement

Contrary to our expectations, our evidence does not suggest any clear-cut relationship between the type of global interest and the pattern of American military behaviour. From 1949 to 1961, the American policy of containment was associated with a total arms embargo of the region and an emphasis on regional pacts to deter Soviet aggression. From 1962 to

1968, containment was associated with sales of limited amounts of weaponry to Israel, Jordan, and Saudi Arabia. And, from 1980 to 1982, U.S. containment was associated with the effort to create a 'strategic consensus' between Israel, Egypt, and Jordan, and Saudi Arabia.

If containment was the dominant leitmotif from 1949 to 1961, 1962 to 1968, and 1980 to 1982, what explains the differences in American military involvement? In 1949, the United States hoped to contain Soviet expansion globally through its developing nuclear arsenal and the creation of military pacts in the Middle East. After the Czech-Egyptian arms deal in 1955 made the failure of its policy clear, the U.S. abandoned its search for military security arrangements and its reliance on arms embargos and became directly involved as an arms supplier to Israel, Jordan, and Saudi Arabia. The U.S. attempted to contain the U.S.S.R. by building up its regional military allies and offsetting Soviet military supplies to its clients. Again, from 1980 to 1982 the United States provided huge amounts of arms to Israel, Egypt, and Saudi Arabia to compensate for the revolution in Iran and the Iran-Iraq War, and to prevent the Soviet Union from advancing into the Gulf states from its improved position in Afghanistan. Changes in the pattern of American military involvement in the Middle East can be explained only in part as a response to different American strategies to contain the Soviet Union. Generally, however, U.S. interest in containment did not translate automatically into one or another military policy.

Nor does the policy of détente provide a better indicator of the extent of U.S. military involvement in the region. From 1969 to 1979, U.S. interest in détente with the Soviet Union was associated with limited arms sales to Israel (1969-1970), heavy arms sales to Israel and moderate arms sales to Jordan and Saudi Arabia (1971-1973), and heavy arms sales to Israel, Egypt, and Saudi Arabia (1974-1979). During 1969-1970, the American interest in reducing tension in the Middle East led to a slow-down in its arms supplies to Israel, a slow-down designed to press Israel to make concessions at the bargaining table and to remove the Middle East as an arena of possible superpower confrontation. From 1971-1973, the United States supplied Israel with large amounts of weaponry to compensate for the Soviet build-up in Egypt, notwithstanding its continued commitment to détente at the global level. From 1974 to 1979, the United States gave major military assistance not only to Israel, but also to Egypt and Saudi Arabia. Contrary to our expectations then, détente did not decrease American arms sales to regional allies but rather, in two of the three time periods, was associated with an increase in U.S. arms supplies to selected Middle Eastern states.

c. American Regional Interests and Conflict Management

We began our analysis with the assumption that when U.S. interest in Arab oil or petro-dollars was relatively low, American leaders would devote little attention to solving the Arab-Israel conflict. Conversely, when the United States became more dependent on Arab oil and petro-dollars, it would play a more active role in managing the conflict. Our evidence suggests, however, that the relationship between American regional interests and its strategy of conflict management is ambiguous.

Between 1948 and 1973, American interest in Arab oil was only low or moderate. It managed the conflict, however, by 'benign neglect' from 1948 to 1968 and 1971-1973, and through intense involvement from 1969 to 1970. Perhaps an intense interest in Arab oil and petro-dollars is more strongly associated with an active strategy of conflict management. Here too, the evidence is mixed. Prior to the October 1973 war, the United States appeared relatively content with the 'no-peace, no-war' situation between Israel and the Arabs. In the aftermath of the war, however, the administration committed itself to progress toward a settlement of the conflict through step-by-step diplomacy. On 6 May 1975, just prior to the successful conclusion of Sinai II (1 September 1975), Secretary of State Kissinger observed that failure to progress toward a settlement might lead to unfortunate consequences for western economies: "We do have the conviction that a prolonged stalemate in the Middle East involves a high risk of another Middle East War with major consequences for the possibility of conflict with the Soviet Union and with a major impact on the economies of all the industrialized nations, including us."[47] Thus from 1974 to 1979, conflict management under Presidents Nixon, Ford, and Carter was intense, fuelled in part by their estimates of significant American reliance on Arab oil and petro-dollars.

Although the United States was equally reliant on Arab oil and petro-dollar investments from 1980 to mid-1982, the Carter and Reagan Administrations altered their conflict management strategies from intense involvement to 'benign neglect'. American regional interests did not change; they remained high. American global strategy shifted, however, from détente to containment. Preoccupied with containing the Soviet Union, the American effort to strengthen its regional allies against further Soviet penetration of the region took precedence over its efforts to make peace in the Middle East.

d. U.S. Regional Interests and U.S. Military Involvement

American interest in Arab oil and petro-dollars is consistently related to the pattern of arms sales to Israel and the Arab states if not to strategies of conflict management. From 1948-1968, 1969-1970, and 1971-1973, American interest in Arab oil was low or moderate. During these three periods, the United States imposed a total embargo on arms to the region (1948-1961); supplied limited arms to Israel, Jordan and Saudi Arabia (1962-1970); and sold large amounts of arms to Israel and moderate amounts to Jordan and Saudi Arabia (1971-1973). At first glance, it

138

appears difficult to discern any consistent pattern. What is striking, however, is that at no time during the period from 1948-1973, when American interest in Arab oil was either low or moderate, did the United States provide massive amounts of weaponry to the Arab states. From 1974-1982, American policy-makers attached much greater importance to Arab oil and petro-dollars. During this same period there was a dramatic increase in the volume of American arms sales, particularly to Saudi Arabia and to Egypt. Evidence drawn from the $8.5 billion AWACS sale substantiates the connection between American interest in oil and petro-dollars and heavy arms sales to the Arab world.

During the prolonged debate in Congress over the AWACS sale, Saudi Arabia made it clear that it regarded the AWACS sale as a 'litmus test' of American-Saudi friendship. The administration initially defended the sale in strategic terms; it stressed the contribution that the AWACS would make to the defense of the Gulf against Soviet penetration. When asked why AWACS in U.S. possession could not provide the same strategic benefit, U.S. government spokesmen were forced to acknowledge that they believed they had no alternative but to give the Saudis what they wanted. Informally, the administration argued that a rejection of AWACS would humiliate the Saudi regime and jeopardize its standing in the Arab world. The result could only damage American interests in the Gulf. At best, the Saudis might turn to Western Europe for arms, but at worst, they might seek a rapprochement with the Soviet Union. If the United States refused to provide the arms the Saudis wanted, they might well raise prices while decreasing their production and thus tighten the oil market.[48]

Pressure to approve the AWACS sale was not confined to government officials. In a superb piece of investigative reporting, Steven Emerson examined the lobbying by U.S. corporate giants of members of Congress. These companies included among others Boeing (the main contractor for the AWACS planes), United Technologies, Transworld Airlines, International Business Machines, Intercontinental Hotels, the Ford Motor Co., Transamerica Corporation, and the Kellogg Co. Scores of other related business interests also campaigned heavily to secure passage of AWACS to ensure the protection of existing petro-dollar contracts or to improve the prospects of new arrangements. Thousands of other business interests were indirectly induced to join the campaign as a result of pressure from their domestic suppliers, purchasers, or business partners. Emerson documents a pattern of extensive lobbying by airline trade associations, health care management firms, rice growers, banks, construction firms, and other commercial interests from nearly every state who pressed hard for the sale.[49] In a series of ads that appeared in the *Wall Street Journal* and *The New York Times* during the AWACS debate in Congress, Mobil Corporation spelled out the importance of Saudi Arabia: "Even without regard to Aramco and the large U.S. oil companies, American business holds well in excess of $35 billion in contracts for work with Saudi Arabia.

The U.S. business relationship with Saudi Arabia has resulted in jobs here for hundreds of thousands of men and women...Saudi Arabia is far more than oil — it means trade for America, jobs for Americans and strength for the dollar."[50]

The contribution of recycled petro-dollars to the development of new weapons systems was also an important factor in governmental interest in arms sales to the Arabs. The AWACS sale, for example, represented a significant recycling of dollars expended on oil imports. Weapons bought by the Saudis in 1981 alone were expected to provide 112,000 jobs for Americans over the subsequent five years. Arms sales also reduce the unit costs of defense items for a manufacturer by extending production runs and spreading the cost of development outlays. It has been estimated that for every $1 billion worth of weapons that the United States exports, the Pentagon saves $70 million in unit costs. During the AWACS debate, some analysts estimated that future production of the radar-aircraft would be jeopardized if the sale to Saudi Arabia were not consummated.[51]

If major arms sales to Saudi Arabia appear to be strongly related to American perceptions of its dependence on Arab oil and petro-dollars, the same explanation does not hold for American arms supplies to Egypt. Increased arms sales to Egypt from 1974 to 1979 would seem to be better explained by the need to maintain a regional balance in the face of increased arms sales to Saudi Arabia and Israel. From 1980 to 1982, a shift in American global interests from détente to containment also provides an additional explanation for American arms sales to Egypt as well as to Saudi Arabia and Israel.

Conclusions And Implications

We set out to examine the linkages between American interests and foreign policy behaviour. Since policy is probably a function of both global and regional interests, it is hardly surprising that an exclusive focus on either set of interests produced only mixed results. An examination of American global interests revealed that during the three time periods in which the United States pursued its interests in détente — 1969 to 1970, 1971 to 1973, and 1974 to 1979 — the United States moved from active involvement to benign neglect and back to active involvement in its management of the conflict in the Middle East. This suggests that American interest in détente was not associated in any consistent fashion with particular conflict management strategies. Nor was détente a better predictor of American military commitment in the region. Again, during these three phases of détente, U.S. military involvement shifted from a pattern of limited arms sales to Israel, Jordan, and Saudi Arabia in the first phase, to one of heavy supply to Israel and moderate supplies to the Arab states in the second phase, to heavy arms sales to Israel and the Arab states during the third phase. At no time, however, was détente ever associated with American efforts to create military pacts or a 'strategic consensus'.

When we looked at American regional interests, we also found no meaningful relationship between the salience of Arab oil and/or petro-dollars and U.S. conflict management strategies. U.S. interest in Arab oil was low to moderate from 1948 to 1973, but its conflict management strategies moved from benign neglect (1948 to 1968) to active involvement (1969 to 1970) and back to benign neglect (1971 to 1973). Although U.S. interest in Arab oil and petro-dollar investments was significantly stronger from 1974 to 1982, this did not produce any consistent policy of conflict management. From 1974 to 1979, the U.S. was actively involved in managing the Arab-Israeli conflict; from 1980 to mid-1982, the conflict was placed on the back-burner; in the latter half of 1982, there was an increase in American involvement — largely in response to Israel's invasion of Lebanon.

We did find two sets of relationships, however, between interests and behaviour that held largely constant throughout. First, our evidence suggests a strong relationship between the intensity of American interest in Arab oil and petro-dollars and American military commitments to the region. Low salience of Arab oil and petro-dollar investments was associated either with an arms embargo or with limited arms sales to Israel and the Arab states (1948 to 1970), while high salience of Arab oil and petro-dollars was associated with heavy arms sales to Israel and the Arab states (1974 to 1982). When the United States considered itself both energy self-sufficient and economically vibrant, it was less likely to supply the Arab states with large amounts of military equipment. Alternatively, when the United States perceived itself as heavily dependent either on Arab oil and/or petro-dollars, it was more inclined to supply both Israel and the Arab states with large amounts of sophisticated weaponry.

American interest in containment was also linked to its conflict management strategy of benign neglect. When the United States regarded Soviet ambitions and intentions with unremitting hostility and expressed a strong interest in containing the Soviet Union, it pursued a policy of benign neglect towards the Arab-Israeli conflict (1948 to 1968, 1980 to 1982). Even when the special American envoy, Philip Habib, worked to end the crisis precipitated by Israel's invasion of Lebanon in June 1982, American involvement was designed primarily to prevent further violence. Habib's mediation was largely reactive; it differed from previous American attempts to expand the peace process by resolving fundamental issues.

When both sets of interests reinforced each other, the links to American policy were even stronger. The cumulative effects of containment and low salience of Arab oil and petro-dollars (1948 to 1968), for example, produced a consistent strategy of benign neglect; but when American interest in détente and Arab oil was high, from 1974 to 1979, the United States was actively involved in the peace process. And, with respect to arms transfers, a combination of American interest in containment and high

141

salience of Arab oil and petro-dollars (1980 to 1982) resulted, as expected, in heavy arms sales to Israel and the Arab states, while détente and low salience of Arab oil and petro-dollars (1969-1970) were associated with limited arms sales.

The pattern is far less clear when global and regional interests do not work in the same direction. For example, when U.S. interest in détente is accompanied by low salience of Arab oil and petro-dollars, there are competing theoretical expectations. Détente predicts intense involvement while low salience of Arab oil and petro-dollars should generate benign neglect. Yet when these two interests operated simultaneously (1969-1970), policy was one of intense involvement. Since 1980, American global and regional interests have also operated at cross-purposes. American interest in containment suggests a conflict management strategy of benign neglect, while the high salience of Arab oil and petro-dollars predicts active involvement in managing the conflict. The data reveal that when American leaders expressed intense interest in both containment and Arab oil and petro-dollars, policy alternated between benign neglect (1980-June 1982) and intense involvement (the 1 September 1982 Reagan Peace Plan).

If, as current market conditions suggest (circa March 1983) we are entering a phase in which there is a decrease in the salience of Arab oil and ultimately petro-dollars, and if this continues to be accompanied by a renewed American commitment to containment at the global level, then we should expect a corresponding decline in American interest in orchestrating a comprehensive Middle East peace settlement — in short, a return to the pattern that characterized the era from 1948-1968.

FOOTNOTES

[1] Among the more notable exceptions to this somewhat sweeping generalization is William Quandt, *Decade of Decisions* (Berkeley: University of California Press, 1977).

[2] For a detailed account of both the bureaucratic and organizational process models, see Graham Allison, *Essence of Decision* (Boston: Little, Brown & Co., 1971). For a critical assessment of decision-making literature see Robert Jervis, *Perception and Misperception in International Politics* (Princeton: Princeton University Press, 1976), and Janice Stein and Raymond Tanter, *Rational Decision Making: Israel's Security Choices, 1967* (Columbus: Ohio State University Press, 1980).

[3] Daniel Yergin details the historical development of these two competing sets of images of the Soviet Union which he describes as the Riga vs. the Yalta axioms. See his *Shattered Peace* (Boston: Houghton Mifflin Co., 1977).

[4] Quandt, *Decade of Decisions*, p. 14.

5   The decision to characterize U.S. conflict management strategies during certain historical periods as 'intense involvement' and during others as 'benign neglect' was based upon qualitative rather than quantitative indicators and relied heavily upon the judgements of decision-makers themselves as well as foreign policy analysts. Periods of intense involvement vs. those of benign neglect can also be distinguished using such quantitative indicators as the frequency of visits by senior government officials to the Middle East, their bureaucratic rank, as well as content analyses of the speeches of various senior U.S. decision-makers.

6   The categorization of U.S. military commitments in the Middle East as limited or moderate vs. heavy was based upon judgements by U.S. decision-makers and foreign policy analysts as well as on the magnitude of arms sales to the region. Again, a purely quantitative approach, discriminating between arms sales above or below a pre-determined value in constant dollars for a given year could have been adopted.

7   Quoted in Bernard Reich, *Quest for Peace* (New Brunswick, N.J.: Transaction Books, 1977), p. 22.

8   Nadav Safran, *Israel: The Embattled Ally* (Cambridge, Mass.: The Belknap Press of Harvard University Press, 1978), p. 19.

9   Quoted in Reich, *Quest for Peace*, p. 26.

10   Quoted in ibid., p. 29.

11   Quandt, *Decade of Decisions*, pp. 63-4.

12   *Ibid.*, pp. 64-8.

13   For a detailed account of these negotiations see Laurence L. Whetten, "The Arab-Israeli Dispute: Great Power Behaviour," *Adelphi Papers* 128 (Winter 1976/77) (London: International Institute of Strategic Studies, 1977).

14   Quandt, *Decade of Decisions*, pp. 128-64 offers a good summary of these developments.

15   *Ibid.*, pp. 208-9.

16   Leslie Gelb, "U.S. Working on New Peace Plan to Broaden Camp David Accords," *The New York Times*, 12 August 1982.

17   Quoted in Reich, *Quest for Peace*, p. 23.

18   Quandt, *Decade of Decisions*, pp. 66-7.

19   *Ibid.*, pp. 94-7.

20   *Ibid.*, pp. 98-100.

21   *Ibid.*, p. 101.

22   *Ibid.*, p. 163.

23   See Table 1a and 1b: U.S. Department of Defense, *Foreign Military Sales and Military Assistance Facts*, December 1980.

24   *Aviation Week and Space Technology* (1973): 16-19.

25   See Table 1a and 1b: U.S. Department of Defense, *Foreign Military Sales and Military Assistance Facts*, December 1980.

26   *Ibid.*

27 *Ibid.*
28 George F. Kennan, "The Sources of Soviet Conduct," *Foreign Affairs* 25:4 (July 1947): 572.
29 *Ibid.*, p. 576.
30 John Lewis Gaddis, *Russia, the Soviet Union and the United States* (New York: John Wiley & Sons, 1978), pp. 251-5.
31 *Ibid.*, p. 255.
32 Quoted in Robert Kaiser, "U.S.-Soviet Relations: Goodbye to Détente," *Foreign Affairs* 59:3 (1981): 500-21.
33 *Ibid.*, pp. 511-2.
34 For a more extensive discussion see Safran, *The Embattled Ally*, pp. 578-9.
35 Quandt, *Decade of Decisions*, p. 13.
36 *Strategic Survey* (London: Institute of Strategic Studies, 1972), p. 33.
37 For a precise tabular account of the systematic increase in the price of OPEC oil from 1973-81, see William Quandt, *Saudi Arabia in the 1980s* (Washington: The Brookings Institute, 1981), pp. 178-9.
38 Fred Singer, "Limits to Arab Oil Power," *Foreign Policy* 30 (Spring 1978): 58, and U.S. Department of Commerce, *Statistical Abstract of the United States, Bureau of the Census* (1980), Table 602.
39 Quandt, *Saudi Arabia*, pp. 178-9.
40 *The New York Times*, 5 March 1982.
41 U.S. Department of Commerce, *Highlights of U.S. Export and Import Trade* (December 1977), pp. 3-4.
42 *The New York Times*, 5 March 1978.
43 *Petro-Impact*, 2:1 (1979): 1-2.
44 *The New York Times*, 8 June 1982.
45 *Institutional Investor* (June 1980): 67.
46 Preliminary research suggests that changes either in the pattern of American conflict management or the level of military commitment occurred seven times from 1948-82.
47 Quoted in Oded Remba, "America, Oil Power and Western Response," *Middle East Review* (1975-76): 8.
48 Robert W. Tucker, "Appeasement and the AWACS," *Commentary* 72:6 (1981): 25-9.
49 Steven Emerson, "The Petrodollar Connection," *The New Republic*, 17 February 1982, pp. 18-25.
50 Quoted in Fredelle Z. Spiegel, "The Arab Lobby," American Professors for Peace: Background Paper, November 1981, pp. 1-2.
51 *Canadian Middle East Digest* 6:3 (March 1982): 3.

THE POLITICS OF ALLIANCE POLICY:
EUROPE, CANADA, JAPAN, AND THE UNITED STATES FACE
THE ARAB-ISRAEL DISPUTE

Janice Gross Stein
Department of Political Science
The University of Toronto

The Arab-Israel conflict has been central not only to the politics of the Middle East but to alliance politics among the western industrialized states as well. As a policy issue, it has dominated the politics of the Fertile Crescent for the last half century if not longer. And interested outsiders bring to the conflict a history of past involvement as well as strong current interests. The Europeans particularly have a long tradition of involvement in the Middle East which predates the origins of the Arab-Israel conflict. Canada, Japan, and especially the United States, the other principal members of the western alliance, although relative newcomers to the Middle East, have responded to the intensity of the conflict in a strategically important but volatile region. Precisely because it has been and continues to be so important, because it is a central rather than a marginal issue, policy toward the Arab-Israel conflict mirrors the strengths and strains within the western alliance. The management of the Arab-Israel conflict is an important benchmark of policy coordination within the alliance.

The turbulence and trauma of Middle Eastern politics in the last decade, it is often held, have had a strong impact on western policy toward the management of the Arab-Israel conflict. As the politics of oil grew in importance, as the stakes increased, policy on issues critical to the Arab-Israel conflict has changed substantially and, equally important, division within the western alliance has grown. The optic of energy-dependent Western Europe is considerably different from that of the superpower and leader of the western alliance, and it is not surprising to find exasperation and temper on both sides of the Atlantic.

I propose to dispute both these contentions. At best, arguments of substantive change in policy and consequent exacerbation of tension within the alliance are considerable exaggerations. Using policy toward the Arab-Israel conflict as the test case, similarities among alliance members continue to be greater than their differences, this despite the varying degrees of energy dependence on and political involvement in the Middle East. Second, policy has evolved considerably on only one of the central issues in the Arab-Israel conflict, the Palestinian dimension, and even though the evolution has not been symmetrical, change has taken place on both sides of the Atlantic. Differences are not substantive but procedural.

If these conclusions are justified by the evidence, they have considerable implications for alliance policy toward the Arab-Israel conflict. They dictate judicious consideration of common concerns and careful coordination of policy to enhance shared interests. The record of this last decade shows unilateralism to be a suprisingly ineffective strategy, both in the Middle East and within the alliance. We turn now to a careful tracing of the argument and evidence which generate these rather sobering conclusions.

To assess the scope of change in alliance policy toward the Arab-Israel conflict in the decade of the nineteen-seventies, we need a base line of comparison. A brief historical retrospective is unavoidable. We begin with an examination of Canadian, European, Japanese, and American approaches to conflict management from 1967 to 1973. The roots of the divisions within the alliance, divisions which became apparent after the war in 1973, can be traced to this period. Although 1967 seems a somewhat proximate basis for subsequent comparison, it does mark the exacerbation of the conflict after more than a decade of relative quiescence. Following the crisis over Suez in 1956, a crisis as much for the western alliance as for the Middle East, the Arab-Israel conflict stopped short of all-out war until 1967. The years between 1967 and the outbreak of war again in 1973 can serve as a benchmark, then, for comparison of approaches to conflict management by the United States, Canada, the EEC, and Japan at the end of the decade.

What the analysis omits is as important as what it includes. By design, it does not consider the intersecting economic crises which accompanied the last escalation of the Arab-Israel conflict, nor does it examine changing relationships between the two superpowers. Both these factors which had significant impact on the development of the conflict within the Middle East — and on the alliance — are treated elsewhere in this volume. Nor does the analysis extend to an examination of alliance policies toward the Middle East generally. Rather, the focus is sharply on the Arab-Israel dispute, and particularly on differences in approach to its management and resolution and their consequences for cohesion or division within the alliance. Although these limits are adhered to in the body of the analysis, the conclusion does speculate on the consequences of the deteriorating relationship between the superpowers for alliance approaches to the settlement of the Arab-Israel dispute.

The Alliance and the Dispute: the Roots of the Division

In May of 1967, after Egypt requested the withdrawal of the United Nations' peacekeeping force and blockaded the Straits of Tiran, war again seemed likely in the Middle East. This time, however, the crisis was not compounded by serious disagreement among the allies. Britain and the United States were largely agreed in their approach to the crisis — unlike 1948 or 1956 — and had no need this time of a Canadian "honest broker". President Johnson consulted extensively with members of the alliance in the weeks preceding the outbreak of war and, although General de Gaulle differed somewhat in his approach to the management of the conflict, the scope of the divergence would not become apparent until after the war had ended. Although the escalation of the Arab-Israel dispute and the crisis created by the outbreak of war were severe, consultation and coordination among the allies were effective and free of strain. The contrast to 1956 could not have been more striking.

Cooperation among the allies continued in the immediate post-war period through tacit division of responsibility which facilitated the international management of the Arab-Israel dispute. Under British leadership, with the approval and support of the United States, the Security Council passed the omnibus resolution which would set the parameters of the debate for the next six years. Resolution 242 was a delicate compromise, arduously achieved through five months of international bargaining. In its English version, it called for "withdrawal of Israeli armed forces from territories occupied in the recent conflict," "termination of all claims of belligerency and respect for and acknowledgement of the sovereignty, territorial integrity, and political independence of every state in the area and their right to live in peace within secure and recognized boundaries free from threats or acts of force," and "a just solution of the refugee problem."[1] Deliberately vague in its outline of the terms of a comprehensive settlement of the dispute, it avoided either an explicit demand for full withdrawal or for full peace.[2] The resolution was to become the benchmark of policy for all members of the alliance. Indeed, Japan's first diplomatic involvement in the Arab-Israel dispute came when its representative on the Security Council expressed support for Resolution 242. Although not then a member of the Council, Canada affirmed the broad consensus of the western alliance when it accepted the resolution as the official statement of Canadian policy toward the dispute.

With the advent of a new administration in the United States in 1969, President Nixon began an unprecedented effort to achieve a comprehensive settlement of the dispute. Nixon read the lessons of 1967 differently than did his predecessor and, repeatedly emphasizing the dangers of renewed escalation in the "Balkans of the twentieth century", attached considerable urgency to a reduction of the conflict.[3] Skeptical of the capacity of the disputants themselves to reach agreement, the United States began discussions with the Soviet Union to design the outlines of a general settlement. Simultaneously, parallel four-power negotiations, which included France and Britain as well, began in New York. The participation of the two European powers in these discussions in 1969 met a long-standing demand for a formal role in the management of the conflict. Indeed, during the war in 1967, President de Gaulle had insisted on an autonomous role in the negotiating process and vigorously opposed a Soviet-American condominium.

The French approach was in striking contrast to that of Canada and, even more so, to that of Japan. Canada was deeply involved in a reassessment of its traditional international role as "helpful fixer". The newly-elected Prime Minister Trudeau urged a tighter linkage between

147

domestic interest and foreign policy and heightened emphasis on national independence. The relevance of the Arab-Israel dispute to matters of domestic concern was marginal and the reduced attention to mediation and peacekeeping further decreased the salience of the Arab-Israel dispute as a foreign policy issue. Japan too had no diplomatic ambitions in the Middle East. Neither Canada nor Japan had been a power in the region in the past and both were content with a passive rather than an activist approach to conflict management. At the end of the 'sixties, the western alliance encompassed both active mediators, struggling to design a comprehensive settlement of the dispute, and passive observers. This divergence in responsibility created little strain within the alliance.

It was not the four-power meetings, however, but the parallel Soviet-American discussions which produced proposals for a comprehensive settlement in December, 1969. These proposals were aborted by an escalating war of attrition along the Suez Canal, a war which provoked military intervention by one and diplomatic activism by the other superpower. For the first time in the history of the conflict, the Soviet Union committed its own combat personnel to Egypt's defense and, in so doing, sharpened and polarized its competition with the United States in the region.[4] Responding to Soviet military involvement and its attendant dangers, the United States abandoned its attempt at comprehensive settlement, concentrated on terminating the fighting between Egypt and Israel, and first proposed a partial settlement, achieved incrementally, as an appropriate approach to conflict reduction.[5] The polarization of the Arab-Israel dispute by the superpowers signalled the eclipse, at least temporarily, of the preferred European approach to the reduction of the conflict; the search for a comprehensive settlement was no longer the basis of American strategy.

Even before President Nixon abandoned the comprehensive approach, however, the European contribution to its development had been more apparent than real. Despite the formality of British and French participation in negotiations in the spring and summer of 1969, it was the bilateral Soviet-American discussions that produced the outline of a package settlement. The limited impact of the two European powers suggested limits to the capacity of Western Europe to influence the development of the conflict. France, at its own initiative, no longer sold sophisticated equipment to Israel and, consequently, was no longer a major supplier of any of the front-line states. Britain withdrew formally and finally from the Persian Gulf in 1971 and thereby ended its long military presence within the region. The old imperialism seemed no more than a historical remnant. Even as their political and military influence in the Middle East declined, however, the economic dependence of Western Europe grew. The two seemed in almost inverse relationship.

In 1970, the production of American oil peaked and the United States entered the international market as an important consumer. That same

148

year, Libya challenged the autonomy of resident oil companies and, in 1971, oil producers meeting in Teheran first suggested that they would interrupt supply in an effort to improve the terms of trade. As the dynamics of the international oil market began to shift, it is not altogether surprising that the European approach to the management of the Arab-Israel dispute shifted. Excluded by the superpowers, the foreign ministers of the European Economic Community met to consider a common diplomatic posture.

The shared consensus of the EEC did differ in emphasis from the previously agreed-upon Resolution 242. The Community called for a withdrawal by Israel, with minor adjustments, from all the occupied territories; the preservation of the security and territorial integrity of all states within the region through the creation of demilitarized zones and the stationing of United Nations' forces; the internationalization of Jerusalem; and a solution of the refugee problem through repatriation in stages or compensation under the supervision of an international commission.[6] One year later, the EEC announced its intention to implement a Mediterranean policy through a series of bilateral agreements with all Mediterranean states. In these actions, the Community signalled a change in the tone if not the substance of its approach to the management of the Arab-Israel dispute.

When the failure of the four-power talks and the comprehensive approach became apparent, members of the Community, led by France, preferred a collective posture to national articulation of positions on the issues in dispute. By formulating joint policies through a coordinating process within the Community, the weakness of even the strongest individual member was adumbrated by the weight of the group. The joint document concealed the range of opinion that did exist among members and, even more important, insulated individual states from pressure to modify their position independently of the others. Second, the EEC distinguished itself, through its continued emphasis on a comprehensive settlement, from the United States; President Nixon was then pursuing a partial settlement along the Canal to be implemented in phases. Third, the substance of the European position differed marginally from that of the United States. The EEC gave greater priority to international guarantees and, consequently, placed less emphasis on negotiations between the participants both to determine the status of Jerusalem and to secure mutual recognition.[7] Fourth, the Community paid less attention to Soviet involvement and the ensuing superpower competition than did the United States. Finally, by developing a strategy of bilateral economic arrangements, leaders within the Community attempted to outflank the conflict through commercial and trading relationships with members of the region who were not "front-line" participants in the dispute. Europe moved from individually- to collectively-formulated positions, from participation in international negotiations with the superpowers to a regional forum, to a divergence in emphasis and approach from that of the United States, and to a broadening of the instruments of policy.

It is worth noting that this revision in policy antedates the withdrawal of Soviet military personnel from Egypt in 1972 and the consequent reduction in the danger of superpower confrontation. Competition between the United States and the Soviet Union outside of Europe did not invoke alliance solidarity; this interpretation of the limits to the scope of the alliance would bedevil European-American relations in the ensuing decade, not only in the Middle East but throughout the third world. Second, the shift in approach antedated the outbreak of hostilities in the Middle East in 1973 and the accompanying oil embargo. If logic dictates that cause cannot follow consequence, the change in the European approach cannot be traced directly to the intersecting crises of the 'seventies; the optic shifted before oil was embargoed. The relationship between energy-dependence and policy position is more complicated than their simple equation would suggest. At most, in an explanation of the shift in the European approach, the politics of oil were relevant principally through anticipation. Third, the change that did occur was limited in substance; the Community distinguished itself through approach and technique rather than through content. And, what is even more striking, Europe would continue to diverge from its American ally in degree but not in kind, principally in approach rather than in substance, throughout the traumas of the 'seventies.

October, 1973: An Alliance under Stress

In 1973, war came to the Middle East unexpectedly and with unprecedented ferocity. Not only the fighting but also its consequences were severe. Within three weeks of the Egyptian-Syrian attack, supplies of oil had been curtailed to some members of the alliance and, the United States, locked in fierce competition with its counterpart superpower, had initiated a world-wide nuclear alert in response to a Soviet threat of military intervention. In Europe, Canada, and Japan, the heightened threat to international security and the international economy provoked concern, if not alarm, and sharply oscillating, poorly coordinated, initial responses. Policy varied considerably within the alliance.

Canadian policy was most consistent with its prewar posture. In his first official statement, issued while the fighting still continued, the Minister for External Affairs condemned the resort to force by Egypt and Syria, reaffirmed Canada's support of Resolution 242, and restated Ottawa's longstanding refusal to tamper with the text through addition or subtraction.[8] This initial statement reflected Canada's traditional approach to international conflict management: strong support for the resolutions of the United Nations and peacekeeping and an emphasis on negotiations between the parties to a conflict.

150

Within the European Community, collective action disintegrated under the pressure of the oil embargo which accompanied the renewal of fighting. Confronted with intersecting security and economic crises and heavily dependent on imported oil, members scrambled to secure supplies and, in so doing, exacerbated relationships within the Community and within the alliance as a whole. Despite this almost visceral resort to unilateralism and the very dissimilar positions adopted initially by members of the EEC, however, the broad outlines of the collective strategy developed earlier would quickly become apparent.

Initially, divergence of opinion did appear to be considerable. While Holland, like Canada, condemned the use of force by Egypt and Syria, France justified the attack as the repossession of occupied territory. Indeed, disagreement within the EEC was so sharp that Holland and Denmark refused to authorize Britain and France to present a collective position in the Security Council debate at the United Nations. Tension within the Community was compounded by the low priority accorded alliance concerns by critically important European states and their consequent inattention to the competition between the superpowers. Despite the Soviet airlift of equipment to Egypt and Syria, Britain, France, and, to a lesser extent, even Germany refused to cooperate with the United States either in the transfer of military equipment to Israel during the war or in its diplomatic initiatives immediately after the war.[9] There was disagreement not only within Europe but between Europe and the United States.

Within a month, however, the EEC had coordinated policy sufficiently among its nine members so that it could issue a collective declaration of policy. While the statement issued on 6 November reiterated established policy themes, there was one significant change. The Community renewed its emphasis on the inadmissability of the acquisition of territory by force, repeated its demand for withdrawal by Israel from all occupied territory, reiterated the right of every state in the Middle East to secure and recognized boundaries, and again urged the creation of demilitarized zones reinforced by international guarantees.[10] What was new was the European treatment of the Palestinian question. The EEC no longer called for a just solution of the refugee problem, as it had in the earlier statement, but for the recognition of the legitimate rights of the Palestinians. Although much remained the same, the new emphasis on Palestinian collective rights would become the leitmotif of European policy. Indeed, it would be the single change of substance for the rest of the decade.

The reaction of Japan, the most heavily dependent on imported oil, was even sharper than that of the EEC. On 22 November, the Chief Cabinet Secretary issued a statement deploring Israel's occupation of Arab territories and calling for total withdrawal, respect for the integrity and security of all countries in the area, accompanied by guarantees, and the recognition and respect of the just rights of the Palestinians. The statement

151

concluded with the warning that Japan would "continue to observe the situation in the Middle East with grave concern" and, depending on future developments, it might have to "reconsider" its policy toward Israel.[11] The shift in the tone and substance of Japan's policy, a pronounced shift, brought no immediate reply from the oil-producing states; supply restrictions were not lifted. Very shortly thereafter, Deputy Prime Minister Miki began a seventeen day visit to eight Arab countries where he pledged US $127 million to restore the Suez Canal and multi-million dollar commodity and product aid credits. Even before Miki left the Middle East, supply restrictions against Japan were removed.

The thrust of American policy, quickly becoming pivotal in the management of the conflict, was considerably different in its approach. Secretary Kissinger, now seized with the dispute, focused his attention on the process rather than the substance of a settlement. He emphasized a gradualist approach which began with the easier rather than the more difficult issues, built on small successes, and worked through postponement of failure. While Europe and Japan urgently emphasized the solution and elimination of the conflict, the United States concentrated on its management — and transcendence — through incrementalism. Kissinger argued strongly that even the modest objective of management, if it were to be achieved, required the decoupling of economic from political issues and a sharply circumscribed role for the Soviet Union. Moreover, he considered cooperation within the western alliance an important structural requisite for the effective management of both the Arab-Israel conflict and the Soviet-American competition.

Europe, to put it mildly, was not overwhelmed by the wisdom of Kissinger's strategy. The difference essentially was one of approach, not only to the management of the conflict, but also to a series of political and economic issues which, although not formally part of the Arab-Israel agenda, nevertheless accompanied the escalation and internationalization of the conflict. The complexities of energy dependence in the "north" and the terms of technology transfer and the supply of financial and commercial services to the "south" were difficult enough, but the relationship of this broader set of policy issues to the Arab-Israel conflict was itself a matter of some dispute. Oil producers in the Middle East urged and some in Europe accepted a link between the two sets of issues, while the United States led those who insisted on decoupling rather than linking the two agendas. When war in the Middle East created a new international agenda, the western allies differed in their approach to handling of the issues: some supported linkage and a comprehensive solution while others suggested decoupling and an incremental, partial approach to the conflict in the Middle East.

To resolve these differences, members of the alliance tacitly agreed to an initial division of responsibility. The United States would handle the specifics of the dispute in the Middle East and the attendant east-west competition, while Europe concentrated on restructuring and stabilizing relationships with the newly powerful oil-producing states. This initial approach seemed sensible: building on the relative strengths of Europe and the United States, it would utilize American political and military capabilities to de-escalate the conflict and, simultaneously, insulate the energy-dependent from the passions of the dispute in the Middle East. This insulation, it was hoped, would facilitate the orderly rearrangement of international energy and financial markets. The approach was more difficult, however, to realize than to conceive. Especially in the immediate post-war period, it was more difficult to decouple economic from political issues than the United States had anticipated. But, when the issues were linked, the results of the linkage were far less than Europe and Japan had expected. If linkage seemed to be necessary, it clearly was an insufficient approach to the complex of policy issues which now dominated allied discussion and behaviour, public as well as private. A look at the voting record at the United Nations, the public forum *par excellence*, documents the differences and similarities among the allies in their approach to the management of the Arab-Israel conflict.

The Arab-Israel Dispute Internationalized: Voting at the United Nations

In the years which followed the October War, Arab participants in the conflict expanded the arena and shifted the emphasis of the dispute. Although a solution to the Palestinian problem had always been important, it was to become the overwhelming focus in multilateral meetings. Particularly at the United Nations, Arab leaders insisted that the Palestinian question be approached as a national and political issue, not as a refugee problem. Moreover, they made it clear that they considered voting on resolutions in the General Assembly to be a valid indicator of the policy position of members. A review of the voting records of the EEC, Canada, Japan, and the United States is useful, then, to isolate changes in policy as well as differences within the alliance. Examination of the turbulent session of the General Assembly in 1974 can provide the benchmark for subsequent detailed comparison of votes from 1975, the twenty-ninth General Assembly to the meeting of the thirty-fourth Assembly in January, 1980 and the last session for which valid statistics are currently available.

The first regular meeting of the General Assembly after the October War provided tangible evidence of the changing terms of the Arab-Israel debate. Two quite distinct issues were at the center of the discussion. Resolutions introduced before the Assembly affirmed the right of Palestinian self-determination and, secondly, asked that the Palestine Liberation Organization be recognized as the sole legitimate represen-tative of the Palestinians and be invited to participate in the work of the Assembly as well as its committees. Since Resolution 242, the previous

153

embodiment of policy for the western allies as well as for Arab governments and Israel, made no such provision, submission of these resolutions to a vote created a dilemma for most members of the alliance.

The EEC, Japan, and Canada abstained on the resolution which affirmed the Palestinian right of self-determination, national independence, and repatriation, recognized the Palestinians as a principal party in the establishment of peace and requested that the PLO be contacted on all matters relating to Palestine. The United States opposed the resolution.[12] Canada's explanation of vote is valid for other members of the alliance as well. Ottawa's Ambassador to the United Nations noted that the text made no reference to the earlier Resolution 242 as a framework for negotiation and, consequently, ignored the interrelatedness of the complex of issues which constitute the Arab-Israel dispute. However, Canada considered representation of the Palestinian people to be an essential component of a peaceful settlement of the dispute. Consequently, it abstained.[13] Canada agreed with its European allies: Resolution 242 was a necessary but insufficient basis for discussion of the Arab-Israel dispute. Specifically, it was incomplete in its failure to make provision for Palestinian participation in the process of negotiations which must follow.

Voting on the second resolution highlighted a different issue and a second, quite distinct trans-Atlantic coalition which would vote together repeatedly over the next several years. In its opposition to granting the PLO permanent observer status, the United States was joined by Canada and most of the EEC; France and Italy abstained, however, as did Japan.[14] In the debate that followed, Japan made its position explicit. Its representative argued that the Palestinian question was at the heart of the Middle East problem and that PLO participation in the debate was essential.[15] Japan added, however, that it would be helpful if the PLO were "to work in a constructive spirit for a political settlement through peaceful means."[16] Opposition to the resolution by members of the alliance stemmed both from general principle and particular circumstances. Some refused, as a matter of principle, to prejudge the issue of the appropriate representation of the Palestinians.[17] More important, others objected to specific characteristics of the PLO, particularly its unwillingness to forego the use of terrorism and accept the legitimacy of Israel within the Middle East.[18] Differences in approach to the PLO cut across Europe and created a coalition which spanned the Atlantic. Divergence of opinion on this subject would remain substantial throughout the decade as alliance members moved beyond the issue of representation to consider the suitability of the PLO as a partner in the negotiating process. And in the ongoing debate, a core of Europeans would switch their vote to determine a majority either in Europe or across the ocean.

One additional resolution is worthy of attention. During the thirtieth meeting of the General Assembly in 1974, a resolution condemning all forms of racial discrimination *inter alia* declared Zionism to be racist.

Introduction of the resolution in this form suggested a deliberate attempt to delegitimize one of the principal parties to the dispute. Members of the western alliance were virtually unanimous in their opposition to such a strategy; only Japan abstained. In voting against the resolution, alliance members established the parameters of their approach to conflict resolution: divided on the legitimacy of the PLO as the representative of the Palestinian people and, more to the point, on its suitability as a negotiating partner, they were agreed in their opposition to the delegitimization of Israel.[19]

The pattern of voting in the subsequent five Assemblies documents the scope of divergence as well as consensus among the allies in their approach to the dispute. Inspection of the record on some forty-nine resolutions dealing with the Arab-Israel dispute, all put before the Assembly, suggests a rather complicated pattern of voting within the alliance (Table I).[20]

TABLE I

Agreement within the Alliance

	1975	1976	1977	1978	1978
	N=5	N=11	N=10	N=14	N=9
EEC	.20(1)	.81(9)	.80(8)	.78(11)	.44(4)
The majority of the EEC and US	.60(3)	.45(5)	.60(6)	.50(7)	.66(6)
The majority of the EEC and Canada	.60(3)	.90(10)	.80(8)	.71(10)	.77(7)
US and Canada	.60(3)	.45(5)	.80(8)	.78(11)	.88(8)
When US and a majority of the EEC disagree:	(2)	(6)	(4)	(7)	(3)
Canada and a majority of EEC	1.00(2)	1.00(6)	.50(2)	.43(3)	.33(1)
Canada and US	.00(0)	.00(0)	.50(2)	.57(4)	.66(2)
Japan and a majority of the EEC	.20(1)	.72(8)	.80(8)	.50(7)	.44(4)
Japan and US	.00(0)	.27(3)	.40(4)	.21(3)	.22(2)
Japan and Canada	.20(1)	.63(7)	.60(6)	.28(4)	.33(3)
When US and a majority of the EEC disagree	(2)	(6)	(4)	(7)	(3)
Japan and a majority of EEC	.50(1)	.66(4)	1.00(4)	.57(4)	.66(2)
Japan and US	.00(0)	.00(0)	.00(0)	.00(0)	.00(0)
	% N	% N	% N	% N	% N

Immediately apparent is the low level of consensus in the difficult first years which followed the October War. In 1975, for example, the EEC was deeply divided and voted together on only one of five resolutions, and the United States and a majority of the Community agreed only marginally better than half the time. In a new trend, when the United States and the EEC disagreed in their approach to the Arab-Israel dispute, Canada voted with the Community; one year later, Canada was even more strongly in agreement with a majority of the EEC.[21] These data suggest a considerable reorientation of Canada's policy, but inspection of the record for the subsequent three years shows a return to Canada's more usual position of balance between allies in disagreement. Although Canada no longer considered itself an "honest broker" within the alliance, although it abjured its activist role of the 'fifties, it continued to distribute its vote even-handedly, if not within the Middle East, at least within the alliance.

Japan, on the other hand, never voted with the United States when America disagreed with the EEC. Indeed, Japan's disagreement with the EEC, when it occurred, can be explained largely by its approval, along with a large part of the third world, of resolutions which the Community, much less the United States, could not support or opposed. The level of agreement between Japan and other members of the alliance was significantly lower than that among all other allies. On issues relating to the Arab-Israel dispute, Japan was singular in its failure to do as the others.

During these five years, what did vary was the level of cohesion within the EEC and the shifting coalitions which resulted. After 1975, cohesion improved markedly. In the United Nations, EEC members demonstrated the capacity to follow a collective policy on the Arab-Israel dispute. Closely associated with improved policy coordination within the EEC was disagreement with the United States. When the EEC did not vote together, however, a trans-Atlantic coalition was almost always present, a coalition which included at a minimum the United States, Canada, Belgium, Germany, the Netherlands, the United Kingdom, and Denmark. The evidence of these five years does not support an argument of intensifying trans-Atlantic division. On the contrary, almost as often as not, a majority of Europeans voted with the United States. Divisions within the alliance existed not only between the United States and Europe, but also within Europe itself. A suggestion of a European and an American perspective on the Arab-Israel dispute appears to be a considerable oversimplification of the complexities of alliance policies in the Middle East. Examination of the substance of policy as well as the pattern of voting also supports this pattern of trans-Atlantic consensus as well as difference.

The Arab-Israel Conflict: the Terms of a Settlement

For the past thirty years, a settlement of the Arab-Israel conflict has been of international concern, but in the nineteen-seventies, it received priority on the international agenda. A canvass of the substance of allied positions on the appropriate terms of a settlement shows surprising consensus within the alliance by the end of the last decade. There was little disagreement within Europe or between Europe and the United States on the broad parameters of a resolution to the conflict. The problem lay elsewhere.

The United States, Canada, the EEC, and Japan all supported the security, territorial integrity, and political independence of all the states in the Middle East. In so doing, they explicitly upheld Israel's right to exist within the region. Indeed, Prime Minister Miki of Japan, in one of the earliest criticisms of Resolution 242, suggested in 1975 that the resolution was deficient in its failure to refer explicitly by name to the state of Israel.[22] And the Nine, in their important declaration issued in Venice, affirmed Israel's right to existence within the region as essential to a settlement.[23]

Second, although there were minor differences in language, the EEC as well as Japan, the United States, and Canada supported the withdrawal of Israel from the occupied territories. Japan, in its statements at the United Nations, demanded total withdrawal from all the territories captured in 1967, as did Italy, France, and Germany.[24] In Venice, the Community used somewhat more circumspect language: it called on Israel "to put and end to the territorial occupation...as it has done for...Sinai."[25] The analogue of Sinai is, of course, to a total withdrawal. The position of the United States was a little different. As long ago as 1969, the United States called for a return to the 1967 borders with only 'minor' rectifications. Canada's position was most open-ended: it argued that final borders must be settled through a process of negotiation. Although these differences in language suggested shadings in policy, there was overwhelming concensus for virtually complete withdrawal.

From this shared consensus sprang common opposition to any unilateral change in the status of the occupied territories which would prejudice the outcome of negotiation between the parties to the conflict. There was unanimous opposition, for example, to the establishment of settlements by Israel, expressed frequently at the United Nations and more recently in the Venice declaration of the EEC. Equally, there was widespread opposition to intemperate and one-sided criticism of Israel, criticism which tended to dominate debate at the United Nations in the latter half of the 'seventies. This opposition to unbalanced attack was reflected in the trans-Atlantic coalition which appeared persistently during these years.

Finally, there was widespread consensus within the alliance that the Palestinian problem required a political and territorial solution. A textual analysis of the vocabulary of western leaders would isolate differences in language which, however, indicate only minor differences in substance. Addressing a town meeting in Clinton, Massachusetts after only two

157

months in office, President Carter spoke of the need for a 'homeland' for the Palestinians.[27] Canadian statements were models of linguistic acrobatics, arguing that the future of the Palestinian people was a central element in the Middle East conflict and that an enduring solution must provide "...a territorial foundation for political self-expression by the Palestinian people consistent with the prinicple of self-determination."[28] A report prepared for then-Prime Minister Clark, urged Canada to lend its support to the Palestinian right to a homeland. One year later Canada called explicitly for a homeland within a clearly defined territory, the West Bank and the Gaza Strip.

Opinion in Europe was little different. Germany, strongly committed to the unification of its own people, spoke of the right to self-determination of the Palestinians.[30] At the conclusion of a tour of the Persian Gulf, the president of France, in an official communiqué issued in March of 1980, similarly endorsed the right of the Palestinian people to self-determination. Britain referred formally to the "national identity" or "personality" of the Palestinian people. European leaders refrained, however, from endorsing the creation of an independent Palestinian state. Britain and France abstained when such a proposal was put to the Security Council,[32] and the French foreign minister explained that the political form of self-determination was beyond the competence of outside powers to determine.[33]

Collectively, the position of Europe was little different from that of its individual members. Indeed, a review of the series of formal statements issued by the EEC points to a steady evolution in Community thinking during the decade. In November of 1973, the EEC spoke of the "legitimate rights" of the Palestinians. Four years later, in June of 1977, Community leaders explained that the right to a "homeland" was a component of these legitimate rights[34]; in so doing, they joined their colleagues across the Atlantic. At their meeting in Venice in 1980, leaders of the Nine reiterated that the Palestinian people must be given an opportunity to fully exercise its rights to self-determination.[35]

This examination of opinion on both sides of the Atlantic points to a surprisingly broad consensus within the alliance by the end of the decade on the terms of a settlement to the Arab-Israel dispute. In their meeting in Venice, the Nine argued that a settlement must be based on two principles: the right to existence and security of all states in the region, including Israel, and justice for all peoples, which implied recognition of the legitimate rights of the Palestinian people.[36] No member of the western alliance quarrelled with this statement. The broad consensus on ends — the security of Israel and a political solution to the Palestinian problem — did not extend, however, to the means to reconcile and achieve these objectives.

Disagreement within the alliance stemmed not from the components of a comprehensive settlement of the dispute but from important differences over negotiating methods and participants. Europe and the United States differed, not for the first or only time in the nineteen-seventies, in their assessments of the most effective approach to the management and resolution of the conflict. Two issues were central to these divergent assessments. The first, a disagreement over the practicability of an immediate and comprehensive settlement, was institutionalized in the code words "Camp David" and "Geneva". Second, members of the alliance differed on the suitability of the PLO as a participant in the negotiating process. These two issues were present, in one form or another, in all the resolutions which provoked different votes on the two sides of the Atlantic. Beneath this disagreement over strategy and tactics, moreover, lay a difference in the appreciation of the independent role of Europe as a conflict mediator. As on so many other issues, the Middle East was again a harbinger of things to come.

A Step-by-Step Approach to Camp David

After the October War, Europe, Canada, and Japan accepted the pre-eminent role of the United States in engineering a settlement of the Arab-Israel dispute. Britain and France, participants in the negotiations in New York in 1969, had shown neither capacity to nor interest in defining a new role for themselves following the failure of the four-power talks. The outbreak of war, accompanied by a near-confrontation between the two superpowers, underlined the special resources needed to mediate the Arab-Israel dispute. Cognizant of their limited capabilites, the allies seemed almost to prefer an allocation of responsibility which provided some distance from the enveloping and dangerous dispute. Unrestrained by the need to set and meet concrete negotiating objectives, Europe and Japan were free to outline their view of a comprehensive settlement with little attention to the obstacles to its immediate achievement or to the required negotiating procedures. Canada was more restrained: it emphasized its role as peacekeeper rather than peacemaker and focused some attention on the process of negotiations as well as the substance.

It was the United States which assumed principal responsibility for the de-escalation of the conflict. Kissinger opted for a partial, incremental approach whose objective was a reduction in the probability of renewed warfare and its attendant dislocations and dilemmas. Very much preoccupied with the possible rather than the desirable, American diplomacy succeeded in disengaging the military forces of the combatants and engineered a series of partial agreements between Egypt and Israel, the two most forthcoming participants in the negotiating process. Although the pace was often painfully slow, the approach was designed to build the basis over time for a series of interrelated agreements. Given the real obstacles to agreement and the slow progress toward even modest objectives, the United States was not terribly sympathetic to demands for an immediate and comprehensive settlement; it considered such an approach irresponsible and a recipe for failure. Only after the second round of agreements between Egypt and Israel in 1975 did Secretary Kissinger consider that the process was by now cumulative in its results, creating a basis for broader agreement. Preliminary exploration of the outlines of such an agreement ended with the electoral defeat of President Ford.

Under President Carter, the United States shifted completely to the preferred strategy of the Community and Japan and concentrated on the negotiating dynamics of a comprehensive settlement. It consciously strengthened its relations with front-line confrontation states and indirectly offered incentives to the PLO to encourage it to modify its position and join the negotiating process. The Carter Administration also reopened discussions with the Soviet Union in an effort to ensure its cooperation should the Geneva Conference be resumed; superpower consensus is a structural requisite of a comprehensive settlement. For a brief period of time, from January to November 1977, there was agreement between the United States and Europe not only on the substance but also on the strategy and tactics of settlement.

A comprehensive approach to conflict resolution, tried again for the first time since 1969, was similarly disappointing in its outcome. It produced consensus among the allies but no progress in the negotiations. American overtures to the PLO were not reciprocated, the reintroduction of the Soviet Union antagonized two of the principals in the negotiating process and, in frustration, President Sadat launched his unilateral initiative. He did so not only to deprive his more militant Arab allies of their veto, but also to exclude the Soviet Union from the peace-making process. The president of Egypt considered the Soviet Union obstructive, a hindrance rather than a help.

After some initial confusion, the United States adjusted its approach and returned to the vigorous pursuit of an agreement between Egypt and Israel which would simultaneously provide at least a framework for progress on other fronts. The ensuing Camp David accords and peace treaty between Egypt and Israel exchanged full withdrawal from the Sinai for some demilitarization of the desert area, limited force zones, and normalization of relations. The agreements were comprehensive — all outstanding bilateral issues between the two signatories were resolved — and partial — in their creation of a loosely defined framework for further open-ended negotiation with other participants who had not yet joined the process. It was a signal moment in the long and tortured history of the Arab-Israel conflict.

Approaches to Conflict Management: Procedures and Participants

Contrary to American expectations, Camp David got mixed notices from some members of the alliance. The dilemma of the allies in 1978 was similar to that of 1973 with, however, one important exception. The agreement between Egypt and Israel did significantly reduce the probability of major war in the Middle East, at least in the short-term and, consequently, virtually eliminated the possibility of an oil embargo. In engineering the agreement, therefore, the United States met one of the principal demands of energy-dependent Western Europe and Japan. Strong Arab skepticism and opposition to the proposals for Palestinian autonomy, however, again created a policy problem for western leaders who could not simultaneously support the American attempt at conflict reduction and meet Arab criticism. Particularly strong opposition came from the PLO who was given no formal role in the forthcoming series of negotiations. Again, a partial and evolutionary approach was grossly insufficient to satisfy Arab and particularly PLO demands. Yet an evolutionary approach seemed the only possible alternative to comprehensive policies which could not succeed.

Reaction to this dilemma was considerably different on each side of the Atlantic. Canada, as well as the United States of course, was strongly supportive of Camp David and the ensuing treaty. Officials in Ottawa considered the treaty to be the most significant development in the thirty year history of the conflict.[37] Canada was careful to add that a comprehensive peace treaty between all Arab participants in the conflict and Israel was essential if peace were to be permanent and stable, but insisted that the settlement between Egypt and Israel was a valuable first step and deserving of international support. Even after almost a year of frustrating deadlock in the autonomy discussions, a special report prepared for Ottawa reaffirmed the importance of negotiations between the parties; Arab opposition to Camp David, it concluded, must go beyond general statements to concrete alternatives.[38] In its analysis of the peace-making process, Canada placed as much emphasis on the evolutionary component of the negotiating process as on the substantive content of the agreement.

In Europe, however, the general reaction was guarded. Even before the peace treaty was concluded, Europe's leaders were reserved in the support they extended to President Sadat. After his visit to Jerusalem in November of 1977, the EEC, meeting in Brussels, issued a statement commending the initiative but reiterating the importance of an "overall" settlement which would meet the "rights and concerns of all the parties involved."[39] Ten months later, after the meeting at Camp David in September of 1978, the foreign ministers of the Nine commended President Carter as well as the leaders of Egypt and Israel but again reiterated their hope that the conference was a major step toward a comprehensive peace.[40] Commenting on the peace treaty which grew out of Camp David, the EEC underscored the urgency of a comprehensive settlement, a settlement which would require Palestinian participation and international endorsement.[41] The flush of enthusiasm was considerably less on this side of the Atlantic.

Within the boundaries of their collective response, there were shadings of difference among members of the EEC. Britain was supportive of American mediation as was Germany which had special obligations to Israel and strong commercial interests in Egypt. France, generally less well-disposed toward the United States and a heavy importer from and exporter to the Gulf states, not surprisingly was critical. Unhappy with American dominance of the peace-making process, France supported an enlarged Geneva Conference or an international conference at the United Nations where it would be better able to exercise independent influence. In his perspective, President Giscard d'Estaing differed little from his predecessor a decade earlier; de Gaulle too had protested superpower domination and demanded four-power talks which would recognize the role of France in the international community. At the thirty-fourth meeting of the General Assembly, in December of 1979, France alone among members of the Nine abstained on two resolutions which declared Camp David illegal, condemned all partial agreements and separate treaties which violate the rights of the Palestinian people and contradict the principle of comprehensive settlement, and called for the reconvening of the Geneva Conference.[42]

France was the principal exponent of a new European initiative which could provide a "third way", an alternative to American or Soviet mediation in the Middle East. Touring the Persian Gulf in the spring of 1980, the president of France urged Arab states to look to Europe as a military and diplomatic alternative to either superpower. At French prodding, the EEC considered introducing an amendment to Resolution 242 in the Security Council which would recognize the legitimate rights of the Palestinians and provide formally for their self-determination; the French foreign minister argued that passage of such an amended resolution would help to break the impasse in the autonomy negotiations.[43] President Carter was vehement in his opposition to a European demarche which would compromise the Camp David process. Indeed, the alliance was treated to the rather unusual spectacle of one ally threatening to veto a resolution introduced by the others.[44] Deterrence of an ally is apparently easier than deterring an adversary for, under threat of an American veto, the EEC abandoned its project of a revision to Resolution 242 and decided instead to issue a collective statement at its summit meeting in Venice in June of 1980.

Members of the Community were not agreed on the thrust of the proposed statement. West Germany, Holland, and Denmark pressed for a limited initiative which would complement rather than challenge negotiations going on under American auspices. Deliberately, they sought to reduce division within the alliance. France, on the other hand, supported a strongly-worded statement, insisting that an independent

162

diplomatic role for Europe was more important than smoothly equili-
brated relations with the United States. At stake in the debate were not
only European relations with the Middle East, or even the future of the
American effort at mediation, but, more important, divergent perspectives
on the international role of members of the alliance.

The statement finally agreed to at Venice was a compromise. Its
treatment of Palestinian participation in the negotiating process, an issue
we shall examine in a moment, was designed to avoid explicit challenge to
the United States. The EEC was unequivocal, however, in its emphasis on
an independent European role in the mediation of the conflict. Citing
traditional ties and common interests, the Nine offered to participate in a
system of concrete and binding international guarantees within the
framework of a comprehensive settlement. In addition, the EEC decided to
launch an independent effort at mediation, quite distinct from the
negotiations going on between Egypt and Israel. The statement concluded
with the announcement that a mission would be dispatched to the Middle
East to establish contact with all the parties to the dispute, with a view to
determining the form of a subsequent European initiative.[45]

This difference in perspective was not new to the alliance. Not for the
first time, Europe urged a comprehensive settlement while the United
States insisted on the value of gradual and limited progress over time
which would have cumulative consequences. Not for the first time, Europe
offered to guarantee a settlement reached under international auspices.
And not for the first time, Europe rebelled against American domination
of the diplomacy of conflict resolution in the Middle East. Indeed, careful
reading of the record at the beginning and the end of the decade of the
'seventies would find much in common and little difference. True, in 1969,
Britain and France participated with the United States while in 1980,
Europe collectively demanded an independent and direct role in mediating
the dispute. This demand had as much to do, however, with shifting
dynamics within the alliance as it did with the contours of the Arab-Israel
dispute. The decade-old difference in perspective, temporarily submerged
during active periods of mediation under Kissinger and Carter, re-emerged
as a continuing disagreement both over the appropriate process of conflict
resolution and the proper role for Europe in that process.

A final issue, which arose directly from these competing perspectives,
was the role of the Palestine Liberation Organization in the negotiating
process. On this issue, unlike the others, there was significant change in
policy which did create distinct differences within the alliance. Alone
among the western allies, the United States committed itself formally to
refrain from recognition of and negotiation with the PLO until it
recognized Israel's right to exist and accepted Resolutions 242 and 338.[46]
Early in the Carter administration, officials suggested informally that
acceptance of the United Nations' resolutions would be sufficient to
initiate a dialogue with the United States. This effort to encourage

discussion met with no success, however, and ended when the Egypt-Israel dialogue accelerated. The framework for Palestinian autonomy agreed to at Camp David made no provision for the participation of the PLO.

Canadian policy was also somewhat reserved. Traditionally, Ottawa was unwilling to pronounce formally on the issue of the appropriate representation of the Palestinians, but argued strongly that the Palestinians must be represented in the negotiations. It viewed the policies of the PLO, however, as unhelpful to the peace process; indeed, until the PLO was prepared to accept Resolution 242 and the legitimacy of Israel, Canada could not envisage its constructive participation in negotiations.[47] Unlike the United States, however, the reevalution of Canadian policy toward the conflict, undertaken in 1980, recommended a broadening of contacts with the PLO to encourage "moderation and realism and...open acceptance of the legitimacy of the State of Israel."[48] Here the criterion of policy was encouragement of constructive participation in the negotiating process.

Given their emphasis on the urgency of an immediate and comprehensive solution, policy was considerably different within Europe and Japan. Although Japan did not officially recognize the PLO nor give its office in Tokyo diplomatic status, as early as 1976 it urged a direct Israel-PLO dialogue.[49] Most members of the EEC similarly withheld formal diplomatic recognition from the PLO although they acknowledged its receipt of observer status at the United Nations. Most, however, authorized the establishment of PLO information facilities if not the opening of offices in their capitals.[50] Individually, moreover, some of Western Europe's leaders talked informally and formally with representatives of the PLO. Among the first to do so was the former foreign minister of France, Jean Sauvagnargues, who met with Yassir Arafat in Beirut in 1976. German policy was more reserved: it established as the criteria of recognition renunciation by the PLO of terrorism and acceptance of the existence of Israel.

In the wake of the Camp David accords, Arafat led the PLO in a major attempt to secure official recognition from Western Europe. From the perspective of the PLO, such recognition was important if the United States were to be outflanked, the autonomy negotiations discredited, and the validity of a comprehensive strategy reestablished. Responding to this initiative in the summer of 1979, the former German chancellor, Willy Brandt, and the current chancellor of Austria, Bruno Kreisky, met with Arafat in Vienna under the auspices of the Socialist International in an effort to mediate the Israel-Palestinian dispute. Although the mediators were not present in their capacity as governmental representatives, it was the first semi-official attempt by West Europeans to resume an active and direct role in the management and resolution of the conflict. Despite the cordial tone, however, the meeting ended with no change in the official position of the PLO.

Although no progress was made in these initial diplomatic contacts, the quasi-official discussions presaged a change first in French and then in EEC policy toward the PLO. In March of 1980, the French cabinet issued a communique at the end of President Giscard's tour of the Persian Gulf. Arguing that a settlement must be based on the two principles of security and self-determination, the communiqué called for the participation of the Palestine Liberation Organization in negotiations on this basis.[51] The Venice declaration of the Nine, issued three months later, followed this outline closely: with only slight modification of language, modification designed to avoid provocation of the United States, it insisted that the PLO be "associated" with the negotiations.[52] This new demand for "association" was a considerable change in policy: Europe no longer insisted on acceptance by the PLO of Resolution 242 or the existence of Israel as a condition of participation in negotiation of a settlement. The United States responded that the PLO was not a suitable participant in the negotiating process until it met both these conditions.[53]

So matters rested by the end of the decade. To decade-old differences between the United States and Europe on procedures appropriate to the management of the Arab-Israel dispute were added new differences on suitable participants in the process of conflict management. These newer issues would carry over into the 'eighties and the administration of a new president in the United States. Paradoxically, although the incendiary potential of the Arab-Israel dispute was somewhat less at the end of the decade than it was at the beginning, differences among the allies persisted. These differences in approach assume added importance, however, because of the substantially greater involvement of the United States in the peace-making process and the consequent implications for alliance cohesion.

The Arab-Israel Dispute in Alliance Politics

By the end of the nineteen-seventies, the scope of American involvement in the management of the Arab-Israel dispute was unprecedented. For the first time in the history of the conflict, the United States was not only patron or mediator, but a visible 'partner' in the ongoing negotiations. After an initial interregnum, the Reagan administration committed itself even more fully to active involvement in conflict resolution. In his peace initiative of September 1982, President Reagan moved closer to a strategy of comprehensive settlement, the preferred approach of Europe, but insisted again that the PLO would have to formally recognize Israel's existence before it could be admitted to the negotiating process. Indeed, the Reagan plan gives no official role to the Palestine Liberation Organization.

Inevitably, the United States becomes the target of those who are opposed to its strategy of conflict resolution and disagreement within the alliance, while long-standing and not substantially greater in scope, acquires new significance. While older disagreements on processes narrowed, newer differences over participants translate directly into divergent assessments of the roles of Europe and America within the alliance. These differences have significantly greater consequences for the alliance than they do for the Middle East. Indeed, with only mild exaggeration, European approaches to the resolution of the Arab-Israel dispute can better be explained by the dynamics of the alliance than by the dynamics of the dispute.

At the core of the European approach are the two concepts of comprehensive participation and comprehensive settlement. Comprehensive participation through "association" of the PLO with future negotiations can, Europeans suggest, serve three distinct purposes. First, meeting the Arab demand for PLO participation is as important, if not more important, than the negotiations themselves: it can prevent an Arab turn to the Soviet Union should American mediation fail.[54] The argument has some credibility at the margin. France, Britain, and Germany can supply some of the military needs of some of the Arab states. Egypt, Iraq, and Saudi Arabia, for example, have diversified their military suppliers in the last several years. The scope of arms purchases in the Middle East is of such magnitude, however, that on a longer term basis, Europe does not have the military resources to substitute for the Soviet Union and the United States. Europe can complement but not supplant the superpowers. The 'third way' seems unlikely in practice.

A second, more modest objective of European strategy is moderation of the position of the PLO to create a framework for negotiation with Israel. Such an objective is attractive and important as a strategy of conflict resolution,[55] yet the timing of major statements by the EEC casts some doubt on its likely effectiveness. European leaders met in Venice, for example, directly after the congress of al-Fatah in Damascus, the first to be held in nine years. Far from moderating its position, al-Fatah, the central constituent unit of the PLO, declared in its final communique: "Fatah is an independent national movement, whose aim is to liberate Palestine completely and to liquidate the Zionist entity politically, economically, militarily, culturally, and ideologically."[56] Even after this statement was issued, the Nine pressed for the inclusion of the PLO with no accompanying demand that it moderate its policies. Again, in the summer of 1982, after the trauma of the war in Lebanon, the PLO did not officially change its position, yet European leaders again reiterated their suggestion that the PLO be associated with peace negotiations. It seems unlikely that unconditional acceptance of the PLO will advance the process of conflict resolution. More important, it will not encourage the PLO to take the steps necessary to alter its position, privately and then publicly.

If the first two purposes are either ill-conceived or badly-executed, a third objective is still more modest. The EEC, recognizing the limits both to its capabilities and to its influence, designed its initiative principally to press the United States to bring pressure on Israel to make concessions in the ongoing negotiations. The Reagan plan has made this objective largely irrelevant, but Europe has succeeded in distinguishing its position from that of the United States. It is very likely that such a separation was an important, if implicit, objective of European leaders. Europe's approach responded as much to its own interests and its need for independence from the United States as it did to the realities within the region. Its strategy reflected serious doubt about the quality of the leadership of successive American presidents as well as American capability and determination to move the principal parties toward concession and settlement. Policy also responds to a resurgent and restless Europe which seeks international outlets for its growing aspirations.

The Arab-Israel dispute has shown itself remarkably resistant to national and international solution for most of this century. It is not surprising, therefore, that a complex and intractable conflict of such major proportions defies solution; the obstacles to agreement are both serious and real. Precisely because the answers are not obvious, because almost all the principal approaches are flawed, alliance coordination and cooperation is especially important. Cooperation should be easier in the 'eighties, moreover, because differences between the United States and Europe have narrowed considerably. The Reagan plan moves the United States closer to the substance of the European position even though it explicitly does not support an independent Palestinian state. The United States still views the process of conflict resolution quite differently than do its European allies.

Members of the alliance must adjust their strategies if they are to advance their collective interest as well as those of the participants in the dispute. An alliance strategy toward the Arab-Israel conflict must build on the strengths and resources of its members to encourage the principal belligerents to compromise. The war in Lebanon in the summer of 1982 has made such compromise both more urgent and more likely. Europe has historic economic and cultural ties to important states in the Middle East who themselves exercise influence on frontline Arab participants in the dispute. Abjuring declaratory politics, Europe can insist on moderation, acceptance by Palestinians and Israelis of the legitimacy of the other, and a commitment to formal peace premised on national reconciliation. The new government in France is particularly suited to this task for President Mitterand has unique ties both to Israel and to the Arab world. Particularly with respect to the Palestine Liberation Organization, Europe can use its diplomatic resources and political capital to encourage the change in position which is one of the essential prerequisites to a break in the current impasse. European diplomatic recognition must be recognized as the valuable resource it is; it must be deployed rather than expended. Similarly, the United States must use its extraordinary access to Israel to

167

insist on a national and territorial solution to the Palestinian problem, and to encourage and reward the necessary concessions both on the substance and the process of negotiations.

The United States must also acknowledge the strong European interest in and ties to the Middle East as well as its determination to participate actively in the mediation of the conflict. In cooperation with their allies, American leaders must design mechanisms to consider, consult, and coordinate joint strategy to resolve this as well as other disputes. Through cooperation rather than competition, consultation rather than declaration, through division and sharing of responsibility, the western allies can use their resources collectively to reward concession and encourage moderation. Common sense and common interest dictate a strategy which builds on the differential strengths of members, deliberately emphasizes consensus rather than difference, pays heed to what is common rather than what divides, shares responsibility rather than foments competition, and harmonizes rather than distinguishes policy. A touch of common sense would serve both the Middle East and the western allies well in the difficult decade to come.

FOOTNOTES

[1] United Nations' Resolution 242 was passed by the Security Council on 22 November, 1967. In addition to the three clauses cited, the resolution also called for guarantees of freedom of navigation through international waterways in the area and guarantees of territorial inviolability and political independence of every state in the area. For a full text of the resolution, see United Nations, Security Council Documents (UN.S/), 30 November, 1967, p.8.

[2] The French translation of Resolution 242 used the article "the" before the word "territories" — withdrawal from *the* territories — thereby requiring a total withdrawal by Israel from the territories captured in 1967. This difference between the French and English version subsequently engendered considerable controversy.

[3] This phrase would recur frequently in President Nixon's speeches. During the War of Attrition in 1970, for example, the President painted a grim portrait: "I think the Middle East now is terribly dangerous. It is like the Balkans before World War I — where two superpowers, the United States and the Soviet Union, could be drawn into confrontation that neither of them wants because of the differences there..." See interview of President Richard Nixon on television, 1 July 1970, *Department of State Bulletin*, 27 July 1970, pp. 112-113. William Quandt, subsequently deputy and then head of the Middle East office of the National Security Council, attests to the intense American interest in engineering a settlement during this period. See William B. Quandt,

Decade of Decisions (Berkeley: University of California Press, 1977), pp. 72-104.

4 Estimates of the Soviet commitment vary, but it is generally agreed that the Soviet Union sent SAM-3 missiles with combat crews to man the sites while Egyptian crews were undergoing training. In addition, Russian air combat units, equipped with MIG-21J fighters, provided air cover for Egypt's heartland. Soviet personnel, both in advisory and combat roles, numbered about 20,000. More important than the size of the Russian presence was the commitment of combat forces beyond the Warsaw Pact area, the first time the Soviet Union had so deployed forces since World War II.

5 For a detailed examination of superpower attempts to end the wars in the Middle East, see my "Proxy Wars — How Superpowers End Them: The Diplomacy of War Termination in the Middle East," in *International Journal*, September, 1980.

6 For a detailed discussion of the working paper prepared by the foreign ministers of the then six members, see Hans Maull, "The Strategy of Avoidance: Europe's Middle East Policies after the October War," in J.C.Hurewitz, ed. *Oil, the Arab-Israel Dispute, and the Industrial World* (Boulder, Colorado: Westview Press, 1976, 110-137), p. 118.

7 The Rogers' formulation, the result of Soviet-American discussions and known as Rogers' Plan A, differed in its emphasis on a formal end to the state of war and negotiation through indirect talks using the Rhodes formula. The role of the four powers — Britain and France as well as the United States and the Soviet Union — was restricted to their promise "to exert their efforts to help the two sides adhere to the provisions of the agreement." See *Arab Report and Record*, 1-15 December 1969, pp. 521-522. Differences were largely those of modalities rather than substance. For a full text of the proposals, see the speech by Secretary of State William Rogers, *The New York Times*, 11 December 1969.

8 See the statement by the Minister for External Affairs, Mitchell Sharp, to the House of Commons, 16 October 1973, *Statements and Speeches*, Department of External Affairs, Information Division, Ottawa.

9 Britain, for example, refused to permit the United States to use its bases in Cyprus for the airlift of supplies to Israel during the fighting. Germany, with considerably stronger security ties to the United States, permitted the use of its facilities as long as cooperation was not made public.

10 For the text of the resolution, see *Bulletin of the European Community* 10, 1973, p. 2502.

11 The statement by the Chief Cabinet Secretary of Japan was reported in *The New York Times* on 24 November 1973. For a complete text see *Keesing's Contemporary Archives*, 26 November-2 December 1973, 26228.

12 Resolution 3236 was approved by the General Assembly by a vote of

89(Y) -8(N) -37(A).

13 Statement on Resolutions 3236 and 3237 by Ambassador Saul Rae, Press Release No. 35, Canadian Delegation to the United Nations, 22 November 1974.

14 Resolution 3237 was approved by the General Assembly by a vote of 95(Y) -17(N) -19(A).

15 See the statement by Shizuo Sato, Permanent Representative to the United Nations' General Assembly, *United Nations' Monthly Chronicle* XI, 11 (December, 1974), pp. 105-106.

16 *Ibid.*

17 See, for example, the reply by the Minister for External Affairs to a question in the House of Commons, House of Commons Debates, *Hansard*, 12 November 1974, p. 1260, Ottawa, Canada.

18 This was the thrust of the American objection. The United States subsequently undertook formally to engage in no negotiation with the PLO until it accepted Resolutions 242 and 338 and the legitimacy of Israel. See the text of the Memorandum of Understanding between the United States and Israel, 4 September 1975, in *The New York Times*, 17 September 1975.

19 Resolution 3379 was approved by the General Assembly by a vote of 72(Y) — 35(N) —32(A). In 1979, the same issue arose again with somewhat different results. A resolution put before the General Assembly declared "hegemonism" unacceptable and again condemned "racism including zionism." An attempt to delete the reference to Zionism was defeated by a vote of 79-26 with 33 abstentions; the EEC, Japan, Canada, and the United States all voted in support of deletion. When the amendment was lost, however, only Canada and the United States, along with Australia and Israel, opposed the resolution; Europe and Japan abstained. Members of their delegation explained subsequently that they were reluctant to stand against a general condemnation of discrimination. Their abstention should not be construed, therefore, as acceptance of the equation of Zionism with racism.

20 The list was constructed by examining all resolutions put before the General Assembly and selecting only those dealing specifically with the Arab-Israel dispute. Selection of these resolutions is, however, by no means obvious; there is often considerable discrepancy among analysts. Proposals to establish a nuclear-free zone in the Middle East, for example, were omitted since they do not touch directly on the conflict while resolutions dealing with the United Nations Relief Works Agency (UNRWA) and its responsibilities to the Palestinians are included. To calculate agreement, votes on each of the resolutions are compared annually and the percentage of agreement calculated. When the EEC is divided, the position of the majority of its members provides the point of comparison. Of particular interest is voting by Canada and Japan on

resolutions where the EEC and the United States vote differently. Such resolutions are a subset of the larger number in any given year.

21 A somewhat different analysis compares Canadian voting on 16 resolutions from 1967 to 1972 with its pattern from 1973 to 1976 on 28 resolutions. While the number of resolutions included in the comparison differs from this analysis, the findings are similar for the years 1975 and 1976. While Canada voted with the United States 81.2% of the time before 1973, it did so only 33.3% after the October War. Similarly, Ottawa voted with the EEC only 37.5% from 1967 to 1973 but 88.8% of the time from 1973 to 1976. See Lawrence Grossman, "The Shifting Canadian Vote on Mideast Questions at the United Nations," *International Perspectives*, May-June 1978.

22 Prime Minister Miki made this point in his maiden address to the Diet of Japan in January 1975. For a partial text of the speech, see Kazushige Hirasawa, "Japan's Tilting Neutrality," in J.C. Hurewitz, *op. cit.*, p. 144.

23 The text of the Venice Declaration is reprinted in full in *The New York Times*, 14 June 1980. See Article 4.

24 See, for example, the statement of Shizuo Saito, Japan's Permanent Representative to the General Assembly, on 18 November 1974 in *UN Monthly Chronicle* XI, 11 (December 1974), pp. 105-106; his statement explaining Japan's position on the draft resolution before the Security Council on 26 January 1976, in UN Monthly Chronicle XIII, 2(February, 1976), p.11; and the address by Ichiro Hatoyama, Minister for Foreign Affairs to the General Assembly, 27 September 1977, in *UN Monthly Chronicle* XIV, 10 (New York: United Nations Office of Public Information, November 1977), pp. 75-76.

25 See the text of the Venice Declaration, *op. cit.*, Article 9.

26 See the Venice Declaration, *op. cit.*, Article 9 and the text of the report prepared by R.L. Stanfield, the Special Representative of the Government of Canada and Ambassador-at-large, submitted to the Government of Canada on 20 February 1980. Hereafter, this document is referred to as the Stanfield Report. Stanfield was explicit in his criticism of one-sided resolutions which are counter-productive in their consequences. See p.14 of the Report.

27 Comment of President Carter to a town meeting in Clinton, Massachusetts, 16 March 1977. See *The New York Times*, 17 March 1977.

28 See, for example, M. Fernand Leblanc, Parliamentary Secretary to the Minister for External Affairs, "Canada and the United Nations' Resolution Concerning Israel and the Middle East," *Statements and Speeches*, No. 77/12 Department of External Affairs, Information Division, Ottawa.

29 See the Stanfield Report, p.7.

30 West Germany's Foreign Minister, Hans Dietrich Genscher, spoke of

the right of self-determination of the Palestinian people as early as 1974. Most recently, in an interview with *Frankfurter Allgemeine Zeitung* on 12 March 1980, he applauded French recognition of that right and urged other states to follow suit.

31 The Government of France issued an official communique on 11 March 1980 at the conclusion of the visit of President Valery Giscard d'Estaing to the Middle East. The communique called on all the parties to the dispute to recognize that a lasting settlement "must be based on two universal and complementary principles which are for each state the right to security and for each people the right to self-determination. Each state in the region, in particular the state of Israel whose preoccupations in this field are legitimate, should be able to live in peace within secure, recognized and guaranteed frontiers, which implies a withdrawal by Israel from the territories occupied since 1967. The Palestinian people, whose aspiration is to exist and organize itself as such, should be able to exercise its right to self-determination within the framework of a peaceful settlement." See *Le Monde*, 12 March 1980, translation by the author.

32 The draft resolution before the Security Council on 30 April 1980 affirmed that "the Palestinian people should be enabled to exercise its inalienable national right of self-determination, including the right to establish an independent state in Palestine." Other articles in the draft resolution called for guarantees of the sovereignty and territorial integrity of all states in the Middle East, and withdrawal by Israel from all the territories occupied in 1967. The draft resolution also affirmed the right of the Palestinians to return to their homes or receive compensation. See *The New York Times*, 1 May 1980. The United States vetoed the resolution.

33 Interview with Foreign Minister Jean Francois-Poncet, *The Washington Post*, 30 May 1980. The Foreign Minister added that "we do not exclude a Palestinian state if the Palestinians want a state."

34 Statement by the EEC, 6 November 1973, *Bulletin of the European Community* 10, 1973, point 2502. Statement of 29 June 1977 in *Bulletin of the European Community* 6, 1977, p. 62.

35 See the Venice Declaration, *op. cit.*, Article 6. Two months earlier, the larger Council of Europe had issued a statement supporting the Palestinian right to self-determination. Their statement differed, however, from that of the Nine, in the accompanying demand that Resolution 242 be amended to incorporate explicit recognition of the right to self-determination. For a partial text of the resolution approved by the Council of Europe on 23 April 1980 in Strasbourg, France, see *Le Monde*, 25 April 1980.

36 Venice Declaration, *op. cit.*, Article 4.

37 Interview with senior officer of the Department of External Affairs, Middle East Division, December, 1979.

38 See the Stanfield Report, *op. cit.*, p.8.
39 See the statement by the Ministers of Foreign Affairs of the European Economic Community, 22 November 1977, Brussels, in *Bulletin of the European Community* 11, 1977, p.52: 2.2.4.
40 Statement of the Foreign Ministers of the European Economic Community, 19 September 1978, in *Bulletin of the European Community* 9, 1978, pp. 53-54: 2.2.8.
41 Statement of the Ministers of Foreign Affairs of the European Economic Community, 26 March 1979, Paris, in *Bulletin of the European Community* 3, 1979, p. 86: 2.2.74.
42 See the text of Resolutions 3465B and 3470 put before the General Assembly in December, 1979, in *Resolutions and Decisions Adopted by the General Assembly During Its Thirty-Fourth Session* (United Nations, New York: Department of Public Information, 1980), pp.15, 20-21. Japan also abstained while all other members of the EEC, as well as the United States and Canada, opposed the two resolutions. In both cases, the trans-Atlantic consensus was greater than the cohesion within Europe.
43 See the statement by the Foreign Minister of France, Jean Francois-Poncet, on 29 May 1980 in *The New York Times*, 30 May 1980.
44 The President was explicit in his threat to veto European action in the United Nations: "We will not permit in the United Nations any action that would destroy the sanctity of and the present form of U.N. Resolution 242. We have a veto power that we can exercise if necessary to prevent this Camp David process from being destroyed or subverted and I would not hesitate to use it if necessary...To summarize, we have a good basis, the issues are clearly defined, Israel and Egypt both want a peace settlement. We are asking the European allies not to get involved in it for the time being." See *The New York Times*, 31 May 1980.
45 See the Venice Declaration, *op. cit.*, Articles 2, 5, and 11. The tone of the declaration was much less provocative of the United States than the statement issued, for example, by the Council of Europe six weeks earlier. Members of the EEC, also members of the Council, had approved or abstained on a resolution which termed Resolution 242 inadequate in its treatment of the Palestinians as refugees, condemned Israel's settlements as a violation of international law, and argued that the Camp David accords could not serve as the basis for a comprehensive settlement in the Middle East. Simultaneously, however, the Council of Europe explicitly called upon the PLO to acknowledge Israel's right to existence, security, and independence. In all respects, then, the Council statement was considerably stronger than the declaration issued at Venice six weeks later. For a partial text of the statement issued by the Council of Europe, see *Le Monde*, 25 April 1980.
46 This undertaking was given to Israel in a Memorandum of

173

Understanding on 4 September 1975 as an inducement to sign the second disengagement agreement with Egypt. For the text of the Memorandum, see *The New York Times*, 17 September 1975.

[47] Interiew with senior officer, Middle East Division, Department of External Affairs, Ottawa, January 1980.

[48] See the Stanfield Report, *op. cit.*, p.10. Prime Minister Clark, who commissioned the report but was defeated at the polls before its final submission, argued that Canada would be prepared to recognize the PLO only if it were prepared to renounce terrorism and recognize the right of Israel to exist. See the interview of Prime Minister Clark by the Canadian Broadcast Corporation on 9 October 1979, reported in *The Globe and Mail*, 10 October 1979. Prime Minister Trudeau has not repeated these conditions, however, but has reverted to the earlier Canadian position that representation of the Palestinians is a matter for the Palestinians themselves to decide.

[49] More recently, it was reported that Japan had considered a meeting between a special government envoy, former Foreign Minister Sunao Sonoda, and Yassir Arafat during a twenty-five day tour by Mr. Sonoda to oil suppliers in the Middle East. The purpose of the meeting was to prepare for a visit by the leader of the PLO to Tokyo later in 1980. The proposed meeting was strongly supported by the Ministry of International Trade and Industry but vigorously opposed by the Foreign Ministry. The dispute was ultimately resolved by then Prime Minister Ohira who ruled against the meeting and for continued delay in recognition of the PLO. A detailed discussion of the policy debate within Japan is found in *The New York Times*, 28 February 1980, citing "official sources".

[50] The PLO is represented officially, for example, in Bonn and London and has established information offices in Brussels, Paris, and Luxembourg. No such official representation exists in North America. Austria recently went one step further and extended special diplomatic status to the PLO on 10 March 1980.

[51] For the text of the communique, see *Le Monde*, 12 March 1980.

[52] See the Venice Declaration, *op.cit.*, Article 7.

[53] See the statement by Secretary of State Edmund Muskie in *The New York Times*, 14 June 1980.

[54] See statement by President Valery Giscard d'Estaing, *Le Monde*, 6 March 1980. In his discussions with the Sultan of Kuwait, the President urged the Gulf States to pursue a policy of non-alignment with the superpowers and turn to Europe as a dependable alternative. In an effort to expand French influence in the Gulf, France has increased its sale of tanks to Saudi Arabia and is currently negotiating the sale of approximately 80 Mirage F-1 planes to Qatar. It is already an established supplier of Libya.

[55] In his report to the Government of Canada, Stanfield explicitly set the

moderation of the policy of the PLO as the principal objective of communication with its leaders: "In my view, Canada should broaden contacts with the PLO on issues affecting negotiations and the peace process, with a view to encouraging that Organization towards greater moderation and realism and towards open acceptance of the legitimacy of the State of Israel. This will require frank communication and discussion." See the Stanfield Report, *op. cit.*, p.10. The Council of Europe, in its resolution of 23 April 1980, made a similar demand of the PLO. See n.45 above.

[56] See the communique of the Fourth Congress of al-Fatah, issued on 2 June 1980 in Damascus. The statement continues: "It [al-Fatah] also aims at establishing a Palestinian democratic state on all the Palestinian soil... This struggle will not stop until the Zionist entity is liquidated and Palestine is liberated." The full text of the communique is found in *Al-Liwa*, 2 June 1980, Beirut.

CANADA-MIDDLE EAST RELATIONS:
THE END OF LIBERAL-INTERNATIONALISM

David B. Dewitt and John J. Kirton

Departments of Political Science, York University
and University of Toronto respectively.

Within Canada's broad and demanding foreign policy agenda few areas have so engrossed the Canadian government and people as the Middle East. Since 1947, debates over the partition of Palestine, the ongoing Arab-Israel conflict and recurrent crises in areas such as Lebanon and Cyprus have constituted a continuing focus of Canadian concern. Moreover, in its skillful response to these dilemmas, Canadian policy towards the Middle East has provided most observers with an archetypical example of Canada's profound commitment to an enlightened, liberal-internationalist ethos.[1] These observers have portrayed Canada as a stable middle power with no direct strategic and economic interests, historical commitments and animosities, or distinctive policy and instruments of influence in the region. They have thus highlighted Canada's continued leadership and participation in peacekeeping, its evenhanded mediatory role in search of peaceful settlements, and its generous contributions to promote functional accommodations, all through its favoured vehicle of the United Nations. In so doing they have identified the foundation of Canadian behaviour as a systemic concern with promoting global stability, United Nations legitimacy, and western and Commonwealth solidarity and, equally, the deep, reinforcing internationalist commitment of the Canadian public and policy community itself.[2]

Although official declarations and independent analyses have largely underscored the preeminence of this liberal-internationalist portrait, they have at the same time contained elements which challenge its central vision. Taken together these elements emphasize how Canada's reflexive neutrality, rendered precarious by Canadian insensitivity to Arab perceptions and shifting global coalitions, has given the country a steadily decreasing influence in the region. They point as a cause to the heavy constraints imposed by Canada's lack of knowledge of, and derivative interest in, the Middle East itself and its overriding preoccupation with maintaining harmony between, and special relationships with, a dominant United Kingdom and United States. And they often note Canada's resulting dependence on a specific historic interpretation of Judaism and Zionism, kept alive by the penetrative influence of a well-organized, Jewish lobby within Canada.[3]

During the past decade and a half, the debate between liberal-internationalists and its critics has dominated scholarly and public commentary on Canada's relations with the Middle East. Yet while this debate has flourished the Canadian government has steadily been adopting a new approach which neither of these conventional perspectives adequately describes. This new approach, introduced in 1968 by the Liberal government of Pierre Trudeau and sustained during the brief 1979-80 Conservative government of Joe Clark, lowered Canada's interest in mediating the Arab-Israel conflict, shifted emphasis from political to proliferating economic activities, and expanded Canada's direct bilateral relationships with several key states in the region. From this new focus flowed a growing Canadian involvement and, indeed, influence in the Middle East, and a defined policy grounded in the specific, multifaceted interests of Canada and its Middle East partners. Not suprisingly, the new approach reduced the Canadian government's concern with the evolving consensus about the Middle East in multilateral or alliance forums, and enhanced its responsiveness to a wider range of international actors, the vigorous debates within its domestic society, and its own struggle to define Canada's overarching national interests. These assaults on the once-dominant liberal-internationalist edifice provoked considerable friction, and proved unable to prevail over the traditional instincts in a few policy areas. Yet by the 1980s the slow but revolutionary shift to this new approach was largely complete.[4]

The Decline of Liberal-Internationalism, 1968-1973

When Pierre Trudeau succeeded Lester Pearson as Prime Minister of Canada and head of the Liberal Party in the spring of 1968 few areas of Canadian foreign policy were more integrally linked to the two-decade long success story of "Pearsonian", or liberal, internationalism than the country's role in the Middle East. From the 1947 United Nations partition plan to the June 1967 war, Canada had tried to foster a solution, through the United Nations, to the dominant Arab-Israel conflict. To be sure, Canada had established diplomatic relations with some Middle East countries, developed trade and investment with a few, and pursued limited cultural, educational, and aid programs. But these bilateral activities remained secondary and supplementary to multilateral incentives and commitments.

The immediate post World War II desire to build a strong United Nations, and the ensuing East-West conflict provided the overarching context within which Middle East affairs had been handled. Thus, the 1947 partition plan had involved Canada, not only because it had been viewed as a country without an imperialist or colonialist past, but also because it had wished to establish the legitimacy of the UN as an effective international instrument, to mediate differences between the United States, Great Britain, and France, and thereby to preserve harmony within the Atlantic alliance. Similarly, the Suez crisis of 1956, the previous sale of arms to combatants, and participation in ensuing peacekeeping efforts had all been based upon Canada's concerns with international order, the stature of the United Nations, and Soviet-American competition.

Yet by the mid 1960s signs of new tendencies had begun to appear. A concerted effort to establish ongoing ties with the Arab states of francophone North Africa had been motivated by Canadian internal affairs, and given added force by the assertion by the province of Quebec of a direct international role. Within the Department of External Affairs, which largely controlled Canada's Mideast policy, the internationalist verities had begun to be challenged by increasing disenchantment over UN procedures concerning financing and the UN forces in Cyprus. And finally the precipitous withdrawal of the United Nations Emergency Force (UNEF) prior to the 1967 war had shocked Canadian leaders and the public into a fundamental reappraisal of what had come to be known as the "helpful-fixer", middle power role.

These strains reflected a much broader debate over, and attempt to redefine, Canada's approach to international affairs as a whole. While Middle Eastern issues were neither a direct component of this quest for redefinition, nor a particularly active aspect of Canadian foreign policy until the end of the 1968-73 period, the philosophy espoused by Prime Minister Trudeau, as codified in *Foreign Policy for Canadians*, had a clear impact on Canadian behaviour in the region.[5] In particular, the new stress on national interest, economic growth, and the need for counterweights as fundamental foreign policy priorities was manifested in a growing reluctance to assume a prominent role in UN efforts to resolve the Arab-Israel dispute, efforts to develop economic ties with major states on the periphery of the region, and a restrained approach to the dilemmas created by the 1973 war and accompanying oil embargo. Canada's general orientation toward Middle East affairs was best summarized by Secretary of State for External Affairs Mitchell Sharp who in November 1969 noted that while Canada's Middle Eastern policy had "largely found expression through the United Nations," there were now "great trading opportunities, particularly with Iran and Israel and...the United Arab Republic."[6]

a) Behaviour

At the United Nations Canada continued to pursue a deliberate evenhanded approach, censuring the attacks of both Israel and Palestine organizations on civilian targets, joining in the Secretary-General's condemnation of Iraq's execution of Jewish citizens, and calling upon Israel to consider withdrawal from its occupied territories and provide assistance to refugees within its borders. Its reduced commitment to traditional mediatory roles was seen in its support for the efforts of the "Big Four" through the UN-sponsored mission of Gunnar Jarring to foster peace in the region, Mitchell Sharp's disavowal of an "honest broker" role for Canada, and the government's establishment of firm conditions for its future participation in peacekeeping operations. At the same time, the legacy of past orientations was evident in the perception of Canada's "special role" on the part of countries in the region, and Canada's statements, as early as May 1973, that it would consider accepting a new truce supervisory role in the Middle East.

Canadian policy towards the region was more active in expanding the bilateral economic co-operation that had begun in the previous period.[7] Co-operation with Israel remained largely functional in nature, comprising, in addition to visits from Israel's Prime Minister and Foreign Minister, the conclusion of arrangements on air transport, extradition, and EDC financing. Despite Sharp's visit to Iran and Egypt, and a Canada-Iran agreement to facilitate joint ventures in the region, Canada's priority partners in the Arab world remained Tunisia and Algeria. In Tunisia a joint commission, established after a 1968 summit visit, operated actively, and CIDA loans were granted. And in Algeria a Canadian embassy was opened in 1971, a long-term wheat agreement concluded, and CIDA aid disbursed.

These new relationships with peripherally-located Arab states were directed at strengthening Canada's relations with the francophone world. They thus had no major effect on Canadian behaviour during the 1973 Arab-Israeli war and accompanying oil embargo.[8] Guided largely by past precepts, Canada responded to the 1973 hostilities by requesting a ceasefire and the submission of the dispute to the UN, and contacting the great powers in support of these objectives. Somewhat later, it stated its willingness to contribute to a peacekeeping force, sought to secure Canadian participation in a prospective operation, and agreed, when finally requested by the Secretary-General, to join for an initial six month period under a fairly stringent set of conditions. Somewhat less successful was its effort to avoid, and determine if it was subject to, the Arab oil embargo announced at the same time. Only with its subsequent opening of an embassy in Saudi Arabia did Canada begin to develop the contact required for a more complete and sensitive appreciation of the region itself.

b) The Determinants of Behaviour

The reduced vigour of Canadian activity at the United Nations, and the somewhat functional nature of its bilateral involvements, reflected the decreasing prominence of external factors in Canadian calculations. Although Canada continued to support the Secretary-General and Jarring's efforts, it increasingly left the initiative to, and took its policy cues from, the "Big Four". And while the visits of Israel's leaders reflected the special sensitivity Canada accorded Israel's views, the pattern of Mitchell Sharp's visits from and to Middle East leaders increasingly suggested the adoption of a broader and more balanced perspective. Moreover, Canada's concentration on fostering stable relations with Algeria and Tunisia, Mitchell Sharp's meeting with the representatives of Egypt, Iran, Lebanon, Morrocco, Algeria, and Tunisia during the 1973 war, and the subsequent expansion of diplomatic representation in the Middle East indicated a slowly growing interest in Arab views.

The diminishing salience and broadening relevance of international factors allowed a considerably greater role for domestic actions, not only through traditional parliamentary channels but also directly from organized interest groups and the general public. Within Parliament Israel continued to receive the firm support of all major parties. The Conservatives and socialist New Democratic Party joined the Liberal government in affirming Israel's right to exist and in Canada's continued peacekeeping involvement. In an active debate over the 1973 war they confined their criticisms of government actions to its presumed deference to Egyptian demands for an inspection of Canada's peacekeeping contribution and the government's apparent inability to determine whether it was the target of an Arab oil embargo. Similarly, the press continued to voice strong support of Israel, although led by Toronto's *The Globe and Mail* it raised several critical questions about Canada's peacekeeping involvement in 1973.[9]

It was among organized interest groups that a broader debate first began to appear. The Jewish community intensified its standard activities, meeting with Mitchell Sharp to press for Canadian support for Jewish emigration from Iraq and a halt to air service between Canada and the Arab world, hosting cabinet ministers at annual dinners, and sponsoring a private sector Canadian economic development mission to Israel. Its views, however, received their first broad counter in an ultimately unsuccessful effort by the editor of the United Church's publication, the *Observer*, Reverend A.C. Forrest, to highlight the pro-Zionist bias of the Canadian press through the pages of his publication, and his testimony before the Senate Special Committee on Mass Media. More importantly, the Arab community in Canada developed a greater level of organization and activity. Operating through such vehicles as the Canadian Arab Federation it unsuccessfully urged Mitchell Sharp to include the Middle East in Canada's foreign policy review and called for greater restrictions on Jewish community financial support of Israel. More importantly, it attracted sympathetic support in Quebec from *Parti Québécois* leader René Levesque and leaders of the Confederation of National Trade Unions, and joined with the latter to meet Palestinian leaders in a tour of the Middle East.

In contrast to these new signs of domestic diversity, the government itself approached Middle Eastern issues with a new coherence, grounded in an altered conception of its central foreign policy interests. Although the government's foreign policy review, *Foreign Policy for Canadians*, contained no separate treatment of Canadian relations with the region, its de-emphasis of Canada's role as a "helpful fixer" and the priority it assigned to economic growth provided clear referents for all ministers and officials to follow. Furthermore, while Mitchell Sharp continued to offer leadership on all diplomatic and UN-related questions, the review's stress on the multiplicity of themes affecting policy outcomes, and the collegial style of decision-making favoured by Prime Minister Trudeau, increasingly legitimized the involvement in Middle Eastern affairs of other ministers, notably those from Industry, Trade and Commerce, and Manpower and Immigration.[10]

The Dominance of the New Approach, 1974-80

It was after the shocks of 1973-4 that these new tendencies in Canada's approach to the Middle East came into direct conflict with, and soon managed to dominate, the traditional liberal-internationalist edifice. The long term results of the 1973 Yom Kippur War and oil embargo, together with the return of an experienced, majority Liberal government in 1974, prompted major modifications in Canada's existing Mideast policy, as well as initiatives in entirely new areas. These changes were first apparent on the issues of peace, security, and recognition at the United Nations, where Canada moved slowly from the pursuit of compromise, stability, and institutional development. They were further evident in the general success of the Canadian government in withstanding Jewish community pressure and American example, both in allowing PLO representatives into Canada and legislating against Canadian compliance with the Arab economic boycott of Israel. Their strongest expression came in the creation of an overall policy of strengthening relations with all states in the Middle East, the development of new bilateral relationships promoting Canadian economic interests, and an adjustment of Canada's arms export policy in accordance with these objectives. The depth and durability of this change was severely tested, and eventually sustained, by a 1979 controversy over moving the Canadian embassy in Israel to Jerusalem. For in this case, after initial confusion, the government ultimately recognized, and deferred to, a much broader set of direct domestic and Mideast interests than the liberal-internationalist approach had defined.

a) Behaviour

Canada's reconsideration of its longstanding commitment to develop the multilateral regimes and institutional structure of the UN began with the classic symbol of "internationalism", peacekeeping.[11] Although Canada accepted the revised arrangements for financing peacekeeping forces at the UN, and extended its participation in UNEF and United Nations Disengagement Observer Force (UNDOF), it increasingly argued that peacekeeping merely preserved an uneasy status quo in the absence of concomitant negotiations among the parties directly concerned. It also insisted that the conflicting parties work toward a comprehensive settlement, that Canadian participation required the consent of all parties,

181

and that Canada's involvement in peacekeeping facilitated co-operative bilateral relationships in the economic sphere. This growing skepticism of the liberal-internationalist rationales for peacekeeping was clear in 1978 when, to the surprise of its major allies, Canada hesitated before joining the United Nations Interim Force in Lebanon (UNIFIL) and withdrew its forces after a short term of only six months.

A somewhat more complex evolution occurred in Canada's diplomatic activity at the UN and, in particular, its votes on the crucial question of Palestinian rights and representation.[12] Canada's basic policy was to "maintain and emphasize a balanced and objective approach, based on the principles embodied in Security Council Resolutions 242 and 338, which Canada supported," and further, to have Canada's words and deeds in specific dimensions of the dispute make Canada's objective approach clear to other countries and the Canadian public.[13] In practice this policy slowly moved Canada, in keeping with international trends, towards a greater recognition of the collective rights of the Palestinians, and the role of the PLO as their representative, outside of the rigidly balanced framework of obligations in Resolution 242 and the approval of all parties to the conflict.[14]

Canada began the period by requesting a postponement of a 1975 UN Crime Congress with PLO representation, which it was to host in Toronto. It also abstained on or opposed UN resolutions affirming the rights of the Palestinian people to independence and sovereignty, granting the PLO permanent observer status, and linking racism with Zionism. However, in 1976 it hosted a UN conference on human settlements (Habitat) with PLO representation. And as early as 1974 it began to approve of, or abstain on, votes favouring PLO participation in UN bodies not exclusively inter-governmental in character, and shift its voting alignment away from Israel and the United States and toward Europe.[15] And despite Canada's appearance in coalitions with Israel containing as few as four members in the late 1970s, by 1980 its position was sufficiently flexible to cause anxiety and action on the part of Jewish organizations.[16]

Of greater importance was Canada's creation of its first comprehensive policy toward the Middle East as a distinct region. In a policy developed in the autumn of 1975 and approved by cabinet in February 1976, Canada gave emphasis, *inter alia*, to its desire for close and mutually beneficial bilateral relations with all Mideast states, to the settlement of regional disputes, and to trade and economic cooperation.[17] In keeping with this emphasis Secretary of State for External Affairs Allan MacEachen toured the Middle East in January of 1976. Building upon the strengthening of Canada's diplomatic relations with Saudi Arabia, Iraq, Jordan, Bahrain, Qatar, and the Emirates during the preceding two years, and the work of a Canada-Iran Joint Commission established by his colleague in ITC during an April 1974 visit, MacEachen stressed the importance of moving beyond the Arab "forest" to deal with the individual state "trees". He also provided aid to Egypt and established a Canada-Saudi Arabia Joint Commission.[18] Propelled by these initiatives and the visit of MacEachen's successor, Don Jamieson, to the Middle East in October 1977, Canadian trade with the region proliferated.[19]

These growing bilateral economic relationships soon increased the government's willingness to adjust its traditional multilateral approach in other areas in a way that sustained these flows. In 1978 it conducted a review of its arms export policy. While reaffirming a restrictive approach, this review placed additional demands on those opposing such sales, and led to a more accommodating response to those with prospective contracts in specific cases. More significantly, the government repeatedly resisted demands for legislation to counter the Arab boycott of Israel. It introduced reporting requirements for firms, and promised to introduce legislation only under the considerable pressure of action by the U.S. and Ontario provincial governments and an impending federal Canadian election.[20]

In many ways the strength of the government's shifting multilateralism, growing unilateralism, and developing economic bilateralism was seen most clearly in the controversy over moving the Canadian embassy in Israel to Jerusalem.[21] Canada's interest in fostering a comprehensive settlement in the Middle East, as well as its expanding relationships with Arab states, led Prime Minister Trudeau to refuse Israeli Prime Minister Begin's request, during the latter's visit to Canada in November 1978, for Canada to move its embassy. However, in a major shift toward the position of Israel's government and parts of the Canadian Jewish community, Trudeau's successor, Conservative Prime Minister Clark, promised in June 1979 to undertake such a move. However poorly timed, this decision did signal a new willingness to engage in unilateral action designed in the minds of its progenitors partly to further the Camp David peace process. And when it became clear that such a move would harm the overall peace process and endanger the wide range of durable bilateral relationships Canada had forged with Arab states, the Canadian government rapidly reversed its position.[22]

b) The Determinants of Behaviour

These substantial shifts in Canadian policy were, in the first instance, permitted and reinforced by a notable diffusion of power in the international system. This diffusion made a broader range of states relevant in the determination of Canadian policy, and shifted Canadian government attention from the United States and Israel to major European powers and specific Arab states in the region. Within the United Nations it was the growing strength and legitimacy of Arab and third world state views, rather than those of Canada's traditional allies or of the Secretariats, that defined the consensus to which Canada increasingly, if slowly, responded.[23] The diminishing impact of the United States, both directly and indirectly, was seen in the failure of its anti-boycott legislation to inspire similar Canadian action, its surprise at Canada's firm reluctance to accept ongoing UNIFIL obligations, and Canada's divergence from its voting pattern at the United Nations. Indeed, knowing that Canada was unlikely to respond positively to U.S. influence, U.S. leaders deliberately confined their response to Prime Minister Clark's announcement of the Jerusalem embassy move to a conversation between Secretary of State Cyrus Vance and Conservative Secretary of State for External Affairs Flora MacDonald at the United Nations. This conversation was designed to communicate American concerns about the implications of a move and hence to strengthen Flora MacDonald's position in the internal Canadian government debate.[24]

Helping to moderate American influence was the increasing importance attached to major European states. Their positions were considered and their views canvassed on the Arab boycott question. Their votes at the United Nations reflected a position which Canada found increasingly compatible. And their representations were heard on the Jerusalem embassy question. Of greatest importance, however, was the more sensitive understanding Canada developed of the views of Arab states, through its expanding network of diplomatic posts, visits, and joint organizations, and its policy for forging relationships with individual states. To be sure, the representations Arab states made on the anti-boycott issue, through the Arab League Information Office in Ottawa, were insufficiently focused and too late to affect Canadian actions. Yet the vigorous, widespread criticisms made by Arab states on the proposed transfer of the embassy to Jerusalem helped secure a rapid reversal in the government's policy.

To an increasing degree after 1973, Middle East questions also became the subject of a well-developed, ongoing debate among a broad range of organizations within Canada. Parliamentary and press interest intensified. Jewish and Arab organizations became more effective. And the provinces and business community developed a major involvement. Partly as a result, the sympathetic understanding in parliament, media, and voluntary associations of Israel's positions began to be effectively offset by new components within these communities somewhat more favourable to the Arab cause. In the forefront of this movement was the business community, which shed its traditional reservations to register its views forcefully on the expanding set of economic issues which were of growing importance to business leaders.

These developments were first evident in parliament and the federal parties. Ongoing debates, question period, comments in committee, and Parliament's unanimous approval of a 1975 resolution, introduced by former Progressive Conservative leader John Diefenbaker and condemning the United Nations linkage of racism and Zionism, showed that all major parties were consistently more supportive of Israel than the government itself. The NDP tended to be the most firm and vocal supporters followed by the Progressive Conservatives. Together with Herb Gray of the Liberal Party, these spokesmen pressed to refuse entry to PLO representatives for, and pressed for the cancellation of, the 1975 Crime Congress. They also sought the rapid introduction of strong legislation, similar to that in the U.S., prohibiting compliance with the Arab boycott, demanded more complete information on boycott activities, and publicized individual cases of alleged compliance. The more moderate position of the Liberal Party was accounted for in large measure by the split within their parliamentary caucus between anglophone members, who were inclined to be supportive of Israel, and francophone representatives, who had greater sympathy for and contacts with the Palestinians.

Partly because of these variations, the general parliamentary consensus operated to impose limits on, rather than determine the direction of, government policy. The exceptions were those instances, such as the 1978 introduction of a firm anti-boycott policy, where the imminence of a close election allowed the parties, as transmitters of other interests, a more salient if short-term influence on cabinet calculations. Apart from caucus discussions, direct parliamentary contact with the executive branch tended to be confined to participation in the annual External Affairs briefing preceding the United Nations General Assembly, requests for information by Liberal members during the Jerusalem controversy, and Herb Gray's request for a Canadian Human Rights Commission investigation of a case of alleged compliance with the Arab boycott.

Although the press and the public also continued to sympathize with the positions of Israel's government during this period, neither was unanimous in its advocacy. Canada's largest daily, *The Toronto Star*, strongly disapproved of the government's postponement of the Crime Congress. Respondents in an opinion poll were almost evenly divided in their evaluation of a UN resolution linking Zionism with racism and a large segment professed no knowledge of the issue.[25] The virtually unanimous support of the Canadian press for strong federal anti-boycott measures and the prominence the daily press gave to the issue were factors in cabinet deliberations on the subject. However, on the Jerusalem issue, the press, with the partial exception of the more cautious anglophone Montreal dailies, strongly opposed a move of the embassy and gave full attention to the criticism of this action voiced by foreign governments.

As press views became more complex the Canadian Jewish community, led by the Canada-Israel Committee and its sponsoring organizations, the Canadian Zionist Federation, the Canadian Jewish Congress, and B'nai Brith, found its freedom of action somewhat circumscribed. Through its professional staff in Toronto, Ottawa, and Montreal, and lay representatives in major Canadian cities, the CIC continued to represent the Jewish community on all Canadian-Israel public affairs, to further understanding between the two states and their citizens, and to conduct education and information programmes to this end. In these activities the CIC had the advantage of an increasingly large and skilled professional staff, and close contacts and information exchanges with allied bodies in Canada, counterparts in the U.S., the government of Israel, and Israel's embassy in Ottawa. Its primary resource, however, was the immediate access it had to Members of Parliament, media, and influential citizens across Canada, through its own committee structure, the sponsoring organizations and, in particular, the 10,000 members of Zionist organizations and 150,000 Jewish citizens in the province of Ontario.[26]

Both directly and through members across Canada, the CIC maintained contact with parliamentarians and the press and was able to arrange letter writing campaigns or consultations as the occasion demanded. In Ottawa, its annual policy conference afforded an opportunity for discussions with cabinet ministers and legislators and the CIC maintained close contacts with cabinet ministers who were sympathetic, the Secretary of State for External Affairs, and senior government officials. Although usually unable to provide more timely, privileged, or reliable information, the CIC benefited from a reputation for reasonableness, sophisticated knowledge of Ottawa's decision-making process, and ongoing communication with responsible officials in External Affairs. Despite this access, however, the CIC, with its limited resources and federal structure, was forced into a careful selection of the issues it forwarded, and ultimately dependent upon events and other organizations to influence and shape government policy.

Within the sphere of high politics, the organization tended to concentrate on the issue of the recognition of the PLO, using, ultimately, the tacit threat of community pressure to prevent such an initiative. In the mid-1970s, the CIC urged the government not to admit members of the PLO to international meetings to be held in Canada. Their meeting with the Secretary of State for External Affairs the day before a crucial cabinet meeting, the careful consideration given by Allan MacEachen to the views expressed in a letter from the CIC's National Director, and the fear of massive demonstrations and legal action by Jewish organizations helped lead to a postponement of the 1975 UN Crime Congress in Toronto. However, despite the widespread distaste for a UN resolution linking racism with Zionism, the forceful views expressed at an emergency National Jewish Leadership Conference in Ottawa, and the supportive actions of the Vancouver City Council, the government proceeded to host the UN Conference on Human Settlements the following year.

By briefing Don Jamieson on its view on the Arab economic boycott, assisting in the creation of an independent Citizen's Commission on Economic Discrimination which presented its findings to Prime Minister Trudeau, and publicly criticizing government statements, the Jewish community succeeded in raising the issue of anti-boycott action in the press and parliament, and slowly moving the government toward modest legislative action. The precedent of U.S. legislation, the onset of a close federal election, and the CIC's successful efforts to secure Ontario government legislation, gave momentum to its efforts. The CIC, through letter writing campaigns, co-ordination of petitions in Montreal and Toronto, and close contacts with sympathetic cabinet Ministers, did exact a promise of anti-boycott legislation from ministers John Roberts and Barney Danson and engender lengthy discussion between CIC and ITC officials over the contents of the proposed bill.

Similarly, despite divisions over priorities and tactics within the Canadian Jewish community, the prospect of a close election to be decided in Ontario enabled prominent individual Jewish citizens to induce Joe Clark to declare his support for the transfer of Canada's embassy from Tel Aviv to Jerusalem during the campaign and to affirm the policy as prime minister.[27] However, in the face of an outburst of domestic and international criticism, the Canadian Jewish community proved unable to prevent the appointment of the Stanfield mission to consider the issue and the acceptance of his recommendation against the move.

In some measure the limited success of the Jewish community was due to the emergence within Canada of Arab organizations somewhat more effective than in previous periods, primarily because of the growing size of the Canadian Arab community. Yet this community still had a primary constituency of only an estimated 19,000 Arabs in Canada, backed by 100,000 Canadian Muslims, of whom 60,000 resided in Ontario, and was increasingly beset by internal divisions.[28] Its primary organization, the Canadian Arab Federation, supported by the Quebec-Palestine Association, did succeed in securing a meeting with Allan MacEachen during the controversy over the Crime Congress, occasionally saw the Secretary of State for External Affairs on other issues, actively wrote or telegrammed on the Jerusalem embassy question, and helped encourage contacts between Canadian government and Palestinian representatives. With organizations such as the Canadian-Palestine Committee, Arab-Canada Chamber of Commerce, and Council of Muslim Communities of Canada, it was also active on the boycott issue. However, only on such relatively non-political issues as the admission into Canada of Lebanese nationals at the time of the conflict in Lebanon did elements of the Arab community have a discernable and direct impact on Canadian policy.

A somewhat greater constraint on both Jewish community influence and Canadian government action came from the growing involvement of provincial governments. The Ontario government's unanimous resolution in the legislature condemning the linkage of racism and Zionism at the United Nations helped to sustain federal government predispositions in the Crime Congress cancellation. Moreover, Ontario's firm anti-boycott policy, promise of legislative action, and subsequent enactment of legislation, were substantial determinants of federal policy on the boycott issue. However, the growing interest of the provinces in general, and the three western provinces and Quebec in particular, in trade and financial relationships with the Middle East, had an important offsetting effect on the Arab boycott issue.[29] And the representations made by the Quebec government on behalf of its business community on the Jerusalem issue contributed to the reversal of policy by the Clark government.

Perhaps the most potent domestic influence as the period progressed came from the business community. The search of Canada's high technology manufacturers for exports, together with macroeconomic and regional development considerations, prompted the government to adopt its less restrictive approach to arms exports in 1978. In contrast, because of the internal divisions and preference for discretion and moderation of the business community, the Canadian Manufacturers Association's opposition to anti-boycott legislation had no major effect on the Ontario government's decision to proceed along these lines. However, business contacts with ITC, and the government's concern with the possibility of a "concerted public media campaign" mounted by the business community and focused on the principle of government interference in the private sector, were important in underscoring the reluctance of the federal government to proceed with similar legislation.[30] And public criticism by Canadian exporters and their vigorous private communications to DEA and ITC over the Jerusalem embassy move helped prompt the government to appoint the Stanfield mission and accept its conclusions.

A similar trend toward broader involvement, balanced debates, and greater influence took place within the government's executive branch.[31] Several new bureaucratic players from economic and functional departments joined the debate over policy, pronounced disagreements within officialdom arose, and, consequently, issues were propelled toward cabinet. Increasingly, the prime minister intervened in support of new economic priorities and in accordance with his personal values and approach to foreign policy, overrode cabinet's emphasis on domestic political considerations.

These trends were first visible on United Nations' issues. Cabinet had routinely approved Canada's hosting of the Crime Congress, and established within the Ministry of the Solicitor-General (MSG) a normal secretariat to deal with implementation. However, Cabinet's involvement increased rapidly as the question of attendance by PLO observers prompted conflicting advice from, and an intense debate among, officials from the MSG, the RCMP, Justice, Manpower and Immigration, and External Affairs. The conflict among these officials, and their failure, under DEA's guidance, to produce recommendations acceptable to cabinet, led to a highly volatile process. Officials produced over a dozen draft memoranda for cabinet, cabinet itself debated the issue on six occasions, and finally produced a decision which bore no resemblance to the recommendation forwarded by officials through DEA.

The issue of PLO attendance at the successor Habitat conference also reached either the cabinet or prime minister through the department and minister of external affairs on at least four occasions. Significantly, however, the prime minister, determined to prevent a repetition of the disorderly decision-making on the issue of the Crime Congress, intervened personally to order a fusion of the two responsible co-ordinating centres in DEA and the Ministry of State for Urban Affairs. By putting representatives of the two bodies on an equal footing, clarifying reporting relationships to cabinet, and fostering an orderly presentation of a firm, functionally-grounded recommendation to cabinet, he reduced the influence of domestic political considerations by individual ministers on the cabinet's final decision.

After Habitat, UN issues continued to command prime ministerial and cabinet attention, but with a stronger reliance on the advice and co-ordination of External Affairs. On the recommendation of the department, Canada strongly supported the initiative that culminated in the Camp David accords. Trudeau and Don Jamieson sent letters to Menachem Begin and Anwar Sadat, pointed to actions that were unhelpful such as settlements on the West Bank, and maintained an open and active dialogue with American officials and states in the region.

In addition, the secretary of state for external affairs rapidly reviewed all Middle East issues at the UN, notably the linkage of racism with Zionism at the Geneva conference on racism, the reappearance of this linkage in the General Assembly deliberations and resolutions, and votes at the General Assembly. And as the issue of PLO representation in the General Assembly, the specialized agencies, and the secretariats politicized these bodies, DEA, particularly through its chairmanship in Ottawa of a Committee on UN Specialized Agencies, began to scrutinize resolutions more closely and provide more detailed advice to participating functional departments.

On peacekeeping issues, the professional calculations of the minister of national defense and the general orientation of the prime minister were decisive. Partly in response to the growing disagreement between an increasingly reluctant DND and a still-committed DEA, recommendations supporting renewal of Canada's participation in UNEF and the United Nations force in Cyprus were regularly sent to cabinet from 1974 through to 1977. However, an intensification of this inter-departmental disagreement over participation in UNIFIL propelled the issue further upward. The matter received the close personal attention of the prime minister and occasioned the rare event of a formal meeting among Prime Minister Trudeau, Secretary of State for External Affairs Jamieson, Minister of National Defence Danson, and the Vice Chief of the Defence Staff acting on behalf of his superior. Although the minister of national defense, also a political leader of Canada's Jewish community, was concerned about the domestic dimension, he was guided by the unanimous advice of his officials and the widespread reservations about the conception of the force, its terms of reference, command structure, prospects for success, and heavy demands on Canada's military establishment. Danson successfully insisted, against a somewhat hesitant prime minister and secretary of state for external affairs, that the British and Australians assume the commitment, that Canada enter for only six months, and that other demands on national defense be set aside for this period.[32]

The increased influence of other departments, External's reconsideration of its traditional internationalist orientation, and the shifting cabinet and prime ministerial consensus were even more pronounced on economic matters. In the autumn of 1975, a memorandum proposing strengthened bilateral relations with all states in the region was prepared with heavy contributions from the ministers with economic portfolios and DEA's economic divisions, and was considered in cabinet committee. Secretary of State for External Affairs MacEachen, after some consultation with his colleagues, did decide in 1976 as a symbolic gesture to establish a joint committee with Israel, but, more importantly, he supported the effort of ITC to secure a "fair share" of Arab petrodollars through participation in trade fairs and acceded to ITC's demand that trade commissioners be withdrawn from South Africa and a trade post be opened in Kuwait.

A similar transition took place over the more difficult question of arms exports. DEA traditionally had taken the lead in defining overall policy, joined with DND to control the advice to cabinet on specific cases, and generally sustained a restrictive policy over the competing and more complex claims of ITC, Supply and Services, and the Export Development Corporation (EDC). In the spring of 1978, however, a government review of policy on arms exports added the minister of ITC to the group which had to be consulted before an export decision was made. As a result, greater attention was given to the desirability of indicating to Canadian firms that they would be given an export license at the time of their bid on a contract. And in at least one case the minister of ITC, supported by the minister of DND, overcame Don Jamieson's initial reluctance to authorize a sale in the event of a successful Canadian bid.

The tensions produced by the new configuration were seen most clearly in the debate over measures to counter the Arab boycott in 1978. Prior to 1978 the management of this issue had been confined to officials and ministers in ITC, DEA, Finance, and the EDC, who had easily reconciled their objectives of securing maximum Canadian exports without acceding to the extra-territorial application of others' laws or provoking a domestic political debate. In 1978, however, the issue became the subject of inter-departmental political discussion and Privy Council Office (PCO) involvement, the most active item in the Cabinet Committee on External Policy and Defence and, ultimately, the subject of intense debate in full cabinet itself. At the cabinet level advocacy for a strong anti-boycott policy came from John Roberts, Barney Danson, and other ministers from constituencies with large Jewish populations in Toronto, Vancouver, and Montreal. The opposition was led by Allan MacEachen and Don Jamieson, and included Minister of Finance Jean Chretien, other economic ministers, and those Quebec ministers aware that a great deal of business from their province went to the Arab world. Although the prime minister, in keeping with his general approach in cabinet, attempted to remain neutral, his dislike of pressure by the Jewish community, reinforced by the substantive arguments advanced by DEA, led him to express opposition to strong anti-boycott measures and force adoption of a compromise policy.

The strength of the new priorities was tested most severely, and ultimately sustained most convincingly, in the debate over the movement of the Canadian embassy in Israel from Tel Aviv to Jerusalem. Israel's Prime Minister Menachem Begin, on a state visit to Canada in November 1978, specifically urged Pierre Trudeau to move the embassy. Canada's prime minister was urged to do so by some of his close associates who were particularly sensitive to his worsening domestic political situation, and also anxious to reward Israel's prime minister who had come so far in furthering the peace process. Yet Trudeau, despite the imminence of an election, accepted the advice of the relevant experts in DEA and refused to alter Canada's longstanding position on the status of Jerusalem. Similarly, Leader of the Opposition Joe Clark, on his tour of the Middle East in January 1979, abided by the advice of U.S. officials, DEA, and the Canadian ambassador to Israel, rather than that of personal advisers and candidates who accompanied him, and rejected Prime Minister Begin's request for a move.

Joe Clark's promise to move the embassy, issued immediately before his meeting with the Canada-Israel Committee during the 1979 election campaign, was a personal decision. It was based on his calculations of Conservative electoral fortunes in Southern Ontario and in those Toronto ridings with large Jewish populations, and the favourable views of his closest political advisers. In reversing his position, Clark overrode the opposition of other Conservative strategists and candidates. His decision to implement this promise immediately upon becoming prime minister was also personal, taken despite the objections expressed in a DEA-PCO briefing paper and the request of Secretary of State for External Affairs Flora MacDonald for a delay. The urgings of Clark's personal adviser Lowell Murray, the more general procedural issue of firm prime ministerial control over the civil service and, less directly, the need to implement an electoral promise, to demonstrate determined leadership to the party and public, and to fulfill an electoral mandate to undertake fundamental change all strengthened Clark's determination to proceed with the move. Moreover, as the consistent reference to the Camp David peace process in the prime minister's public statements indicated, his decision stemmed in part from Clark's personal belief that such an initiative would help to unblock Mideast negotiations, further the peace process, and permit Canada to initiate and improve contacts with Palestinian representatives.[33]

However, very shortly after his announcement of the decision, Clark became convinced of the need to shift ground. He was persuaded by the assessments he had received from the PCO, by the conviction of the secretary of state for external affairs that the ensuing disruption to her department had to be reduced, and by the virtually unanimous views of officials in DEA and elsewhere in government. Flora MacDonald, her closest associates, and after considerable discussion, senior departmental officials developed the idea of appointing a special mission to review the issue. Upon her return from an OECD meeting in Paris, she made such a proposal to the prime minister, who accepted both the proposal and her subsequent suggestion that Robert Stanfield head the mission. Moreover, she also intervened to secure for him a broad and flexible mandate. When Robert Stanfield, in a preliminary report in October, recommended that the embassy not be moved, the prime minister consulted with his political staff, decided to accept the recommemdation, and publicly announced his decision in Parliament.

The New Approach Confirmed, 1980-

On 18 February 1980, the Liberals won a majority in an election and Trudeau returned to prime ministerial responsibilities. His attention was concentrated on the domestic constitutional dispute, the ever worsening economic situation, and the rapidly approaching western economic summit scheduled for July 1980. Trudeau's initial concept of foreign policy as an extension of national interest was strengthened by a heightened awareness that Canada's economic fortunes were tied to the international market place. If Canadian policy were to be effective, especially in third world areas untapped by Canadian entrepreneurs, Ottawa must redress the damage inflicted both by the controversy over the Jerusalem embassy and by Clark's repeated pledge to dismantle Petro Canada, a state commercial instrument which non-OECD countries often saw as necessary for major trading ventures.[34]

The Trudeau government thus actively initiated high-level visits to the Gulf States, Egypt, and Iraq, as well as to Israel. Trade missions from provincial governments, especially Alberta, Ontario, and Quebec, which included senior representatives from the business community, toured much of the Middle East. Major contracts were signed, often with the assistance of IT&C, CIDA, and EDC, for the export of such items as train locomotives to Egypt, automobiles to Iraq, engineering contracting services to Saudi Arabia, and for the purchase of petroleum from the Saudis. Formal meetings of joint bilateral organizations were held with Tunisia and Saudi Arabia. Aid programs to Tunisia and Egypt were

192

renewed or extended, and the government promoted new initiatives in electrical transformer and transporting grids, aircraft supply, natural gas, oil, and agricultural technologies, and the sale of CANDU nuclear reactors.

These economic initiatives coincided with intensive preparations by Canada for a resumption of the north-south dialogue in a summer 1981 meeting at Cancun, Mexico. As part of these preparations, senior cabinet officials travelled widely throughout the Middle East, and Prime Minister Trudeau personally visited a number of countries, including Saudi Arabia and Nigeria, key members both of OPEC and the Muslim bloc. Canada also successfully negotiated Saudi participation in the International Monetary Fund. At the same time, Canada balanced these initiatives towards the Arab world with continuous support for the Camp David peace process, with visits by federal and provincial ministers (including delegations from Alberta and Quebec) to strengthen economic ties with Israel, and in negotiations with Egypt over aid programs.

The active pursuit of bilateralism was further advanced by Canada's decision to decline an American invitation to participate in the U.S.-sponsored Sinai force. Although the force grew out of the Camp David accords which Canada supported, the Canadian position reflected a concern over the lack of UN sponsorship. Far more importantly, Ottawa feared that this American-directed initiative could create political difficulties for Canadian policy abroad, that its participation might rekindle the Arab perception of a pro-Israel bias, a perception which could jeopardize economic gains. Canada also assumed that its participation was unnecessary, given the extent of West European involvement.

The priority given to the expansion of bilateral economic arrangements was confirmed by the failure to propose any anti-boycott legislation or even to table compliance data. Canadian delegations of senior economic ministers, including IT&C's Lumley and Energy, Mines and Resources, Lalonde, also travelled to the Middle East. In addition, when Prime Minister Trudeau visited Saudi Arabia prior to the Cancun conference, he was pointedly informed by his hosts that discussions would focus not on the politics of north-south but on trade, commerce, and investment. The first 18 months of Canada-Middle East relations in the 1980s were governed by imperatives which emerged directly from the high priority of domestic economic development. The peace process and a stable international order, though matters of ongoing concern, were less salient.

Conclusions and Implications

Since the latter part of the Pearson years, Canadian foreign policy towards the Middle East has shifted progressively from the liberal-internationalist approach.[35] Canadian behaviour has been marked by a significant increase in bilateral activity on both state-to-state and private sector levels outside of, and sometimes indifferent to, the concerns of multilateral institutions, especially the United Nations. While the UN remains a pillar of Canadian foreign policy, it no longer dictates the agenda nor the instruments of Canadian policy toward the Middle East. Similarly, while Canada remains concerned with global stability, regional peace, and the western alliance, these considerations no longer dominate Canada's relations with countries in the Middle East. Rather, Canadian foreign policy towards the Middle East, as elsewhere, is increasingly based upon and directly affected by the definition of Canadian national interests, with an emphasis on economic growth and balancing external commitments.

The period since 1974 has seen a further decline in the direct relevance of the United Nations and traditional allies to Canadian policy towards the Middle East. Canada's positions have not coincided consistently — except on the question of Israel's existence — with those of its traditional coalition partners or leaders. It has not followed the American anti-boycott legislation; it has not supported the European Venice Declaration on recognition of the PLO; and it took its Jerusalem embassy initiative largely outside the context of the UN and Camp David. Furthermore, Canada has not maintained its previously automatic and positive response towards peacekeeping, nor consistently voted in the UN with the United States.

Domestic determinants of Canadian foreign policy towards the Middle East have become far more important. Jewish and non-Jewish organizations had been active since before the Second World War, but they have become increasingly articulate in their efforts to gain Canadian support of the Jewish state. Their advocacy on the issues of arms sales, Israel's security, UN voting, the strengthening of diplomatic and economic ties with Israel, and the decoupling of Zionism with racism played an important role in Canadian decision-making. Yet their influence was neither *the* determining factor nor a distortion of the dominant Canadian perception of the day. Rather, they had the good fortune to work within a democratic political system which was sympathetic to their interests, supportive of their rights as citizens to pursue those interests legitimately and responsive to efforts which often reflected the dominant opinion in much of the country. Since 1974, the Crime Congress, Canadian refusal to recognize the PLO, and the initial Jerusalem embassy decision exemplify the success of the Jewish community's efforts, while Habitat, the failure to pass anti-boycott legislation, the reversal of the decision on Jerusalem, balance the pattern. These last two cases underline the increased role of the business community in articulating their concerns over Canadian policy towards the Mideast. They reflect both changing bilateral relationships between Canada and countries of the region as well as Prime Minister Trudeau's concept of foreign policy as an extension of national interests, his tactical focus on economic growth, and his attempt to redress what some have perceived as a pro-Israel imbalance in domestic opinion and official policy.

Over this period political parties and parliamentarians alike have moved from moderate participation under Prime Ministers St. Laurent, Diefenbaker, and Pearson to an increasingly active involvement since the late 1960s. This follows the pattern of increased participation by other sectors of society — Jewish and Arab organizations, religious groups, and the business community. This latter group in particular had an even greater impact upon elected representatives, as foreign policy decision became linked to direct Canadian interests and acquired specific domestic repercussions.

Trends in the government's decision-making process offer further evidence of Canada's thrust beyond liberal-internationalism. With each successive government, Canadian Mideast policy has become increasingly politicized as the prime minister and senior cabinet colleagues have become more involved in policy decisions. While the Department of External Affairs remains a major actor, other departments have been drawn into the arena. DEA has thereby become less dominant, increasingly forced to compete for policy pre-eminence and consequently more insistent in its pursuit of a co-ordinating role in support of overarching national interests. Until the Trudeau era, the focus of Canadian policy on the United Nations underscored the primacy of DEA, and, to a lesser extent, national defense. The expansion of bilateral relations and the politics of oil after 1973 have significantly altered that equation. As a natural progression, once domestic interests expanded and drew a wider range of concerned citizens and their elected representatives into the policy-making nexus, the central structures of government and key personnel, especially cabinet, necessarily became more directly involved.

This demise of a liberal-internationalist foreign policy during the last decade in particular has four major, and perhaps enduring, implications for the conduct of Canada-Middle East relations. First, the emergence of an increasingly broad range of domestic groups who perceive a direct interest between Canada-Middle East relations and their own well-being, and the conflict among many of these groups, suggest an increase in advocacy directed towards political elites. Secondly, this domestic politicization of foreign policy contributes towards "bureaucratic politics" within the government as domestic constituencies generally have bureaucratic "partners" who service their needs. As these constituencies broaden, proliferate, and register demands, government organizations, in responding, become at least partially reflective of societal activity. Thus it is not surprising to see political elites outside the circles of the prime minister and secretary of state for external affairs being drawn into the foreign policy decision-making process, and new departments with identified, specific interests challenging the traditional dominance of the

Department of External Affairs. The most recent attempt by the government to impose direction and control on these new pressures has been the establishment of a reconstituted and greatly expanded External Affairs which has absorbed a number of functions — especially in commerce and trade — previously relegated to other departments.

Thirdly, this new politicization of societal and bureaucratic foreign policy constituencies is compounded further by the increase in provincial activity, with provincial governments acting either as "facilitators," "enablers," or "conduits" of provincially-based private sector interests or more directly as international participants themselves. As they sponsor trade missions, encourage capital transfers, provide export incentives, participate in international meetings, host visiting delegations, or arrange for educational exchange programs, provincial governments introduce a third type of actor to the ever-more complex foreign policy process.

Fourthly, these trends together suggest a profound transition in Canadian foreign policy-making from a narrowly-based political and bureaucratic elite implementing a well-established consensus accepted by a relatively complacent society towards a process penetrated by articulate, interest-based groups reflecting the demands of a more diffuse society. While judgement remains difficult, it also seems that these new forces of domestic diffusion have inspired a counter movement toward greater government control and consolidation. Indeed, the Canada of the 1980s may well exemplify an increasingly strong society with active, articulate constituencies, co-existing with a government apparatus designed to accommodate these new demands while retaining control and co-ordination over the entire policy process.[36] Canadian foreign policy might then be able to reflect Prime Minister Trudeau's initial demands both for a more vibrant participatory democracy at home and a government machine capable of transforming policy from its comfortable liberal-internationalist direction of the past.

FOOTNOTES

[1] See, for example: Peter Dobell, *Canada's Search for New Roles*, (Toronto: Oxford University Press, 1972); Peyton Lyon and Brian Tomlin, *Canada as an International Actor*, (Toronto: Macmillan, 1979), and Michael Tucker, *Canadian Foreign Policy*, (Toronto: McGraw-Hill Ryerson, 1980). Very briefly, liberal-internationalism, as a scholarly perspective, sees Canada's overall foreign policy as a constant, co-operative, multilateral endeavour to enhance widely shared values, through active diplomatic mediation, military peacekeeping and the incremental development of a more institutionalized and just world order.

[2] Tareq Ismael, "Canada and the Middle East," in Peyton Lyon and

Tareq Ismael, (eds.), *Canada and the Third World*, (Toronto: Macmillan, 1976), especially pps. 240-1, and Janice Stein, "La Politique Etrangère du Canada au Moyen-Orient: Stimulus et Réponse," in Paul Painchaud (ed.), *Le Canada et le Québec sur la Scène Internationale* (Montréal: Les Presses de L'Université du Québec, 1977), especially pps. 379-381.

3   Ismael, "Canada and the Middle East," pps. 250, 258, 264-8, Stein, "La Politique Etrangère," Dobell, *Canada's Search for New Roles*, p. 17, and Peyton Lyon, "Canada's Middle East Tilt," *International Perspectives* (September/October 1982): 3-5. These elements correspond to a general "peripheral-dependence" perspective on Canadian foreign policy, which sees Canada as a minor power operating within limits set by a preponderant America, providing uncritical support for American actions and passively promoting those open international regimes and gradual reforms through which America's global pre-eminence is sustained.

4   For supporting evidence of this fundamental shift in approach see Janice Stein, "Canadian Foreign Policy in the Middle East After the October War," in *Social Praxis* 4 (3-4): 271-297; L.A. Delvoie, "Growth in Economic Relations of Canada and the Arab World," *International Perspectives* (November/December 1976): 29-33, and Laurence Grossman, "The Shifting Canadian Vote on Mideast Questions at the UN," *International Perspectives* (May/June 1978): 9-13. This shift corresponds to a "complex neo-realist" perspective on Canadian foreign policy, which portrays Canada's international experience as one of secular, sustained development, reflected in its steadily increasing ability to define, advance, secure and legitimize distinctive national interests and values in a competitive process with adversaries and associates abroad. For a full discussion see David B. Dewitt and John J. Kirton, *Canada as a Principal Power* (Toronto: John Wiley and Sons, 1983).

5   Canada, Department of External Affairs, *Foreign Policy for Canadians*, (Ottawa: Information).

6   Canada, Department of External Affairs, *Press Release*, "Visit to the Middle East," November 19, 1969.

7   L.A. Delvoie, "Growth in Economic Relations," and Antoine Ayoub, "How Should Canada Approach the Many Faces of the Mahgreb," *International Perspectives* (May/June 1972): 36-40.

8   Ismael, "Canada and The Middle East."

9   Press views were, however, not sufficiently unanimous to prevent complaints by Jewish leaders about the anti-Israel bias of several publications, notably the *Montreal Gazette, Vancouver Sun, Edmonton Journal, La Presse*, the *Ottawa Citizen*, and *Le Devoir*.

10   John Kirton, "Foreign Policy Decision-making in the Trudeau Government: Premise and Performance," *International Journal* 33

(Spring 1978): 278-311.

11 This account of peacekeeping is based on Stein, "Canadian Foreign Policy in the Middle East After the October War," and Henry Wiseman, "Lebanon: The Latest Example of UN Peacekeeping Action," *International Perspectives* (January/February 1979): 3-7.

12 On Canadian policy toward the Palestinian question see Paul Noble, "Where Angels Fear to Tread: Canada and the Status of the Palestinians, 1967-1980," paper prepared for the Canadian-Arab Relations Conference, University of Calgary, June 24, 1981.

13 Interview on the Memorandum to the Cabinet on the Arab Boycott of Israel.

14 Stein, "Canadian Foreign Policy," pp. 286-93.

15 Grossman, "The Shifting Canadian Vote."

16 Canada-Israel Committee documents.

17 Interview on the Memorandum to the Cabinet on the Arab Boycott of Israel. See also Stephen Scott, "MacEachen Finds His Policy Acceptable in Middle East," *International Perspectives* (May/June 1976): 3-6.

18 Ibid.

19 Although press estimates vary widely, the International Monetary Fund, *Direction of Trade* indicates a total two-way trade in 1978 of close to $2.5 billion U.S.

20 This account of the boycott issue is based largely on materials contained in files of the CIC.

21 This account of the Jerusalem issue is based substantially on George Takach, "Clark and the Jerusalem Embassy Affair: Initiative and Constraint in Canadian Foreign Policy," unpublished M.A. Thesis, School of International Affairs, Carleton University, 1980; Howard Adelman, "Clark and the Canadian Embassy in Israel," *Middle East Focus* 2 (March 1980): 6-18; Jeffrey Simpson, *Discipline of Power: The Conservative Interlude and the Liberal Restoration*, (Toronto: Personal Library, 1980), pp. 145-59; Yaacov Glickman, "Political Socialization and the Social Protest of Canadian Jewry: Some Historical and Contemporary Perspectives," in Jorgen Dahlie and Lissa Fernando, (eds.), *Ethnicity, Power, and Politics in Canada*, (Toronto: Methuen, 1980), pp. 123-50; and Harold M. Waller, "The Political Process in Canadian Jewish Community Organizations," *Viewpoints* 2 (Fall 1980): 10-19.

22 For the broader conception of the Mideast and redefinition of Canadian policy that justified such a reversal, see Canada, Special Representative of the Government of Canada and Ambassador-at-large (Robert Stanfield), *Final Report of the Special Representative of the Government of Canada Respecting the Middle East and North Africa*, (Ottawa, Canada, February 20, 1980).

23 This judgement is based largely on interview materials.

24 Information about the involvement of the U.S. government is based largely on an interview programme on the American foreign policy process toward Canada, conducted with middle- and senior-level U.S. government officials in the spring of 1981.

25 John Benesh, "Canadian Images of the Middle East: Conflict and Implications for Canada's Middle East Foreign Policy to 1977," unpublished Research Essay, School of International Affairs, Carleton University, 1979.

26 Canadian Jewish Congress, "Brief to the Standing Committee on Justice, Legislature of Ontario," September 18, 1978 and "Brief submitted by the Canadian Zionist Federation, Central Region, to the Standing Administration of Justice Committee in support of Bill 112 'An Act to Prohibit Discrimination in Business Relationships'," CIC files.

27 These divisions are noted in Takach, "Clark and the Jerusalem Embassy Affair," and Glickman, "Political Socialization."

28 Although public estimates of the number of Arabs in Canada vary, these numbers on Canada's Islamic population are contained in Council of Muslim Communities of Canada, "Brief Submitted to Justice Committee on Bill 112," September 6, 1978, CIC files. The figure of 70-80,000 Arabs in Canada is given in Baha Abu-Laban, *An Olive Branch on the Family Tree: The Arabs in Canada*, (Toronto: McClelland and Stewart, 1980), p. 1.

29 "Memorandum to the Cabinet," op. cit., p. 13.

30 Ibid., p. 13.

31 This section is based primarily on interviews conducted in 1975-76, 1978, and 1979-81.

32 The Prime Minister was responding partly to a telephone appeal from UN Secretary Kurt Waldheim, urging Canadian participation in the force.

33 1979-81 interviews. See also Takach, "Clark and the Jerusalem Affair," p. 39.

34 This last section is based on a combination of reports in *The Globe and Mail* and *Financial Post* and interviews conducted in the winter of 1981-82.

35 See *Canada as a Principal Power*, chapter 10, "A Quantitative Overview of Canadian Behaviour Towards the Middle East," especially Tables 1-14 and Figures 1-2, and Parts II-III.

36 Peter Katzenstein, (ed.), "Between Power and Plenty: Foreign Economic Policies of Advanced Industrialized States," *International Organization* 31 (Autumn 1977), Stephen D. Krasner, *Defending the National Interest: Raw Materials Investment and U.S. Foreign Policy*, (Princeton: Princeton University Press, 1978) and Eric A. Nordlinger, *On the Autonomy of the Democratic State*, (Cambridge, Mass.: Harvard University Press, 1981).

ETHNIC INTEREST GROUP ACTIVITY
IN THE CANADIAN FOREIGN POLICY-MAKING PROCESS:
A CASE STUDY OF THE ARAB BOYCOTT

Howard Stanislawski

Department of Political Science, Boston College

Since World War II, Canadian foreign policy toward the Middle East has been shaped by leaders' estimates of the significance of the region and its importance to the Canadian national interest. From 1948 to 1968, Canadians essentially sought to play the "helpful fixer" in Middle East affairs. This approach was epitomized by Lester B. Pearson's role in the formulation of the United Nations Emergency Force (UNEF) in the wake of the 1956 Suez War[1]; for his actions, Pearson was awarded the Nobel Peace Prize. Canada's perception of its own potential as a mediator, of its role as a "helpful fixer", and of the international diplomatic importance of both Canadian intervention and the United Nations as an international body was profoundly influenced by the Suez experience. As Pearson wrote, reflecting on the Suez experience:

> Nothing, I suppose, could better demonstrate than the Suez crisis the extent to which the United Nations had remained a central factor in our foreign policy. Our problem was, and is, one of long standing, how to bring about a creative peace and a security which will have a strong foundation. It remained my conviction that there could never be more than a second-best substitute for the UN in preserving the peace.[2]

In the spring of 1968 a new era in Canadian politics began when Pierre Elliott Trudeau succeeded Pearson as leader of the Liberal Party and quickly won a convincing electoral victory. Trudeau was to remain prime minister continuously until May 1979; then, after a nine-month interregnum under Conservative Party leader Joe Clark, Trudeau again became prime minister in February 1980.

Soon after Trudeau took power, he ordered a full-scale review of Canadian foreign policy to "seek a new role for Canada and a new foreign policy based on a fresh appraisal of this rapidly changing world and on a realistic assessment of Canada's potential".[3] Trudeau was less than totally enthusiastic about Canada's peacekeeping experiences; he sought a new approach to foreign policy issues affecting Canada-U.S., Canada-U.K., and Canada-third world relations. He was not convinced of the continued relevance of the traditional role of "helpful fixer" and he sought to develop coordinated conceptual approaches linking foreign policy considerations to defense and domestic policy. As Janice Gross Stein has pointed out, the completion of the review process, which took two years, signalled a major change in the tone of Canadian foreign policy, replacing the search for role with the maximization of national interest.[4]

The government White Paper resulting from that process listed six major themes of national policy: economic growth, sovereignty and independence, peace and security, social justice, quality of life, and harmonious natural environment.[5] The first of the six themes was to emerge as a major and at times overriding factor in the determination of foreign policy options. The policy review thereby linked Canadian economic growth to the foreign policy-making process, and gave that goal first consideration in a list of priority orientations.

Aside from its interest in countering the growing problem of terrorism on the international level, the government made it clear that it viewed the Middle East as a region with only marginal relevance to Canadian foreign policy-making. With no basic interests, no role to play, and thus little to contribute, the Trudeau government was free to regard the Middle East with very limited policy interest and, at the same time, to allow itself to assess Middle East questions from a fresh perspective. In its emphasis on third world states and their economic development, Canada determined to develop new bilateral contacts that would be mutually beneficial. In reducing the attention paid to the traditional political problems posed by the Arab-Israel conflict, the Canadian government was free to pursue the broadening of ties on a bilateral basis with developing Arab states.

As a consequence of the evolution of the global balance of power and new politicization of the third world, the opportunities available to Canadian diplomacy receded considerably. The role of "helpful fixer" was no longer relevant. The search for role had, in fact, ended, and the conclusions of the White Paper on foreign policy formalized a major shift in Canadian diplomatic efforts. If foreign policy must extend domestic policy abroad and, in particular, meet the most important requisites of domestic policy, then the economic dimensions of foreign policy-making become prominent. Identified as the first of the six major thematic objectives, "fostering Canadian economic growth" provided a major basis for the reorientation of foreign policy and the Middle East was a logical focus for the new look in foreign policy. By the mid-1970s, the development of Canadian foreign policy on Middle East issues had entered a new era.

Ethnic Politics and the Canadian Jewish Community

The Jewish community of Canada has long been highly institutional-ized. The Canadian Jewish Congress, the Canadian Zionist Federation, B'nai Brith, and scores of component organizations have created a highly complex set of communal institutions, commanding the interest and affiliation of large numbers of Canadian Jews. Numbering approximately 310,000 people, the Jewish community is spread throughout Canada, though concentrations of 100,000 each are found in Toronto and Montreal, with approximately 20,000 Jews living in Winnipeg and in Vancouver. Canadian Jewish organizations have long taken their political role seriously, and the representational function has often led to inter-organizational disputes of substantial internal consequence over the years. In the period under examination in this paper, 1975 to 1980, representations to government on behalf of the Canadian Jewish community relating to the Middle East were made by the Canada-Israel Committee, the formal representative of the Canadian Zionist Federation, the Canadian Jewish Congress, and B'nai Brith. Headquartered in Montreal, the CIC maintained a governmental relations bureau in Ottawa and a press liaison operation in Toronto.

In its interventions with government, the CIC's activities and those of any representatives of the Jewish community were circumscribed by a number of important factors. First, Canadian political culture does not readily acknowledge the validity of lobbying. Lobbying is often regarded as an illegitimate attempt to influence governmental officials who embody Canada's broad national interests. Agents of domestic and foreign groups of course exist in Ottawa, but there is little or no overt acknowledgement of their status. There is no requirement that lobbyists register with any governmental agency, though a number of members of parliament have introduced private member's bills to that effect.[6]

Secondly, ethnic groups have tended not to employ organizations or individuals to act as lobbyists in Ottawa. Representations to government are usually undertaken by delegates of ethnic groups on two different levels. Officially, representatives meet with governmental ministers, if such meetings can be arranged. Departmental officials are normally present at such meetings, participating as required. The representational function is thus one of petition vis-a-vis government, and influencing existing policy directions or choices is very difficult. Unofficially, emissaries are sent to speak privately with senior political leaders. In the case of the Jewish community, senior community leaders visited with the appropriate minister and attempted to arrange for a solution to a problem of concern to the community. If the mission did not meet with success, very little was said publicly. "Quiet diplomacy" was the norm, notwithstanding its relative successes or failures.

Thirdly, the general representational function in Ottawa was most successfully fulfilled through various "old boy" networks, crossing governmental, business, and special interest lines. The radical transformation of Canadian society from a basically English-speaking polity with a major French-speaking component, to a highly variegated, multi-cultural, "ethnic mosaic", did not find appropriate expression in the Canadian political or corporate elites. Many saw the ethnic component in politics as an intrusive and less than fully legitimate force, not fully compatible with Canada's national interest.

The illegitimacy of overt lobbying and the absence of professional representation on behalf of ethnic groups circumscribed overt Jewish political activity. In foreign policy, these elements were even more important, and the legitimacy of countervailing economic and bureau-cratic interests presented even greater obstacles to successful representational activity by ethnic interests. In undertaking professional advocacy of issues in Canada's capital, then, the Jewish community and its representative organizations embarked upon a new, uncharted, and somewhat perilous course.

The professional foreign policy elite has had very few points of contact with the general public. Unlike other governmental officers, who view themselves as both representative of and responsible to the public, foreign service officers have tended to see themselves and their policy views as embodying Canada's national interest. They have not developed an apparatus for consulting public opinion on issues of foreign policy. In large measure, this exclusivistic perspective was sustained by the overwhelming apathy of Canadians in foreign affairs. It was also supported by the shared policy perspectives of the very few general international interest groups which existed in Canada. To begin with, then, the determined and educated interest of Canadian Jews in the Middle East distinguished that community from most other segments of Canadian society.

The Jewish community, of course, manifested its interest in foreign policy questions in more detailed ways as well. The development of coordinated policy perspectives, embodied in a professional operation, elevated its intervention in the eyes of the foreign policy elite from that of an uninformed, bothersome, and less than legitimate ethnic interest to that of a highly informed, bothersome, and less than legitimate ethnic interest. Consequently, departmental officials had to reappraise both the interest of the Jewish community in the Middle East policy-making process and their own response. The political activities and involvement of Canadian Jews and Canadian Jewish leaders made explicit to members of the bureaucracy the support which they enjoyed from a broad range of political authorities. As Jewish activism and access to political leadership expanded, the responsiveness of the professional foreign policy elite, of necessity, increased as well. Departmental officials recognized that informed, sophisticated, and politically active Canadians would monitor their actions regularly, and would not hesitate to turn to the political leadership when problems in policy originated in the bureaucracy.

On the political level, the Jewish community has in recent years significantly diversified its support, contacts, and allegiances, as a consequence of changing demographic, geographic, economic, and political factors. As the community grew larger and generationally older, political activism, expressed both in behind-the-scenes involvements and in more aggressive public positions, increased greatly. A high level of political activism reflected a much greater willingness to urge government forcefully to satisfy the policy requests of the Jewish community. Diversified political choices increased the potential size of swing electoral groups and made the development of policy responses to Jewish concerns more attractive to political parties and their candidates. Involvement by Jews at all levels of the political process increased their importance to political leaders, expanded effective communication of Jewish concerns to the public, and increased public and press sensitivity and responsiveness to these concerns. The expertise developed by Jewish organizations, the articulate nature of their representations, the existence of a sound and increasingly important Jewish electoral base, the intensive involvement of Jews in all levels of the political process, their expanding network of contacts, and the willingness of Jewish leaders to articulate their policy interests to both the bureaucracy and political leadership have all worked to increase the involvement of the Jewish community in foreign policy.

The Arab boycott provides a case study of the significance of Jewish community involvement in the policy process and of the broader implications for ethnic interest group involvement in the Canadian foreign policy-making process in the future. Contacts between ethnic leaders and bureaucratic and political leaders were frequent, intense, and broad-ranging. Because they were so, this case can highlight many of the dynamics of domestic influences on foreign policy.

The Arab Boycott

The Arab economic boycott of Canadians and Canadian companies doing business with Israel had its origins in direct (primary) boycott activities undertaken by Arab residents of Palestine under the British Mandate. In an attempt to damage seriously the economic viability of the developing Jewish community in Palestine, Arabs in Palestine and in Arab League countries undertook to refuse to buy or deal with goods manufactured by Jews or to sell land to Jews.[7]

In April 1950, a basic change in scope and policy was announced, extending the boycott from its direct, or primary nature, into secondary and tertiary dimensions.[8] Prior to an Egyptian decree of February 6, 1950, the boycott had tried to prohibit Arab imports of Jewish and after 1948, goods from Israel, regardless of the nationality or ethnicity of its manufacturers. After it issued a decree barring a long list of goods from transit through the Suez Canal, the Boycott Committee expanded its scope "to include shipping services in an attempt (not only) to osbtruct the flow of refugees from Arab countries to Israel", but also to hinder the flow of all trade into and out of Israel.[9] By September 1950, ship and tanker captains were required to provide assurances and allow inspections of log books proving that no cargo would be discharged at any of Israel's ports. A blacklist of vessels contravening these regulations was established, and those ships blacklisted could be denied supplies, fuel, or repair facilities, and their cargo could be seized or impounded. On November 28, 1953, the word "contraband" was defined to include "foodstuffs and all other commodities which are likely to strengthen the war potential of the Zionists in Palestine in any way whatever".[10] By 1955, Egypt had blacklisted more than 100 vessels, including ships of American, British, Dutch, Swiss, Greek, and Italian registry.[11]

In September 1952, the Arab League Council recommended the boycott of all companies with branches in Israel and the surveillance of all sea, land, and air communications and trade contravening the boycott's rules, and detailed guidelines were introduced for the implementation of these new conditions.[12] The extension of the operation of the boycott from a primary to a secondary level also entailed its extension to a new and unprecedented tertiary level.

The basic levels of boycott operations can be defined in the following ways:

1. The *primary boycott* is a direct boycott of Israel and Israel's goods and services by Arab states, firms, and individuals who refuse to do business with Israel. As such, it presents no immediate problem of extraterritoriality or compulsion of uninvolved third party states.

2. The *secondary boycott* is an attempt by Arab states, firms, or individuals to pressure firms of other countries to refrain from dealing with Israel or Zionists, or to end certain relationships with Israel or Zionists, as a condition of trade with Arab states, firms, or individuals. This requirement in effect compels an uninvolved third party state to engage in a boycott against a country with which it may have friendly relations.

3. The *tertiary boycott* is an attempt by Arab states, firms, or individuals to prevent firms of uninvolved third party states from dealing with firms of their own or other similarly uninvolved third party states because of the latter's relationship with Israel or Zionists, as a condition of doing business with Arab states, firms, or individuals. This requirement in effect compels an uninvolved third party state to engage in a boycott against another uninvolved third party with whom it may have no quarrel whatever.

4. A fourth type of boycott, or *voluntary boycott*, (also known as a "shadow boycott" or "chilling effect") is the outgrowth of the secondary and tertiary boycotts. In such cases, firms simply decline to deal with Israel or Zionist-related firms or individuals for fear of antagonizing present or prospective Arab clients.

The secondary and tertiary boycotts constitute direct interference in the economic affairs of uninvolved third party states by the extraterritorial application of Arab laws and regulations to commercial undertakings of those uninvolved states.

While application of boycott regulations will vary in rigour from one Arab jurisdiction to another, there are basic criteria which are common to all states, who subscribing to the Arab League's resolutions, accept the applicability of the provisions of the "General Principles for the Boycott of Israel", published by the League of Arab States, General Secretariat,

Central Boycott Office, Damascus, Syria.[13] Third party firms or individuals seeking to engage in business with Arab states, firms, or individuals are asked to provide information about their activities; alternatively, information about their activities may already have been compiled by the CBO or any of its contributors. Failure to respond to a request for information, or information of activities considered unacceptable under the boycott regulations, or suspected actions that need not be cited, can lead to the blacklisting of the third-party firm. The CBO seeks to invoke boycott restrictions against a firm which:

1. has a main or branch plant in Israel;

2. has an assembly plant in Israel, including firms whose agents assemble their products in Israel, even by special arrangements;

3. is assembling in Israel the major portion of the product it is selling to Arab states;

4. maintains general agencies or main offices in Israel;

5. provides companies in Israel with the right to use its trade names or manufacturing processes;

6. holds shares in companies in Israel;

7. renders consultative services and technical expertise to Israel's factories;

8. has directors or managers who are members of joint foreign-Israel Chambers of Commerce;

9. acts either as an agent for Israel's companies or as a principal importer of Israel's products outside of Israel;

10. takes part in prospecting for natural resources within Israel;

11. declines to answer questionnaires from Arab authorities requesting information on the nature of its relations with Israel;

12. incorporates in its own products components produced by a blacklisted company;

13. utilizes or employs the services or facilities of blacklisted shipping or insurance companies;

14. is pro-Zionist or employs Zionists in high positions;

15. has participated in Jewish organizations or contributed funds to groups active in or on behalf of Israel;

16. directly or indirectly helps Israel's economic growth or war potential;

17. manufactures, anywhere in the world, goods of Israel-made material or components;

18. sells goods anywhere that are identical to goods imported from Israel (to prevent re-export);

19. invests in any blacklisted company;

20. sells stock to citizens of Israel;

21. appoints a national of Israel as a corporate officer;

22. lends money or provides any financial aid in any form to Israel-based entities; or

23. takes part in or supports propaganda activities on behalf of Israel.[14]

All these provisions must be certified before a third party can qualify for commercial relations with Arab states. Documents involved may be as simple as a "negative certificate of origin", stipulating that none of any goods involved in a transaction originate in Israel, in whole or in part, or as complex as a whole series of attestations to any number of the twenty-three items listed above. These stipulations can be invoked in secondary boycott terms or in tertiary boycott terms. Thus, a third party firm can be asked to provide any or all of these assurances about itself; it can also be asked to refrain from dealing with any third party firm which has not passed the same test. Documents required in fulfillment of boycott provisions may be required in the pre-contractual, contractual, or letter of credit phases of transactions. In the latter case, the active assistance of Canadian banking institutions is involved in the collection and transmission of boycott-related documents.

The Arab boycott became a significant Canadian policy concern in the period after 1973. The steep rise in oil prices provided many Arab states with great financial resources, opening that area of the world to Western-produced, technologically-advanced goods and services, and enabling Arab states to intensify their attempt to isolate Israel economically. The Arab oil embargo of 1973-74 provided a dramatic illustration of the dependence of a number of western states on Middle East oil supplies. In the post-1973 period, forced compliance with the Arab boycott has become a more prominent policy concern in western democracies, in general, and in Canada, in particular, as Arab attempts to utilize this anti-Israel instrument became more widespread. The Canadian Jewish community became seriously concerned about the implementation of secondary and tertiary boycotts in Canada, and, beginning in 1974, the Canada-Israel Committee began to include analyses of the boycott and recommendations relating to it in its briefs to the secretary of state for external affairs.

Significant anti-boycott statutes were enacted in various American jurisdictions (thirteen American state statutes, the federal Tax Reform Act of 1976, and the federal Export Administration Act of 1977), and Canadian agitation against the boycott operations increased as well. In April 1975, the Hon. Herb Gray, former minister of consumer and corporate affairs, revealed that the Export Development Corporation, an important federal government agency, had been providing export insurance coverage for a number of Canadian firms in contracts with Arab countries, knowing that these contracts included terms in compliance with the Arab boycott. On May 8, 1975 Prime Minister Trudeau stated in the House of Commons:

> I think it is sufficient to say that this type of practice is alien to everything the government stands for and indeed to what in general Canadian ethics stand for.[15]

However, this statement of principle was not translated into a statement of policy guidelines aimed at combatting application of the Arab boycott in Canada. It did result in increased public awareness of the issue and a heightened determination on the part of Canada's Jewish community to undertake serious political action to urge the government to enact legislation prohibiting compliance with the boycott.

For the next eighteen months, Canadian Jewish organizations mobilized support for anti-boycott legislation in the media, human rights' and civil liberties' associations, trade unions, clergy, and other citizens' associations. Intensified discussion of the issue took place with the federal and provincial governments and opposition parties. On October 21, 1976, the federal government announced an anti-boycott policy, to be administered not by means of legislation, but rather by means of administrative guidelines. This policy, it was stated, would deny government services, support, and facilities to companies for specific transactions containing certain types of boycott clauses. It would also require all Canadians to report to the government on their experiences with boycott requests and would make public the names of firms signing unacceptable clauses. While this policy initially seemed attractive to anti-boycott activists, its subsequent haphazard application by the Department of Industry, Trade, and Commerce, its many loopholes that soon became apparent, and a number of *ex post facto* reinterpretations of the policy for the purpose of widening these escape clauses led to intensified lobbying for comprehensive anti-boycott legislation. The January 1977 report of the Commission on Economic Coercion and Discrimination, a citizens' panel chaired by Prof. Irwin Cotler of McGill University and composed of respected Canadians from all major political parties, served to arouse further large-scale public activity on the issue. Editorials in Canada's major papers were unanimous in calling on the federal govenment to enact serious, comprehensive anti-boycott legislation. Periodic reports in the press focused attention on the ongoing discriminatory consequences of the Arab boycott, notwithstanding the federal government's anti-boycott policy.

In the midst of these demands, the Conservative premier of Ontario, William Davis, announced his intention of introducing provincial anti-boycott legislation, should federal inaction continue. During the Ontario election campaign in the summer of 1977, Mr. Davis committed himself to early introduction of such legislation, and his Liberal Party and New Democratic Party opponents supported that initiative. In December 1977, the first draft of Ontario's anti-boycott bill was introduced. With some revisions, it was reintroduced in the spring of 1978, extensively reviewed in the Justice Committee in September, and signed into law on November 9, 1978.

While initiatives were underway in Ontario, the federal Liberal government of Pierre Trudeau was subjected to continuing criticism by the press and the Jewish community for what they thought was weak policy on the issue. Bureaucratic and business pressures opposed any significant federal anti-boycott activity. Indeed, there had been unremitting business pressure on the Ontario government to refrain from pursuing its initiative. Large-scale bureaucratic and business pressures developed against any new federal anti-boycott initiatives. However, with an election looming in the months ahead, the federal government felt compelled to undertake some action on this issue, and, in August 1978, it announced a significant tightening of the terms of its anti-boycott policy, together with a pledge to enact legislation establishing a compulsory, comprehensive reporting mechanism regarding receipt of boycott requests. This legislation would have required all Canadians to report on their experiences with boycott clauses. Companies agreeing to sign boycott clauses would have been publicly named. While such legislation would not have outlawed boycott compliance, but would only have created disincentives to compliance — the embarrassment of public disclosure — the Jewish community greeted the pledge warmly and awaited its introduction and enactment.

The House of Commons reconvened in October 1978, but Bill C-32, the reporting legislation, was not introduced until the end of December, and was not brought back for second reading and subsequent consideration. Despite the government's pledge to enact the bill, the minister of industry, trade, and commerce, Jack Horner, whose department was to have been responsible for its implementation, repeatedly made clear his opposition to any anti-boycott programme because of possible trade losses. He attacked the Ontario anti-boycott law, arguing that Ontario had already lost trade because of its intitiative; however, he was unable to provide any documentation supporting that allegation, and ministers of the Ontario government asserted that Horner's claims were simply untrue. In the immediate pre-electoral period of March 1979, Horner's statements opposing an anti-boycott initiative embarrassed the federal government, and extraordinary parliamentary manoeuvres were briefly considered to expedite passage of Bill C-32 in one day. These manoeuvres did not succeed, and the bill died on the order paper upon the dissolution of the House of Commons on March 26, 1979.

During the 1979 election campaign, the Liberal Party promised to reintroduce Bill C-32. The Progressive Conservative Party and the New Democratic Party repeatedly, forcefully, and publicly called for the introduction and enactment of comprehensive anti-boycott legislation, along the lines of the American and Ontario statutes. The election of a Conservative government on May 22, 1979, gave rise to expectations that such legislation would be forthcoming within several months of the opening of the new parliament.

Between April 25, 1979 and late October of that year, first the Conservative Party and then the new government found itself in the midst of a major national controversy over the campaign pledge of its leader, Joe

Clark, to move the Canadian Embassy in Israel from Tel Aviv to Jerusalem. That controversy had very significant implications for the anti-boycott policies of all political parties in Canada, as well as for the interest groups involved on all sides of the issue. As a consequence of the Clark government's capitulation to the threats of Arab governments and Canadian corporations dealing with Arab states, the commitment to move the embassy was withdrawn, and, in addition, no anti-boycott legislation was considered during the tenure of the Conservative government. On December 14, 1979, the government led by Prime Minister Joe Clark was defeated in the House of Commons, and, in the elections that followed two months later, the Liberals under the leadership of Pierre Trudeau were returned to power. Since that time, and despite Trudeau's appointment of Herb Gray, the foremost advocate of anti-boycott legislation in the House of Commons, as minister of industry, trade, and commerce, the boycott issue has not been addressed by the Canadian government, or in a serious way, by Canadian Jewish interest groups.

Elites and Interest Groups in the Arab Boycott Controversy

In the course of its activities in pursuit of anti-boycott legislation, Canadian Jewish interest group representatives encountered intensive activity on the part of Canadian elite groups and of other Canadian and non-Canadian interest groups, in some cases in support of the Jewish community's position, but in many cases in firm and active opposition to any anti-boycott initiatives on the part of the Canadian government. The Canadian media — in particular, newspaper editorials, in French and English Canada — were virtually unanimous in their continuing criticism of the government and in their support for anti-boycott legislation. The government nevertheless made use of the media for its own purposes. A copy of a top secret Cabinet document dealing with the boycott, for example, which alleged that the Jewish community had exaggerated its significance, was leaked to *The Globe and Mail* in August 1976. In 1979, during the heated debate over the Jerusalem embassy question, officials in the Department of Industry, Trade, and Commerce leaked selective, at times erroneous, and often provocative information to the press. The media reversed its position and its nearly unanimous opposition to the moving of the embassy contributed to the defeat of anti-boycott legislation as well.

Arrayed against Jewish interest groups on the boycott and Jerusalem issues were Canadian business groups, Canadian banks, and Arab representatives, both domestic and foreign, all of whom sought to link the two issues and convince Canadians of the likelihood of Arab retaliation should Canada proceed to move its embassy and enact anti-boycott legislation. The Canadian Labour Congress and the Canadian Association of Statutory Human Rights Agencies, as advocates of human rights, strongly supported the Jewish community's stance on the boycott and were silent on Jerusalem.

The interest groups arguing against any anti-boycott policies were aligned with the Canadian foreign policy-making elite — a group not substantially sympathetic to representations of public opinion by the Canadian people. In his examination of the influence of public opinion on the formulation of Canadian foreign policy by the foreign policy-making elite, focusing on the Department of External Affairs, Denis Stairs has pointed out that the department has traditionally viewed itself immune to the intrusive opinions of domestic groups or individuals. Since the Department of External Affairs has traditionally seen itself as the guardian of the national interest, it developed a sense of elitism and purpose that led easily to resentment of the intrusion of public opinion, either ill-informed or well-informed, into the policy-making process. Policy could only be harmed by intemperate interests lacking a broad commitment to Canada's national interest and owing allegiances that were, in the department's view, parochial and limited. Unlike other government departments, the Department of External Affairs never considered itself responsive to the perspectives of domestic constituencies.

As foreign policy issues became more complex and more relevant to domestic policy concerns, other governmental departments began to play a more active role in foreign policy formulation. Traditionally, external affairs has held that the department should serve as the coordinating body, drawing on the expertise of departments whose concerns are largely domestic but impinge partly on foreign policy. The reality, however, has often been quite different. Other departments have often played a primary role while external affairs has lent support. As Stairs has pointed out, domestic departments have established constituencies and maintain close — and even symbiotic — working relationships. These close ties have often given these departments a significant political advantage over external affairs in inter-departmental conflict. The political leadership, who ultimately must resolve the internecine departmental struggles, often tend to favour those departments with strong domestic support.[16] External affairs, not surprisingly resents constituency-based political power, as much because of the constituency as the inter-departmental struggle.

Members of the bureaucratic elite — in particular, officials of the Departments of External Affairs and Industry, Trade, and Commerce, and of the Export Development Corporation — were intensively involved in the boycott question from the time it first arose as a policy question in Canada. They made consistent efforts first to prevent any governmental initiative; once initiatives were undertaken, to prevent implementation; once implementation began, to forestall rigorous implementation; when public pressure mounted because of limited implementation, to deny information to the public and to distort information to claim progress where no progress had been made; when forced to deal with public groups interested in the issue, to appear conciliatory despite private opposition to anti-boycott efforts; when asked by political leaders to develop legislative options, to produce proposals that were thin and devoid of substance; and, finally, when faced with imminent legislative action, to leak information to the media to undermine the efficacy of the legislative effort. Materials prepared for cabinet consideration distorted the fundamentals of the problem presented by the Arab boycott. At times, senior civil servants assessed options and made recommendations on the basis of fragmentary and spurious data. Throughout, the bureaucratic elite sought to undermine any efforts the government was prepared to make to combat the boycott. Practices involving certification of religion — clearly contrary to the public policy of Canada — were provided and defended as necessary business practices and as "normal consular functions". As anti-boycott activists began to score some success, senior bureaucrats intensified their private efforts to prevent the implementation of legislation and intervened actively, but anonymously, in the public policy process.

Members of the corporate elite played a similar role. Beginning with occasional private representations to members of both the political and bureaucratic elite, corporate intervention intensified as anti-boycott lobbying developed. Corporate interventions remained consistently private; only those business interests most directly affected by boycott considerations became involved publicly in representational activities. This private pattern of advocacy reflected the traditionally close association of members of the corporate and political elite. It seems that these elites seriously underestimated the public challenge to policy formulation on anti-boycott legislation; in any case, their private representations did retard the development and implementation of government policy and programmes to deal with the boycott issue but were unable to stem widespread public demands for government action. Corporate unwillingness to intervene openly on a policy issue complicated by discrimination and ethical concerns prevented large-scale public pro-boycott action. Governmental policy at first was an irritant rather than a hardship to members of the corporate elite. However, as demands for an expansion of governmental action against the boycott intensified, and as the government responded with policy initiatives, corporate opposition grew and business leaders began to speak out in public. When the Clark government affirmed its intention to move the embassy to Jerusalem, corporate leaders orchestrated large-scale public representations, and, in unprecedented action, began to voice objections to policy proposals in public. Members of the corporate elite resorted to public advocacy, a search for mass public support, and coalition formation in the public arena. The battle was joined both against anti-boycott initiatives and the implementation of the government's policy on Jerusalem.

The political elite was confronted with an unprecedented array of contending influences on a foreign policy issue. The natural inclination of the political elite, bolstered by the forceful representations of the bureaucratic and corporate sectors, was to inaction. Consequently, Prime Minister Trudeau responded to Herb Gray's questioning in April 1975 by condemning boycott practices as immoral, but made no commitment to governmental action. Jewish pressure to act was by itself not difficult to resist, but as public concern rose, as editorial opinion grew forceful and unanimous in demanding action, the government began to press the bureaucracy, much against its will, to consider policy options. The government was embarrassed by bureaucratic participation in and support of discriminatory practices, and by public disclosure of boycott-related incidents which disproved bureaucratic claims. Although the government was now willing to initiate small-scale anti-boycott action, bureaucratic immobilism retarded these efforts to implement policy. Once again, embarrassment caused by disclosures of the Commission on Economic Coercion and Discrimination forced the pace of the governmental response to the boycott issue.

Over the next two years, bureaucratic unwillingness to assist in an anti-boycott effort, coupled with bureaucratic and corporate representations to government, slowed and weakened implementation of the government's anti-boycott programme. Confronted with embarrassing public disclosure of compliance, and pressed by broad media support for anti-boycott action, periodically the government recommitted itself to more effective action. As a federal election approached and the potential electoral importance of the Jewish community became manifest, members of contending wings of the political elite began to vie for that electoral support. The successful passage of anti-boycott legislation in the province of Ontario provided the opposition Progressive Conservative Party with a considerable advantage. This, together with widespread dissatisfaction in the Jewish community with the Liberal government's anti-boycott programme as well as disaffection caused by general economic conditions, made many Jews amenable to Conservative electoral promises. In this atmosphere, federal govermental action became attractive, both to silence the intense and generalized opposition to the government on the issue as well as to appeal to Jewish electors.

During the election period, from August 1978 to March 1979 political activity in search of Jewish support intensified, in particular in metropolitan Toronto. Opposition leader Clark's commitment to move the Canadian embassy in Israel from Tel Aviv to Jerusalem joined the issue of anti-boycott legislation as key campaign questions for the Jewish community. The Liberal Party, in turn, charged Joe Clark with irresponsibility and manipulation of foreign policy for electoral support.

After the election of the Clark government, the new political leadership sought as a priority to subordinate the bureaucracy on policy issues. At his first press conference as prime minister, Mr. Clark publicly asserted this goal of policy preeminence, by reiterating his government's commitment to the movement of the embassy. Almost immediately, a major rebellion began, led by members of the bureaucratic and corporate elites. For the first time in its history, a petition of resignation circulated in the Department of External Affairs as career foreign service officers threatened to resign if the Jerusalem decision were not reversed. Under intense pressure, the determination of the Clark government to assert its preeminence on this issue rapidly dissipated. In the process, its frequently stated intention to institute anti-boycott legislation also eroded significantly. The pro-business orientation of the Conservative Party reasserted itself as members of the bureaucratic, corporate, and political elite pressed for a simultaneous and total reversal of both policy commitments. The bureaucratic-corporate alliance cemented the linkage of these issues and after the defeat of the Clark government in February 1980, it successfully eroded support for more substantial anti-boycott action. National interest, defined in primarily economic terms, once again dominated the making of public policy.

The bureaucratic and corporate elites were bolstered by the active support of various interest groups. On the boycott issue, human rights and labour groups actively supported the Jewish position; they remained silent on Jerusalem. While church groups were largely silent on the boycott, they intervened actively against the Jewish position on Jerusalem.[17] United Nations' Associations and the Canadian Institute of International Affairs did not express their views on the boycott; the UNA did pass a resolution against the Jewish position on Jerusalem in 1979. As has already been mentioned, the media played an important role in both cases, reflecting near-unanimity in support of anti-boycott legislation and against the proposed move of the embassy. Canadian Arab groups were largely ineffective during the entire course of the boycott issue. They captured the attention of government leaders only when they repeated threats made by Arab leaders abroad.

The business and banking sector was very active with regard to the boycott and Jerusalem issues. The Canadian Manufacturers Association, Canadian Export Association, Association of Construction Engineers of Canada and major corporations such as Atco, Canadian Westinghouse, and SNC Engineering engaged in vigorous lobbying, linking these issues to prospective Canadian business activities in the Middle East. Their interventions during the boycott phase were private and highly confidential; although they made consistent efforts to prevent the development of anti-boycott action of any kind, they did not try to mobilize public support until the controversy over the embassy. Business leaders sought to make government policy on the boycott as ambiguous and porous as possible. Canadian businessmen vigorously protested against the limited governmental initiatives that were undertaken in October 1976, even though these protests were made privately. The traditional policy consensus, with only the details subject to *pro forma* public and private bargaining, did not prevail in policy-making on the issue of the Arab boycott. The apprehensions of business leaders intensified as governmental concessions mounted. The public receptivity to the findings of the Cotler Commission renewed and increased public and press demands for substantial anti-boycott action. The banks responded forcefully, confidently, and privately. Only the Royal Bank of Canada initiated significant changes in the way in which it dealt with international letters of credit.

In Ontario, business pressed Premier William Davis hard, urging him to refrain from implementing his electoral commitment to anti-boycott legislation. Despite the ideological affinity between business and the Ontario Conservative Party, which had been in power for over thirty years, the strong commitment of the government to enact such legislation, the political consequences of reversing that commitment, and the absence of effective bureaucratic interests with the power to undermine the bill, defeated the efforts of the business community to prevent legislation.

At the federal level, the political forces seeking anti-boycott legislation continued to provide a strong and highly effective challenge, but just as a significant victory seemed at hand, Joe Clark made his Jerusalem pledge, and the configuration of forces altered dramatically. During the Jerusalem controversy, business groups mounted an unprecedented public campaign, predicting catastrophic economic consequences, including the loss of 55,000 jobs.[18] The Royal Bank of Canada and Bell Canada leaked exaggerated and frightening estimates to the press. Alliances, both tacit and explicit, were formed between Canadian business interests and Arab governments and their representatives, so that statements from one bolstered the credibility of statements from the other. Repeated public statements were made by prominent business groups, such as the Canadian Manufacturers Association and Canadian Export Association. Direct communications between leading corporate figures and senior governmental ministers intensified. In Arab countries, Canadian businessmen met with Canadian journalists and stressed the importance of the Arab states to Canada's economic future, focusing, of course, on the potential that existed for their companies that would benefit Canada as a whole.

In the context of the Jerusalem controversy, Canadian business interests engaged in an unprecedented public lobbying effort to overturn an announced governmental decision in foreign policy. In their frequent representations during this period, business leaders spoke expressly of the negative consequences that would flow both from action against the boycott as well as from the commitment to move the embassy to Jerusalem. They linked the two issues. In fact, some business interests, in meetings with senior ministers and with Prime Minister Clark's special ambassador, Robert Stanfield, predicted a far worse set of consequences for Canada if anti-boycott legislation were enacted.[19] Business leaders found a receptive audience among senior bureaucrats in the Canadian government. The departments of external affairs and industry, trade, and commerce played strong supportive roles in developing these extraordinarily gloomy forecasts. They both initiated and confirmed the estimates of business leaders. This predisposition to accept the worst projections of the economic consequences that would follow from the Canadian initiatives was reportedly even stronger in the ranks of Joe Clark's cabinet. The Conservative Party, after all, had long been closely linked to Canada's corporate elite.

The behind-the-scenes lobbying of business interests in the pre-Jerusalem phase of the Arab boycott issue in Canada was, from their perspective, at best a limited success. An anti-boycott federal programme was in place, albeit one with gaping loopholes. An anti-boycott statute had been enacted in Ontario, but it was relatively easy to circumvent, given an inclination to do so, by signing a contract outside the jurisdiction of that province. Nevertheless, these programmes were seen by business interests as obstructionist and injurious to usual business practices. Business leaders were even more strongly opposed to the government commitment to establish a compulsory, comprehensive reporting mechanism. On this issue, however, the press had long been totally committed and public opinion reflected the perspective of the country's leading editorialists. After the Jerusalem issue became a public controversy, however, business leaders could develop a new, public, assertive, activist lobbying effort, which maximized the formation of coalitions and manipulated public opinion in support of the goals of large corporations. Because of these new tactics, business interests were able both to reverse the Jerusalem commitment and to prevent the introduction and enactment of the long-promised anti-boycott legislation by the Progressive Conservative Party.

The boycott case also illustrates the strength and potency of the influence of Arab governments, working in concert with Canadian corporate and bureaucratic interests, on Canadian foreign policy. Arab leaders successfully set the parameters for Canadian policy. Immediately after Prime Minister Clark reaffirmed his intention to move the embassy, the new minister of external affairs, in one of her first actions, met with Arab ambassadors to assure them of the government's intention to refrain from any quick action on the issue. Arab governments conveyed their opposition to Canadian political leaders directly, indirectly through Canadian interest groups (especially those of the corporate world), and through the skillful use of the pragmatic alliance they forged between the Canadian foreign policy bureaucracy and Arab international interests.

Canadian Foreign Policy-Making and the Arab Boycott

Canadian foreign policy is made in Cabinet and in the bureaucracy. In cabinet, all ministers of the Crown who take a political or substantive interest in any given foreign policy issue are involved, but most important are the views of the minister for external affairs, the minister of industry, trade, and commerce, and the prime minister. Officials of the Department of External Affairs and the Department of Industry, Trade, and Commerce are the principal bureaucratic players. Parliament as a body, and members of parliament individually and collectively, play a relatively small role in the foreign policy process; generally they can only raise interest in controversial or politically divisive issues. In this regard, the foreign policy process functions no differently from any other sector of Canadian decision-making. In their relationship with domestic and international interests, however, those involved in the foreign policy-making process have traditionally functioned quite differently from Canadian policy-makers in other sectors. Representations by domestic interest groups on questions of foreign policy were viewed as legitimate by the makers of Canadian foreign policy only when those representations came from general foreign policy interest groups who shared the political and international orientations of the foreign policy-making elite and from corporate interest groups pursuing economic goals that the foreign policy-making elite considered to be in the Canadian national interest. Consequently, the inclination of foreign policy-makers throughout the controversy over the Arab boycott was to discount the significance and legitimacy of ethnic interest groups seeking to influence policy; bureaucratic leaders discounted and minimized the significance of ethnic interest group pressures. Political leaders generally accepted the appraisals they received from the bureaucracy and tried, insofar as possible, to insulate policy from interested groups. They used the procedure that had always been effective in dealing with ethnic representations — general, pious statements of support, coupled with little substantive action, especially where there were serious countervailing costs. Not once did the bureaucracy initiate any action against the Arab boycott. Only when political leaders felt they could no longer ignore public pressure, did they force action on a reluctant and resentful bureaucracy. We can conclude, then, that the representations of interest groups were effective only when they impressed the costs of inaction upon Cabinet members.

The difference between the response of the federal and Ontario governments to representations for anti-boycott legislation reflects the absence on the provincial level of an actively obstructionist bureaucracy. Premier Davis of Ontario made clear his commitment to legislative anti-boycott action. What remained to be determined, and it took twenty-two months to do so, were the precise modalities to operationalize and implement that political commitment. The relations of Jewish interest groups with the Ontario government were substantially closer in all phases of the process than they were at any time with the federal government; in fact, Jewish interest groups at no point considered themselves to be in an adversary relationship with the Ontario government and its ministers.

On the federal level, adversary politics were the norm, as representatives of interest groups encountered the determined opposition of a strong and effective bureaucracy used to controlling the process of Canadian foreign policy.

In alliance with corporate interests, officials succeeded in preventing implementation of important aspects of the policy statement issued by Don Jamieson in October 1976 and in opposing disclosure of the identities of companies that contravened government policy and consequently forfeited government support for specific contracts. Arbitrary revisions in implementation of anti-boycott policy were made with an almost capricious disregard for political responsibility or the inviolability of political commitments. It seemed to matter little to those drafting reports and implementing policy that they were undermining public and private commitments made by ministers of the government. In almost every policy confrontation with political leadership, the bureaucracy triumphed.

Political leaders, in the initial phases of this controversy saw the issue of the boycott as an inconsequential matter. As Jewish lobbying intensified, and as public support for anti-boycott legislation grew to the point where it embarrassed the government, political leaders agreed to modest initiatives to gain political advantage among groups making representations while paying a minimal price for a modest anti-boycott initiative. As time went on, the obvious insincerity of the bureaucracy in its implementation of anti-boycott regulations proved even more embarrassing to the government, as the country's editorialists were quick to note. As elections approached, federal leaders began to appreciate the resonance and political significance of the boycott controversy. Consequently, in the summer of 1978 they tightened the anti-boycott programme and promised to legislate a reporting mechanism. Some of those who lobbied, particularly some of the Jewish leadership, questioned the government's commitment to legislate. Those who suspect duplicity cite the lengthy delays in the introduction of the bill and the government's unwillingness to bring the bill back for second and third readings. Other ethnic leaders forcefully discount this interpretation, accepting the government's explanations for the process unfolding as it did. Liberal Party and bureaucratic officials maintain that the government certainly intended to enact Bill C-32, and that it did not pass the House because of the vagaries of electoral politics and the timing of the dissolution of the House of Commons.

There can be no doubt that the controversies over legislation to respond to the Arab boycott and the movement of Canada's embassy to Jerusalem produced a process of foreign policy-making quite different from the norm. The alliance of interest groups calling for anti-boycott action constituted an unprecedented challenge to elite determination of foreign policy options. Also unprecedented was the widespread acknowledgement — and support — by non-ethnic groups of the legitimacy of ethnic representation on foreign policy issues of central concern; previously, ethnic interests had been effectively isolated. Canadian political leaders were forced to deal with a wide array of complex, interacting, and contending interests in their responses to the Arab boycott issue, and they were in many ways unprepared for the ongoing public supervision, assessment, and criticism of the intricacies of their policy toward the boycott. Other than Jack Horner, government leaders and spokesmen firmly supported strong anti-boycott action in their public statements and explicitly opposed the discriminatory practices of the Arab boycott. In practice policy was quite different, however, for the government placed few constraints in the path of Canadian businesses seeking to comply with the discriminatory and restrictive trade provisions of the boycott. Federal policy-makers argued repeatedly that Canadians had the right to function that way if they so desired.

The Arab boycott issue introduced major challenges to the system of foreign policy formulation in Canada. The active intrusion of Jewish domestic interest groups in both traditional behind-the-scenes lobbying activity and overt confrontation, the building of broadly-based coalitions, the work with parliamentarians and opposition parties in a mutually-advantageous attempt to dramatize policy divergences with Cabinet, the dramatic alteration in strategic and tactical postures of major corporate interests, and the extensive involvement of Arab governments seeking to influence Canadian foreign policy-making upset the flow of foreign policy-making and contributed to a partial breakdown in the programmatic consensus of political leaders. Newspapers played a significant role in shaping public perspectives on this issue and in conveying to government a public sense of outrage at discrimination against Canadians and urgency of action. In effect, the Arab boycott issue provoked a potent, if preliminary, challenge to the traditional mode of foreign policy decision-making in Canada. Although corporate interests prevailed and prevented the passage of any meaningful anti-boycott legislation at the federal level, there were some modest accomplishments. The system of foreign policy-making was subjected, at least temporarily and partially, to scrutiny and criticism; it was held accountable. In future, challenges by diverse interest groups may be easier. If such challenges are to occur, however, community leaders must accept the reality that on virtually every issue, there are both winners and losers, and the losers must be both willing and able to accept defeat and then reenter the process for yet another round. If Canadians are unable to accept both challenge and defeat as part of the rules of the game, then a truly dynamic and representative foreign policy process remains at best a distant possibility.

FOOTNOTES
[1] See Lester B. Pearson, *Memoirs*, vol. 2, (Toronto: University of Toronto Press, 1973).

2 Ibid., p. 310.
3 Quoted in Janice Gross Stein, "Evenhanded Ambiguity," MS, p. 25.
4 Stein, p. 26.
5 *Canadian Foreign Policy in the Middle East* (Ottawa: Canada-Israel Committee, 1976) p. 23.
6 For example, during the 1978-79 session of the House of Commons, PC Members of Parliament David Macdonald and Walter Baker both called for the registration of lobbyists, and Macdonald introduced a private member's bill to that effect.
7 For more detailed accounts of the origins of the boycott, see Dan S. Chill, *The Arab Boycott of Israel: Economic Aggression* (New York: Praeger, 1976), Donald L. Losman, *International Economic Sanctions: The Cases of Cuba, Israel, and Rhodesia* (Albuquerque: University of New Mexico Press, 1979), and W.H. Nelson and T. Prittie, *The Economic War Against the Jews* (New York: Random House, 1977).
8 Nancy Turck, "The Arab Boycott of Israel," *Foreign Affairs*, 55, 3, p. 474. Also see Report of the Subcommittee on Oversight and Intelligence of the Committee on Interstate and Foreign Commerce of the U.S. House of Representatives, chairman, Rep. John Moss (Washington, DC: U.S. Government Printing Office, September 1976).
9 Chill, p.3.
10 Ibid., p. 3.
11 Nelson and Prittie, p. 3.
12 Chill, p. 2.
13 U.S. Department of State document, Division of Language Services (translation), L.S. No. 34448 T-C/R, Arabic, 1972.
14 See Chill, pp. 4-5. Also see Turck, pp. 475-478, and U.S. State Dept. document cited in n. 13.
15 *House of Commons Debates*, May 8, 1975.
16 Denis Stairs, "Public opinion and external affairs: reflections on the domestication of Canadian foreign policy," *International Journal* (Winter 1977-78), 141-45.
17 Statement by Canadian Council of Churches on Jerusalem, June 8, 1979, reported in *The Globe and Mail*, June 9, 1979.
18 See coverage of the Jerusalem issue in *The Toronto Star*, June 5-30, 1979.
19 *The Toronto Star*, September 15, 1979.

CONCLUSION

David B. Dewitt
Department of Political Science
York University

To paraphrase the Greek philosopher Heraclitus, "Nothing is permanent but change". The Middle East seems, from the vantage point of a North American observer, to be in continuous flux. Subject to western imperialism in the nineteenth and early twentieth centuries, today the sovereign states in the Middle East reflect the tensions between modernity and tradition, between rich and poor, and between competing centres of power and influence. The complex interaction of forces within and outside the region contributes not only to the "permanence of change" but also to the atmosphere of almost continuing crisis.

Yet the essays contained in this volume indicate that the factors at play are neither new to the stage of world politics nor to the arena of the Middle East. They are merely the modern variant of traditional and long-present forces and factors. Indeed, what is remarkable is the resilience and adaptability of the peoples and governments of the Middle East to the combination of internal forces and external powers which continuously sweep through the region. Once again, the Middle East is at the "crossroads of civilization", provoking increased interest from the outside at the very time that local forces are trying to establish control over their own destiny. The clash of interests between competing external powers is exacerbated by the dynamism of indigenous forces which are themselves in conflict. Is the "permanence of change" synonymous with the "permanence of crisis"?

Conflict and turbulence are not unique to the Middle East. On the contrary, politics within the Middle East are profoundly affected by the broader arena of world affairs. Since the closing days of the Second World War, a single theme has dominated much of the thinking of diplomat and scholar alike: growing interdependence among states will lessen the forces of nationalism and hence decrease the likelihood of war. In spite of the cold war between the superpowers, the numerous "brush-fire" conflicts and "wars of liberation", and the escalating arms race, analysts speak of the "global village" and "spaceship earth". Yet while the vision may be well-intentioned, the facts often counter the hope. Over the past 30 years, the number of nation-states has tripled and military expenditures have reached staggering levels as many of these new states pursue security, narrowly-defined. The "distribution of security" continues to dominate the desperate need to establish a more equitable "security of distribution" of the goods and services of mankind. In the past decade, the Middle East has become a central factor in this tension between security and distribution, both as it affects the politics of the international community and, in turn, as it is affected by external factors.

Within the Middle East the search for security takes many forms. As Qureshi notes, the resurgence of a politicized Islam with both revolutionary and traditionalist goals is rooted in an articulated revitilization of the destiny of Islam with an attempt by Islamic leaders to wrest control away from those who mimic western and secular ideas. Islamic leaders consider that only an Islamic society can provide security — and hence prosperity. Thus a resurgent pan-Islam challenges the legitimacy of the nation-state, undermines the security of the state system and, of course, confronts the non-Islamic citizenry of those states. From this perspective, neither non-Muslim states/peoples (e.g., Israel/Jews, Christians, Baha'is) nor predominantly Muslim states which separate the secular from the profane (e.g., Egypt, Lebanon, Iraq, Syria, Jordan) are safe. Because Islamic fundamentalism crosses state boundaries throughout the Islamic world, it can undermine the legitimacy both of the sovereignty of states and the attendant order of the international system. The protracted struggle between Iran and Iraq, the assassination of President Sadat, and the fears of the Gulf states which contributed to the recent establishment of their Cooperative Council, attest to the transcendant quality of the Islamic movement. Fundamentalism strikes at the heart of the other indigenous politico-ideological movement in the Middle East, pan-Arabism.

While pan-Arabism is generally considered a political failure, over the years it provided the practical vehicle for Arab leaders to pursue co-operative if not complementary policies. Within the framework of pan-Arabism, they confronted Israel, the intervention of the superpowers, the dilemmas of modernization, and formulated strategies for the third world and non-aligned coalitions as well as the north-south dialogue. Islamic fundamentalism threatens whatever coherence exists within the Arab world, for it challenges secular authority and state legitimacy and undermines the effort to establish political and socio-economic equivalence with the states of both east and west. For these reasons, as has happened since the ninth century, Islamic fundamentalists will likely accommodate to the exigencies of the day. The differences within Islam and the structure of Arab states will modify and temper the more extreme variants of fundamentalism. Nevertheless, the resurgence of Islam will require modification of policy and likely the ensuing struggle between the secular and the profane will sharpen the atmosphere of crisis within the Middle East.

It is in the context of this struggle that the issues raised by Carmichael and Rudolph become most acute. From an Islamic perspective, the presence of Israel springs not only from Arab weakness, or even from western imperialism, or from the failures of pan-Arabism. To an Islamic fundamentalist, the reality of Israel is an affront to the universalism of Islam. Thus, the struggle against Israel is no longer one of guns or nationalism but rather a clash of values defined by a fundamentalist

Islamic consensus. The issue is not that Israel is a Jewish state, but rather that it is a non-Islamic state in the historic heart of the Islamic world. From this perspective, secular Egyptian, Jordanian, or Syrian control over the area would be little better. The attack on Israel is now two-pronged — one from pro-Palestinian nationalists and the other from Islamic nationalists. In this situation, any accommodation which Israel might reach with Palestinian nationalists would have little impact on Muslim fundamentalists.

In the 1950s and 1960s, various Arab leaders often called for a "jihad" or holy war against Israel. In the shadow of Khomeini, that call becomes real. Ironically, it is a call which threatens states other than Israel, since it invites attack both from outside and from within. This challenge to revolution from within is of little concern to Israel but is directly relevant to all other Middle Eastern countries. This more than anything else may propel other Arab states to join with Egypt in the search for some accommodation with Israel. A compromise satisfactory to Palestinians and other Arab nationalists would strengthen the forces of nationalism and the legitimacy of secular state structures. Otherwise, the continued existence of Israel and the failure to resolve the Palestinian question strengthen the forces of militant Islam. It is one thing for Arab governments to impart legitimacy to pro-Palestinian forces in their struggle to establish a state; it is quite another when nationalist forces fail and religious forces dominate the arena of political action. Israel then becomes but one among many targets in the Middle East.

The third transnational factor in the Middle East — oil — most closely links the region to the broader international community. Like Islamic militancy and armed conflict, oil had been a factor in the region's politics in earlier years; yet unlike the other two factors, the dynamics of oil — its control, cost, distribution, and attendant technology — have affected the fortunes of almost every country in the world. The revolution in the price of oil in the last decade has contributed to crises in balance-of-payments, to escalating inflation, to industrial recession, to over-heated economies, and to overcommitment and over-ambitious modernization projects; to arms races in the third world and to conflict among OECD members. As one of the primary resources for fuels and synthetics, and as a principal earner of hard currency, oil has become a leading factor in international affairs and key petroleum exporting countries which have imposed state control over oil-related policies have emerged as significant actors on the world stage. They have played an important role in the Arab-Israeli conflict and have had a major impact on north-south diplomacy and on international economic and monetary stability. These issues focus upon the security of distribution.

The past ten years have been punctuated by the elevation of international economic issues to the realm of "high politics". OPEC has played a critical role in escalating the price of petroleum products and, as

Zerker notes, despite growing internal conflict, its member countries remain significant international actors. Even if disagreement continues and, indeed, increases, if internal conflict impedes coordinated action, and conservation and new technologies lessen the degree of dependence of consuming states, key suppliers such as the Gulf states will remain of critical importance as sources of oil and direct investment abroad, and as purchasers of OECD-produced goods and services. Yet, the oil exporting countries face serious internal challenges.

The economic and diplomatic benefits which accrue to oil producing and exporting countries may extract a high cost, both internationally and domestically. There is increasing concern about the consequences of petro-dollar recycling, and international monetary instability has become a central topic for discussion at the annual western economic summits of the seven major OECD first ministers. Management of oil revenues in an obviously fragile monetary system is extraordinarily difficult, especially in light of the increasingly large demands of debt servicing. Not only must the OPEC members worry about the real value of currencies they receive for their resource, but leaders of these states also face the political consequences of sociological and technological spin-offs which go along with the rapid change in their economic capacity. These policy-makers must try to design and control the difficult relationship between economic and political factors. While all political leaders face this challenge, the dilemma is particularly acute in oil producing and exporting countries. We need only refer to the overthrow of the Shah of Iran and to the various domestic "incidents" in Saudi Arabia, Kuwait, and Bahrain to understand the scope of the challenge.

At the same time, consumers in the industralized world cannot assume that a significant decrease in the price of oil will necessarily end their struggle with inflation and recession. Lower oil prices very likely will undercut the development of alternate energy sources and technologies, which before the rise in oil prices were considered uneconomic but are now price competitive. Government tax revenues and the international value of currencies could be adversely affected. Furthermore, a decrease in OPEC revenues will be felt directly by those production and service industries increasingly dependent on sales to these producing countries. The complexity of the political economy of oil is a central problem for the entire world and the attendant uncertainty is a critical component of the ongoing crisis in the Middle East.

Unlike the past, when empires and great powers imposed their will upon the governments and peoples of the Middle East, today the relationship between those within and those outside the region, while not yet balanced, is far less asymmetrical. Some argue that the two superpowers retain unmatched capability to penetrate and dominate the Middle East. With the exception of Afghanistan, however, — and the final chapter of that story has yet to be written — and despite very specific and direct interests in the area, neither the United States nor the Soviet Union has been able to guarantee its interests or impose its will upon the states within the Middle East, much less consolidate well-defined and controlled spheres of influence. Although the reasons are many and varied — as suggested in the chapters by Steinberg and Marantz — two stand out: (1) growing capabilities within the region and, on some issues at least, policy coordination among member states and (2) the increasingly diffuse international system with many centres of power. These two factors constrain the activities of the superpowers as well as the broad set of relationships between the countries of the Middle East and the rest of the world.

The growing involvement of many of the OECD states further exacerbates the complexity of an already diffuse and varied region. As Stein notes, the deteriorating relationships between the United States and the Soviet Union and the multiple initiatives by a range of interested outsiders may confuse the ongoing peace process and alter the delicate balance within the region. The inability of the two superpowers to achieve a consensus on their interests in the Middle East, the decline in superpower hegemony, may have adverse consequences on the active pursuit of conflict resolution. This is especially so if the local participants no longer think that their patrons or guarantors are either able or willing to enforce policies of mutual interest. The expansion of bilateral relations between Middle East countries and OECD states did not, Stein suggests, result in a fundamental rift between Canada, West Europe, Japan, and the United States over Mideast policy. Yet it does indicate competition — and hence possible conflict — between these states over access to the resources and markets of the area. Senior British officials have disagreed with a number of Western European countries over policies in the Middle East, and European spokesmen have voiced uncertainty over the willingness of the Americans to protect European interests in the Fertile Cresent and the Gulf. Competition has also been evident in differing, often conflicting, responses to both the Camp David accords and the recent Reagan proposal, as well as to Israel's war with the PLO in Lebanon in the summer of 1982.

The involvement of a large number of principal powers in the Middle East may also contribute to the peace process as long as there is underlying consensus both on the legitimate existence of Israel and the need to satisfy the legitimate rights of the Palestinian people. The two superpowers establish the outer limits of "acceptable military action", but the principal powers, who combine political stature with economic and diplomatic presence, may be able to introduce a note of self-interested moderation in a process too often defined by extremes. While not exact analogies, both Zimbabwe and Namibia offer hopeful precedents to the significant and positive roles that principal powers can play.

Canada exemplifies a principal power with a relatively new role in the

Middle East. Its rapidly expanding bilateral relationships grow out of the surplus petrodollars of OPEC states and the declining hegemony of the United States. The oil-producing states have attracted Canadian entre-preneurs whose goods and specialized services are marketable throughout the third world, both among the less developed and the newly industrializing. Canada has pursued its interests aggressively, often in collaboration with other principal powers, in turn-key projects in Saudi Arabia or complex aid programmes in Egypt and Tunisia. In the longer term, expansion of Middle East-OECD relations will increasingly tie each to the other and build common interest in stable political and economic relations. This may well prove to be the single most important effect of petrodollar diplomacy. If peace is to come to an increasingly modern Middle East, then full reciprocal recognition and acceptance of "normal" diplomatic relations among all states is the minimum requisite. The prospects of peace are increased not by superpower competition played out in the Middle East but rather by the identification of a mutuality of interests in peace and prosperity. Even though the superpowers dominate the arms bazaar, the principal powers may provide the incentives and the means to bring the states of the Middle East into full politico-diplomatic partnership with the western world.

The fate of the Palestinian people remains one of the central, and perhaps the most difficult, impediment to the creation of a stable and peaceful order in the Middle East. The Palestinian question, which plagues not only the Arab-Israel conflict but spills over into the region and the general international community, can be resolved only by the parties directly in confrontation. While external parties can facilitate, mediate, and guarantee, the necessary compromises involving people, land, and security rest within the Middle East community. Peace can be built if, and only if, the people and their governments within the Middle East decide that it is in their interests. External powers can assist or hinder; internal forces ultimately are responsible.

A NOTE ON THE CONTRIBUTORS

D.J. Carmichael is associate professor of political science at the University of Alberta. He has contributed articles to *Terrorism: An International Journal* and to the *Canadian Journal of Political Science*.

David B. Dewitt is associate professor of political science at York University. His most recent publication is a co-authored volume with John J. Kirton, *Canada as a Principal Power: A Study of Foreign Policy and International Relations* (Toronto: John Wiley & Sons, 1983).

John J. Kirton is associate professor of political science and coordinator of the International Relations Programme at the University of Toronto. A specialist in Canadian foreign policy, he has contributed to the *International Journal* and is co-author, with David Dewitt, of *Canada as a Principal Power*.

Paul J. Marantz is associate professor of political science at the University of British Columbia. He has contributed articles to *International Journal*, *Orbis*, *Current History*, and *Problems of Communism*. He is now completing a book on "Changing Soviet Perspectives on East-West Relations, 1917-1982."

Saleem Qureshi is professor of political science and associate dean of arts at the University of Alberta. A specialist in the politics of Islam, he has recently contributed articles to the *International Political Science Review* and *World Development*.

Ross Rudolph is associate professor of political science at York University. A specialist in the political thought of Thomas Hobbes, he is now completing a book on "Hobbes's Philosophic Politics."

Howard Stanislawski is lecturer in political science at Boston College and at the John F. Kennedy School of Government, Harvard University. He has contributed articles on the Middle East to *The New Republic*, *Middle East Focus*, and *Le Devoir*, and is now completing a comparative study of Canadian and American anti-boycott legislation.

Janice Gross Stein is associate professor of political science at the University of Toronto. She has contributed articles to *International Journal, Canadian Journal of Political Science, Journal of Strategic Studies*, the *Jerusalem Quarterly*, and *Etudes Internationales*. She is co-author of *Rational Decision Making, Israel's Security Choices, 1967* (Columbus: Ohio University Press, 1981), which received the Edgar S. Furniss award, and is currently completing a book on *The Psychology of Deterrence in the Arab-Israel Conflict*.

Blema Steinberg is associate professor of political science at McGill University. She has contributed articles on Soviet and American foreign policy to the *Canadian Journal of Political Science, Orbis, International Interactions*, and *The Jerusalem Journal of International Relations* and is now completing a book on "American Foreign Policy in the Middle East: The Search for Peace."

Sally F. Zerker is associate professor of economics and social science at York University, and editor of *Middle East Focus*. Her latest publication is *The Rise and Fall of the Toronto Typographical Union, 1832-1972: A Case Study of Foreign Domination* (Toronto: University of Toronto Press).

INDEX

230

231